ERRATA

Page 159: On line one, $\kappa(b)$ should read $K(b)$.

Page 161: In third paragraph, $'$ denotes matrix transpose.

Page 180: In equations (A3.7) and (A3.8), κ should read K.

Page 195: In equation (A6.1), N refers to the cumulative normal distribution.

Page 198: In equation (A6.5), dJ should equal $+\frac{1}{E}$ in default.

Page 205: On line six, Ei should read E_i.

Page 209: In equation (A7.9), K should read K.

Page 215: In equation (A8.1), κ should read K.

Page 243: Ninth line from the bottom should begin $\left(1-\ell\right)^{2/\eta-1}$

Pandora's Risk

KENT OSBAND

Pandora's
Risk

*Uncertainty at the
Core of Finance*

Columbia University Press
Publishers Since 1893
New York Chichester, West Sussex
Copyright © 2011 Columbia University Press
All rights reserved
Library of Congress Cataloging-in-Publication Data
Osband, Kent.
Pandora's risk : uncertainty at the core of finance / Kent Osband.
p. cm.
Includes bibliographical references and index.
ISBN 978-0-231-15172-6 (cloth : alk. paper) — ISBN 978-0-231-52541-1 (ebook)
1. Financial risk management.   2. Financial risk.   I. Title.
HD61.O83 2011
658.15'5—dc22
2011002618
∞
Columbia University Press books are printed on permanent and durable
acid-free paper.
This book is printed on paper with recycled content.
Printed in the United States of America
c 10 9 8 7 6 5 4 3 2 1
References to Internet Web sites (URLs) were accurate at the time of writing. Neither
the author nor Columbia University Press is responsible for URLs that may have
expired or changed since the manuscript was prepared.

To those who fear more to pretend to know
than to admit they don't

CONTENTS

PREFACE

The revelation came one lazy summer evening. I had just dozed off when two goons broke into my house, threw a sack over me, and whisked me away. In an instant that felt like an eternity they took me to their lair and hauled me trembling before their leader.

Suddenly I heard His voice. "Have no fear, my son. I have brought you here for blessing, not punishment."

"Is that your escort service?" I asked.

"Those are your guardian angels. You arrived safely, did you not?"

"And the sack?"

"A spacesuit. You wouldn't survive the journey without one."

"Why no eyeholes?"

"None can look at me and live. But l will let you glimpse my hand. Do you see it?" Two slits miraculously appeared in the sack. Through them I saw the most wondrous hand I had ever seen. It was the color of . . .

"Do not tell anyone the color," He said. "You people torment each other enough in my name already. Just watch as I show you." He turned His hand to reveal enormous emeralds, with more facets than I could count and a different number cut into each one.

"They're dice!" I cried. "And you're playing them. Einstein must have been stunned."

"He was. But so was Bohr when I showed him what I am about to show you. What do you see next to my hand?"

"Nothing. It's pitch black."

"It is a black hole. No light can return once it enters. But watch this." He thrust His hand into the black hole and pulled it back out. The dice were perfectly aligned and displayed the number 622,487.

"Fantastic. Hawking was right. You do sometimes throw dice where they can't be seen."

"Keep watching." Again He threw the dice and pulled them back from the abyss. The number was exactly the same: 622,487.

"What a coincidence," I said. "Nothing has changed."

"You are not watching carefully enough."

I looked again. Diamonds had replaced emeralds, with more facets than before. "You changed your dice!"

"And what does that imply?"

"The risks have changed."

I heard murmurs of approval. "Congratulations," He said. "You have passed the first test. Not many people in finance do."

"I'm surprised. It's so obvious."

"Not when you don't see the dice. Then you have to infer change from the evidence. That's murky. Most of finance presumes the risks are clear."

"Why not just announce every change?"

"Because that would break Pandora's bargain."

"Bargain? With Pandora? I don't understand."

"I don't expect you to. Just relay my useful message."

"The message that You change your dice without telling us? How can that be useful?"

"Because knowing the right question is better than answering the wrong one."

"But how do You expect us to find the answer?"

"By using the organ I gave you for experimentation, discovery, and delight."

A dirty thought crossed my mind. He must have read it. "You fool," He thundered. "I meant your brain!" Lightning bolts flew and a mighty wind knocked me down. I knew my end was near.

Suddenly a woman's voice broke in. "Stop, Prometheus! He's just a man. What do you expect?"

The heavens stilled. "That's better," she said. "And stop impersonating the gods. They'll have you arrested and your liver eaten out."

"They have and they do."

"Yes, but why aggravate the charges?"

"You're right, Pandora. Men are not worthy of our gifts."

"Not yet, but they will be. We give to make them worthy. Has man not proved worthy of the fire you gave?"

"Yes, it has created far more than it destroyed."

A gentle hand helped me to my feet and removed the sack covering my head. I saw an ancient but strikingly beautiful woman. Her eyes sparkled. "Hello," she said. "I am Pandora. And if you look up you'll see Prometheus, the titan you mistook for a god."

My mind raced too fast for words. "Pleased to meet you," I finally mumbled.

"I doubt it. More likely you mourn the havoc we've allegedly wreaked on the world, through fire, famine, pestilence, and the curse of labor."

"Actually, I wasn't so worried about the fire. Prometheus is on our side."

"Unlike me?"

"Yes, unlike you. You opened the box. You shouldn't have. Zeus told you not to."

"We made a deal. It was a bargain for mankind."

"Pandora, you're sick. You get too curious, unleash all kinds of evils, and then call it a bargain because we're left with hope?"

"There was good in the box too. Countless discoveries. Treasures at the edge of imagination."

"Great. So you let them slip away as well. Oh, I forgot. We can hope to find them again. Thanks a lot."

Pandora winced. "Stop," said Prometheus. "You're torturing her with a lie. The story doesn't even make sense. But whenever Pandora hears it, it is as if the eagle eats her liver too."

"What do you mean the story doesn't make sense?"

"Think about it. What was the point of the box?"

"To keep bad things away from mankind."

"Was it working?"

"Yes, until Pandora opened the box and the bad things rushed out."

"Men knew nothing about the contents before?"

"I don't see how they could have."

"So why was it good that hope stayed in the box? Why didn't hope rush out to find mankind, the way the bad things did?"

I was stumped. "I don't know. I wasn't there."

"And yet you judge. . . . Pandora, tell him what life was like before you opened the box."

"It was serene," she said. "Too serene. Prometheus brought men only the fire outside. They had none in their bellies. No hunger for adventure, no thirst for discovery. Opening the box opened their eyes to opportunities."

"And people fault you for that?"

"They fault me for the risks. Opportunity always comes with risk. Without risk they hadn't even needed hope. It was locked away in the box."

"Locked? The box was locked?"

"Of course it was locked. Otherwise risk would have nudged it open. Zeus held the only key."

"Which you stole like Prometheus stole fire?"

"I never stole," said Pandora. "I bargained. Zeus handed it to me fair and square, in return for my pledge to guard the box for all eternity."

"For what purpose? To keep hope inside?"

"No, to keep the risk that emerged from getting back in."

"And why did Zeus demand that?"

"To remind men that they are not gods."

It took me a while to digest this. Pandora's version fit the evidence better than the original did. Only I still didn't understand the bargain. "What does it mean to keep risk outside the box?"

"It means that men will never fully know the risks they face. They will have to guess, and face the new risks their guesses impose. No man will ever fully master his universe."

"Can men recapture certainty by averaging over a large number of events?"

"Not fully. Averages aren't always relevant. Some of the information they average may pertain to the old set of dice."

"And what do you want me to do with this insight?"

"Explain it to others. Explain that risk always comes with uncertainty, and that uncertainty twists and magnifies its effects."

"Man has known that for nearly a century. Uncertainty is central to quantum physics."

"It is not yet central to finance. The core equations of standard theory match those of pre-quantum physics. They presume that the risks are known, or that the market consensus implicitly reveals them."

"Behavioral finance doesn't. It emphasizes the irrationality of markets. It's a respected field as well."

"Yes, finance theory is a wonderful game. Every fact is snipped to support either standard finance or its behaviorist rival. However, both camps assume that rational traders exploit risk to the fullest."

"What's wrong with that?"

"Because traders don't see risk to the fullest. They observe some things and have to learn about the rest. Learning implies error and the correction of error."

"So you don't see markets as either stupid or wise but somewhere in between."

"In *transit* between. Learning is a process, not a place. It leaves big tracks in market prices: extra volatility, fat tails, and other peculiarities. Theorists tend to wrestle with each of these puzzles separately. Learning provides a unifying explanation. Also, it points policymakers in the right direction."

"Which is?"

"Never assume the markets know, but make it easy for them to learn."

"Don't policymakers realize that already?"

"No!" bellowed Prometheus, and nearly bowled me over again. Pandora steadied my shoulder.

"Prometheus gets very emotional about this," Pandora said. "He is very sensitive to cycles of pain and recovery."

"Surely his are far worse."

"Unquestionably. But none of his are self-inflicted. Some of mankind's are."

"Do you want me to explain that too?"

"Of course."

It was becoming clear. Clearly wrong. "Pandora, Prometheus, I thank you both. Your cause is noble. I'm just not the right person to make your case."

"This isn't about us. It is about the nature of financial risk."

"I appreciate that. But you need two different books to drive the point home. One should be fiery and funny, with minimal math and maximal intuition. Draw on history where you can. Make up stories where you can't."

"Bravo. Bring out the big picture. And the other?"

"Dispassionate and scientific, with math dominating chat. Derive the core equations of learning and their implications for market pricing. Evaluate various risk measures and regulatory incentives."

"Delightful. Dispense with the drivel. When can you start?"

"I'll send you a list of candidate authors as soon as I get home."

"I meant when can you start writing?"

"Sorry, Pandora, I'm not on the list. These are two completely different genres and I'm no expert in either."

"But your book *Iceberg Risk* combined them, did it not?"

"Yes, it was the best financial math novel ever written. It was also the worst. I'm not trying that again."

"Why not?"

"Because mathematicians didn't take it seriously and most of the rest couldn't take the math. The risk miscalculations I warned about grew more monstrous than before."

"So take a stab at nonfiction and make the math clearer."

"It won't work."

"You cannot be certain. Now excuse me while I guard the box."

In a flash Pandora was gone. Prometheus bid farewell, and turned his attention to a giant eagle circling overhead. Everything started to spin, and I passed out. When I awoke I was home. A box was open, and risk was all around.

ACKNOWLEDGMENTS

For decades I have been fascinated with financial ignorance. It started with my own, and only gradually expanded to embrace others'. Fortunately some knowledgeable people hired me anyway. I thank Larry Brainard, Andrew Ipkendanz, and Mike Novogratz for providing window seats on the world.

Among theorists, I am considered a practitioner. Among practitioners I am considered a theoretician. These terms are partly insults in each of the circles they're used in. I apologize for having deserved them. Tom Barket, Aaron Brown, Paul Glasserman, Tilmann Gneiting, Henry Milligan, Deborah Pastor, Ken Posner, Stefan Reichelstein, Paul Wilmott, David Wilson, and Gary Witt have in various ways encouraged me to persevere.

Most writers credit their families for tolerating their preoccupation. My family credits my preoccupation for keeping me out of their hair. Still, I draw a lot of inspiration from watching my children Ian, Valerie, Alexander, and Eric grow up with such sparkle and motivation. My wife Annette offered numerous helpful criticisms and encouraged me to redo without despair. I also appreciate the friendship of my former wife, Jan, and the support of my parents, Richard and Shirley.

This book was originally intended to be Part 3 of *Iceberg Risk*, but that book grew too long and my window for writing too short. In hindsight the ideas needed longer gestation. Paul Wilmott and editor Dan Tudball provided an incubator in *Wilmott* magazine. They also infected me with their vision of making quantitative finance clear and user friendly.

I made another false start on the book in 2005. Brian Lee helped me sift through a lot of literature but I couldn't bring it together. The drafts sat for years in my computer, gathering electronic dust.

The spark that finally caught fire came from Myles Thompson. A cofounder of Texere, which had published *Iceberg Risk*, he had joined Columbia to build its Business School press, CBSP. In May 2008 we sat discussing the gathering storms in finance theory and practice. After Hurricane Lehman slammed ashore, I realized a calling had found me. Myles realized it too and shepherded the manuscript to approval.

Preparing the manuscript for publication became an unexpected joy. Bridget Flannery-McCoy of CBSP helped keep me on track. Copy editor Carrie Nelkin helped scrub and polish drafts. Designer Milenda Lee created an inviting layout and production editor Michael Haggett set high standards throughout. I am responsible for any roughness that remains.

Special thanks go to an old friend and mentor, Barbara Stein. She has long encouraged me to explore the realm where spirit meets science and right brain meets left. Our conversations sparked most of the mythological allusions and at least one of the mathematical models. I hear in her the voice of Pandora.

ABBREVIATIONS

AIG	American International Group
ARCH	Autoregressive Conditional Heteroskedasticity
BET	Binomial Expansion Technique
bps	basis points
CorBin	correlated binomial distribution
CDO	Collateralized Debt Obligation
CGF	cumulant generating function
CRRA	constant relative risk aversion
CVaR	Conditional Value at Risk
DXY	U.S. dollar index
ECB	European Central Bank
EIS	elasticity of intertemporal substitution
EMA	exponential moving average
FX	foreign exchange
GAO	U.S. Government Accountability Office
GARCH	Generalized ARCH
GDP	gross domestic product
HLOC	high/low/open/close prices
i.i.d.	independent, identically distributed
IMF	International Monetary Fund

MSE	mean squared error
NegBin	negative binomial distribution
NPV	net present value
OECD	Organisation for Economic Co-operation and Development
PIIGS	Portugal, Italy, Ireland, Greece, Spain
RRA	relative risk aversion
SAMURAI	Self-Adjusting Mixtures Using Recursive Artificial Intelligence
SEC	Securities and Exchange Commission
S&P	Standard & Poor's
SMA	simple moving average
SPX	S&P 500 Index
SRE	standard relative error
TSE	Toronto Stock Exchange index
VaR	Value at Risk

Pandora's Risk

1

Introduction

This is a book about the most important risk we face in finance. It's the risk that comes from learning about risk. I call it Pandora's risk in honor of legend's prime culprit. If she hadn't opened the box of wealth and woe, we'd have no hunger to learn.

Other fields involve learning too. Since the observer never fully understands the observed, there's always something to learn. Occasionally, learning overturns some core beliefs. That's how scientific revolutions occur.

Finance stands out in that the core objects of study are themselves observers. Market participants rarely know the true value of what they're trading. Markets grope for knowledge by aggregating individual beliefs. But beliefs are constantly shifting.

Twentieth-century finance theory treated learning as a sideshow. It assumed that the market consensus largely captured the true risks. Error was dirt around the edges. If the dirtballs got big enough, speculators should arbitrage the discrepancies and clean things up.

In reasoning this way, theorists missed something that every market practitioner knows. Most speculators don't trade on changes in risk. They trade on changes in *beliefs* about risk. Those aren't the same. Sometimes they're not even close.

This confusion pervades financial risk analysis. For example, the global banking regulations known as Basel sanctified nearly unlimited leverage for loans to top-rated credits. They brushed off as minor detail the difficulty in rating safety. The disregard helped stoke the greatest debt bubbles in world history.

Most financial analysts incline to downplay Pandora's risk. They want to impress their superiors with what they know. Their superiors in turn want to persuade investors and regulators that risks are under control. Few want to advertise their uncertainty.

Results betray them. Risk bounds have to be continually reset, even when the nominal investments don't change. Despite these adjustments, losses breach extremes far more frequently than standard models suggest. When stricken, most standard setters seek comfort in the crowd.

It doesn't have to be that way. Uncertainty is our friend as well as our enemy. It encourages us to agree with each other, or act as if we agree, even when there's no objective basis. The consensus encourages real trade and investment, which turns the fictions of belief into material facts.

Better appreciation of uncertainty can also help us think outside the box. As Mark Twain is alleged to have said, "It ain't what you don't know that gets you into trouble. It's what you know for sure that just ain't so." Every financial crisis brings reminders.

This book is dedicated to changing mindset. I want professional analysts to realize that uncertainty is core to finance, not peripheral. The market isn't some knowledge machine grinding out approximately ideal prices. It is a learning machine that continually errs, corrects itself, and makes new errors.

The scale of error makes us moan. Societies rend and nations lose their way over mania that later looks idiotic. Long-term inevitabilities get obscured by noise.

The scale of error correction makes us marvel. Capital markets forge consensus vision out of the dreams of millions of people, temper it in the fires of observation, and harness resources and will toward realizing it in practice. No one who has not witnessed huge capital markets would believe they exist.

Never has it been more important to keep both tendencies in mind. The world as a whole is the richest it's ever been, and growth is nearly the fastest. Yet debt imbalances are outpacing gross domestic product (GDP) and appear unsustainable. Financial analysts who can't draw the connections endanger those they serve.

On the practical side, this book offers some approximations to help track uncertainty. Mostly they're just stylizations of what traders already do. They aren't perfect. They can't be. The best model would require an infinite number of calculations every instant.

There is a broader lesson here. Every practical application makes do with error-correcting approximations. Sometimes these approximations work terribly and unleash a plague of market demons. Eventually the error correctors kick in and help rectify the mistakes.

From a learning perspective, both apostles and foes of free capital markets should curb their enthusiasm. On the one hand, markets deal in consensus beliefs rather than truth. Following like lemmings can lead us off the cliff. On the other hand, markets are awesome error-correcting mechanisms. Stifling what regulators don't want to see or hear often transforms downturn into disaster.

Confusion about the strengths and weaknesses of markets has fomented some rotten regulation. It lets some big excesses go unchecked, while exaggerating the importance of minor signals. It encourages statistical fraud. From a learning perspective, we need to simplify the regulatory framework and encourage more fiduciary responsibility.

Other overheated disputes pit orthodox finance against behavioral finance. Orthodox finance tells us how markets should operate, given well-informed participants acting in their own rational self-interest. Behavioral finance emphasizes the abundance of counterexamples and links them to human irrationality. Treating the market as a rational learning machine can help transcend the divide.

Last but not least, a learning perspective can improve portfolio management services for retail investors. Standard approaches expose them to far too much risk in crises. As we shall see, this is remarkably easy to mitigate. While it won't completely level the playing field with wealthy investors, it will reduce the "Dooh Nibor" (reverse Robin Hood) effects that prevail now.

The Context of Finance

To appreciate the importance of learning in finance, let's go back to basics. Life forces a trade-off between risk and reward. By venturing out to eat, I expose myself to being eaten. Brains evolved in large part to raise the munch-to-munched ratio. Risk analysis is what they do. Financial risk analysis is simply a special case, focused on investments.

Broadly speaking, financial risk analysis makes three kinds of assessments. The first kind rates the pleasure or pain of the possible outcomes. The second kind forecasts the relative likelihood of these outcomes. The third kind estimates the uncertainty fogging our projections.

In practice it is hard to say where valuation ends and risk or uncertainty estimation begins. Imagine, for example, a strawberry. What is eating it worth? On reflection, that depends on ripeness, flavor, and other qualities not evident on sight. Perhaps the strawberry is harboring a stomach bug. Or perhaps a stomach bug one already has will make the strawberry unpalatable. That happened once to my youngster, leaving a red stain on the carpet as memento.

We could, if we wanted, distinguish a host of specific strawberry-eating experiences, assign likelihoods to each, and gauge our uncertainty. Both brain and gut would soon tire of the effort. To simplify, we bundle choices and outcomes, define a bigger action like "buying a strawberry and eating it," and compare that action to other actions in terms of rewards, risks, and uncertainty.

For more complex risk analysis, consider the joint action of planting a strawberry field, tilling it to harvest, and marketing the crop for profit. Here we have to guess both the strawberry yield and the future price per strawberry. Granted, we might lock in one or both with a futures contract, but that just transfers the risk analysis to someone else.

For still more complexity, consider the purchase of a strawberry farm. Now we must analyze a succession of strawberry fields, one year after another. The further we peer into the future, the more wobbly our estimates will be. We will not know what strawberry-growing innovation might appear, what pests might infest the area, or whether future customers will prefer blueberries. We will not know the future tax regime on strawberry fields or the option value of selling the farm to a real estate developer.

Next imagine a giant agribusiness. It operates many farms producing many different products, runs various processing plants, and engages in a host of trading operations. Diversification and vertical integration lower some product-specific risks but heighten exposure to macroeconomic risks.

Finance weighs risks against rewards in search of higher or more secure profit. When finance gets it right, it raises the average munch-to-munched ratio and encourages productive investment. Occasionally finance gets things spectacularly wrong and wreaks havoc. Sometimes, too, it cannot resist munching on the people it is supposed to serve.

These contrasts between treasure and trouble, between promise and peril, naturally fascinate observers. They inspire envy and dread, admiration and contempt. Finance is awesome and awful.

One of the strangest features of finance is its self-absorption. Its most earthshaking decisions can seem divorced from studies of the earth. Most financiers are most concerned about what other financiers will think. This adds another layer of risk, but a strange, self-referential one. To invoke Keynes, a financial market is like a beauty contest aiming to pick not so much the greatest beauty as the one the judges will pick.

This makes financial markets terribly prone to herding. They can chase after bad ideas or run too far too fast after good ones. Those who resist can get trampled in a stampede.

However, there is a positive side to this. To appreciate it, let's transform our imaginary herd of cattle into a hive of bees. The bees go out looking for nectar. Not knowing where it is, each starts looking on its own. When one bee finds it, other bees find out. Perhaps they hear directly. Perhaps they notice telltale pollen on the discoverer's feet. Perhaps they just follow the buzz. Soon a swarm forms. The swarm becomes a better indicator of pollen than any individual bee. That is the wisdom of the hive.

As best we can tell, the wisdom of the hive generally outweighs the horrors of the herd. Economies with financial markets tend to be much more productive and innovative than those without. In the twentieth century, Communist states tried to prove the superiority of market-light planning. They failed miserably. The Soviet bloc collapsed. Only China thrived economically, and only after it reversed course and let markets guide planning.

Note that this is an empirical inference about financial markets, not a theoretical one. Note too that our confidence falls far below the standards of proof in natural science. We have observed a few dozen market-phobic industrializing societies, not a few trillion. We haven't rerun Soviet experience substituting different planners.

But that is the norm for financial risk analysis. Our inferences come from relatively few experiments, most of them poorly controlled. Consequently our conclusions are more tentative than in natural science and prone to more frequent and bigger readjustments.

Learning About Learning

Market learning is now a mainstream topic in economics. Pastor and Veronesi (2009) have recently surveyed the developments. I too have tried to popularize these themes in the narrower circle of finance practitioners interested in theory (Osband 2002–2005, 2008).

However, financial risk analysis still treats learning risks as peripheral. It is stuck in a mindset akin to that of physics in the early twentieth century, which clung to classical mechanics despite the accumulating refutations. Arguably it's stuck worse. Whereas physicists never blamed dumb matter for messing up theory, finance theorists frequently blame dumb traders.

How can we best change mindset? I wish I knew. Rigorous treatments get dismissed as dry or incomprehensible. Popular treatments leave professionals unconvinced. This book will try something in between. It will lead a study tour.

Our tour will visit some of the biggest financial risks in the world and explore major uncertainties at their core. We will watch markets unite, stretch, and defy beliefs. We will witness the damage that comes from ignoring uncertainty. We will look for neat ways to rebuild.

As the tour guide, it's my responsibility to keep things lively and not too long. I will mix topics and approaches that don't normally get mixed and draw analogies that don't normally get drawn. I will ignore most caveats and keep intimidating terminology to a minimum. Where models scream out with policy advice, I will let them.

To those prizing neat results, I offer a few delights. We'll expose the statistical confusion implicit in conventional risk measures and discover superior alternatives. We'll decouple safety from certainty. We'll link market turbulence to learning.

In return, I'm going to ask a lot from participants. Readers ought to have a sound grounding in economic history, finance theory, and statistics. They should be interested in economic policy. They should enjoy mathematical modeling. They should love thinking outside the box.

If you're rusty in these areas, that's okay. I'll try to keep the exposition clear and provide references for deeper study. I will route most of the math to the Appendix so that it doesn't overwhelm the flow.

One thing I won't ask is complete agreement. Some of what I'm saying is surely wrong; I just don't know which some. For fairness, I will let two august critics weigh in at the end of every chapter.

If you're not sure it's worth investing the time, skip to the Conclusions in Chapter 12. If they all make perfect sense, you don't need to read the book. If none makes any sense, you won't want to read the book. I'm aiming for the persuadable middle.

Itinerary

Money (Chapter 2): Every day people sell real goods and services for ciphers simply because everyone else does. It's never certain that money will keep its magic, and sometimes it doesn't. Yet modern civilization is unimaginable without it. We'll uncover Mahserg's Law and watch it at work.

Wealth (Chapter 3): Financial wealth discounts future earnings in ways that have long puzzled theorists. We will see that the most plausible explanations invoke uncertainty. Forced to look backward into the future, people discount heavily for tiny fears of disasters and prize perceived safety.

Debt (Chapter 4): Debt trades current money for future money with interest. If wealth grows fast enough, debt can potentially be repaid indefinitely out of rollover. This tempts self-financing bubbles of debt. We'll examine a model in which patently worthless debt stays low-risk for long periods before blowing up. The model is too close to reality for comfort.

Banking (Chapter 5): Banks tend to be more interested in borrowing short to lend long than in facilitating payments. This makes the financial system more fragile and cycle prone. Regulators have inadvertently exacerbated the risks. To better appreciate the dynamics, we'll model credit spreads and debt stocks as a predator-prey game.

Safety (Chapter 6): Many credit markets behave as if they're inferring from only a few dozen years of relevant observations. We can best model their beliefs as highly dispersed distributions. The uncertainty calls for much larger contingent reserves on top-rated credits than standard regulations assign.

Regime Change (Chapter 7): Risks often change with little notice, rendering past observations obsolete. We can use dynamic mixtures of simple models to track change robustly. Still, tiny doubts can evolve into big differences. Using a cumulant expansion, we'll see that predictability is severely limited. That's why markets trade so much.

Credit Rating (Chapter 8): Credit rating is far more complex than the simple counting game at its core. Still, uncertainty pervades ratings and deserves more disclosure. This needn't make ratings gyrate wildly. In analogy to magnetism, a mild preference for agreement on relative safety can induce remarkable stability.

Portfolio Derivatives (Chapter 9): Large portfolios are commonly rated for risk as if losses are bound to fall close to the mean. This can be wildly inappropriate, especially for senior debt tranches. Ignorance, greed, and bad regulatory incentives have driven gross misuse verging on fraud. We'll examine some healthier alternatives.

Value at Risk (Chapter 10): Standard Value-at-Risk (VaR) methodology pretends to superior identification of the risks of large market losses. Instead, it indulges the common fallacy of extrapolating from small losses and needlessly sacrifices precision. We can do much better by tracking short-tem volatility and allowing for uncertainty.

Resizing Risks (Chapter 11): Most discretionary traders scan price charts for channels. Orthodox finance theory regards this as voodoo. In fact, the practice provides substantial insight into uncertainty. The extra information can warn of crisis and help investors dynamically resize their portfolios. However, it can never completely tame market risk.

Risk Versus Uncertainty

Before we embark, let me clarify some basic concepts and alert readers to relevant scholarship. For more analytic discussion, see the Appendix. I will start with the distinction between risk and uncertainty.

Financial risk means different things in different contexts. Counterposed to reward, it refers to exposure to possible loss. Counterposed to determinacy, it refers to a spectrum of potential outcomes. Counterposed to uncertainty, it refers to an objective probability distribution independent of the observer.

The juxtaposition of uncertainty to risk harks back to Frank Knight's *Risk, Uncertainty and Profit* (1921), which defined uncertainty as unquantifiable risk and treated it as one of the cornerstones of economics:

Uncertainty must be taken in a sense radically distinct from the familiar notion of Risk, from which it has never been properly separated. . . .

There are far-reaching and crucial differences in the bearings of the phenomenon depending on which of the two is really present and operating. . . . A measurable uncertainty, or "risk" proper, as we shall use the term, is so far different from an unmeasurable one that it is not in effect an uncertainty at all. It is this "true" uncertainty, and not risk, as has been argued, which forms the basis of a valid theory of profit and accounts for the divergence between actual and theoretical competition. (Knight 1921: chap. 1)

John Maynard Keynes (1937) echoed Knight's concern:

By "uncertain" knowledge, let me explain, I do not mean merely to distinguish what is known for certain from what is only probable. The game of roulette is not subject, in this sense, to uncertainty. . . . The sense in which I am using the term is that in which the prospect of a European war is uncertain, or the price of copper and the rate of interest twenty years hence. . . . About these matters there is no scientific basis on which to form any calculable probability whatever. We simply do not know.

The influence of so-called Knightian uncertainty waned for two main reasons. The first was Knight's aversion to quantification, embedded in the very definition he used. The second was the rational expectations revolution, launched in hindsight by Muth (1961) and gaining influence through the work of Lucas (1972), Sargent and Wallace (1973), Sargent (1979), Stokey and Lucas (1989), and others. Rational expectations tended to presume that people correctly anticipate risks.

In my opinion, both Knight and the reaction against Knight went overboard. Knight confused mathematical formalization with precise measurement. Knight's critics confused ignorance with stupidity.

I say that as someone who easily gets confused too. Suppose someone hands me a coin and ask me to check it for fairness. Seeing no obvious blemish, I toss it 100 times and count 52 heads. That's reasonably close to 50 (less than 0.5 standard deviation for a fair coin), and I don't expect perfection in every sample, so I start to say it's fair. Then I wonder. If there's no suspicion of bias, why am I asked to check? Come to think of it, how sure am I that other coins are perfectly fair?

Real life rarely poses questions as crisply as we would like. At one extreme we can stress our inability to know. At the other we can assume a competitive market has zoomed in on the correct odds. This book will focus on the learning process that goes on in between.

Quantification of Uncertainty

Reconciling uncertainty with probability theory is a challenge. A measure should be something we can agree on. If we're uncertain enough, we likely can't. According to game theory, two people who disagree can never fully agree on what they disagree about.

The simplest resolution, which dates back to the Reverend Thomas Bayes (1764), treats beliefs as subjective probabilities. Its main tool is a rule for updating beliefs given new evidence. Known as Bayes' Rule, it is embedded in the concept of conditional probability itself. In effect it operates the laws of probability in reverse. Bernardo and Smith (2000) provide an excellent overview of Bayesian theory.

Probabilistic beliefs are closely related to ideal market prices, as Bruno de Finetti (1931b, 1937) emphasized. Bayesian probability represents the maximum willingness to pay for a claim paying one if the event occurs and zero if it doesn't. Given a complete set of option prices, we can potentially infer an entire spectrum of beliefs. From this perspective, any rational bettor behaves as a Bayesian.

Nevertheless, the application of Bayes' Rule is fraught with controversy. In mingling distorted beliefs with sound ones, it muddies the notion of statistical truth. For generations the statistics profession split into rival camps, with a majority opposed to so-called subjective probability and a minority favoring it.

Mark Twain solved the mystery over who wrote the plays credited to Shakespeare by declaring that it wasn't Shakespeare but someone else by the same name. In that spirit, I declare that beliefs are not probabilities but something else that behaves the same. Only now I have to immediately undercut myself by noting that beliefs about probabilities fly around a lot more than the probabilities themselves. That's why credit spreads oscillate so much more than default risk.

Markets mix objective risk with subjective uncertainty and sometimes mix them up. So do the planners who oversee markets or intercede. Everyday speech adds confusion by referring to both hypotheses and degrees of conviction as beliefs. However, for mental clarity let us try to keep the following division in mind:

Concept	Objective Risk	Subjective Uncertainty
Applies to	observed outcome	imagined cause
Described by	probability	conviction (belief)
Core difference	same for all observers	in each observer's head
Characteristic behavior	relatively persistent but may change	wanders noisily around objective risk
How to measure	actual payoff	maximum willingness to pay
Observations needed for 100% accuracy	infinite	one
Example	credit risk	default perception implied by credit spread

Straightaway, this division creates a problem. Objective risk is usually deduced from principles of symmetry, making certain kinds of events equally likely. If not, we should have enough same-but-different samples (the technical name is "independent, identically distributed," or i.i.d.) to estimate the probabilities to high precision—e.g., a billion trillion subatomic collisions of identical type. How can we obtain that kind of clarity in finance?

The short answer is we can't. While we may liken default or other outlier event to the roll of a die, its measure can't be pinned down nearly as well. Finance deals, in effect, with dice that are not fair, might get switched between rolls, and are subject to freak interference. The objectively measurable risk, if there is one, gets shrouded with subjective uncertainty.

In personal interactions, we can see that others' uncertainty adds to our risk and vice-versa. In financial markets, beliefs reverberate even more strongly on real investment and growth. George Soros (1988) dubbed the feedback loop "reflexivity".

Hence, the division is largely heuristic. However, it does embody one core truth. All knowledge derives ultimately from observation.

What happens if the events of interest are so rare, or our vision so restricted, that even years of observation provide little genuine news? Then we won't know very much. That's far more common in finance than we care to admit. Still, it doesn't change the core updating rules associated with rational learning.

In fairness, let me acknowledge that one can embrace uncertainty without accepting the definition or relevance of rational learning. Nassim Taleb's best-seller, *The Black Swan: The Impact of the Highly Improbable* (2010), falls into this camp. Taleb provides numerous reasons for doubting the rationality of ordinary mortals. He also is skeptical of Bayesian inference, particularly where rare events are concerned (Douady and Taleb 2010).

Instead of debating these points, this book conducts an extended thought experiment. It treats market prices as assessments of subjective probability while portraying objective risk as heavily veiled. It assumes that market participants make rational or near-rational probabilistic inferences based on inherently limited information. It then works out the consequences. I find it remarkable how much weird financial behavior this can explain. Keep reading and I think you'll agree.

～

"Did you hear?" asked Pandora. "Osband agreed to write the book."

"I heard," said Prometheus. "Only the outline seems incomplete. Where's your equation? Where are all the puzzles it solves?"

"Be patient. First he has to motivate the questions. We've had millennia to think about them. And people don't like to think about uncertainty. It makes them anxious. They'd rather fight or flee open risk than have it lurk in the shadows."

"I don't see why. They've done a good job embedding uncertainty into quantum theory."

"That took generations. Even Einstein resisted. And physics doesn't have to grapple with stupidity the way finance does. When atoms don't do what theory predicts, no one says, 'Oh, the theory's fine, that's just atoms being foolish.' In finance it's the gut reaction."

"So how does theory make progress?"

"It splits in two. Finance theorists can win Nobel prizes either for explaining how investors ought to behave or for explaining how they don't. No evidence need refute anything, just get categorized right."

"That doesn't sound healthy."

"It isn't. I hope this book will help mend the rift."

"Then why hive off the math from the intuition?"

"To some people, even in finance, higher math is torture."

"That's ridiculous! Math is relief from torture. I once spent a decade pondering Euclid before I noticed the eagle eating my guts."

"You're super-human. They're not. Look, all he's asking you math types to do is page to the end and come back. It's a minor annoyance, I know, and it's not fair. But the nonmath types can't jump over the math; they look down, get scared, and run away."

"If they can't stand the heat they shouldn't be in the kitchen."

"They are in the kitchen, like it or not. Or they run kitchens. They need to know what's brewing."

2

The Ultimate Confidence Game

Every day we exchange useful goods and services for mere symbols of value, on little more than the conviction that others will do the same. The exchange in turn helps justify the conviction. When crises expose the underlying fragility, other symbols vie to replace. Money proves the power of belief; it fosters massive division of labor and knits economies together.

Financial markets chronically confuse beliefs with reality. That's their job, along with unwinding the confusion and helping make beliefs real. They're so pervasive that we ordinarily take their smooth operation for granted.

To rekindle our sense of wonder, this chapter focuses on the safest thing we know in finance: cold hard cash. What is it? What makes it safe? How does it evolve? As we will see, uncertainty and learning permeate what we think we know best.

Money as Liquidity

To give is better than to receive. This is especially true of money. I give you some ciphers; you give me something I can directly use.

This inequality renders most commerce absurd. When two people trade, neither wants to get ripped off. The values exchanged ought to be approximately equal.

Fortunately, the stores I frequent don't realize that. They encourage people to cart away valuable items or have them delivered. All they demand in return is the deposit of qualified symbols with the cashier. These symbols are nearly always government-issued paper known as fiat currency, or electronic claims to the same. Their direct usefulness apart from trade is negligible.

Sometimes a government desperate for revenue prints fiat currency with wild abandon. As inflation spirals into hyperinflation, people stop accepting it for exchange. They demand another currency or payment in kind. That happened in Germany after World War I, with dire repercussions. It has happened in other countries too, most recently in Zimbabwe.

But none of that seriously worries my providers. Consequently, even though I am no fool, I don't insist on payment in kind for my own goods and services. In fact, accepting fiat currency has a lot of advantages. It is easy to count, easy to transfer, and easy to use for comparisons. Best of all, it's easy to sell quickly, at very low transaction costs and limited wobble in purchasing power. I call that liquid. The real goods and services I offer are much less liquid.

Curiously, these rational calculations on my part encourage others in their apparent foolishness. They confuse my willingness to accept fiat currency with lack of worry. Indeed, some of them dare to claim that they're unusually rational and accept fiat money only because of the apparent foolishness of people like me.

In short, fiat money is the ultimate confidence game. People sell real values for known tokens just because everyone else does. That confidence is incredibly useful. It weaves together a decentralized, global division of labor. It encourages longer-term investment. It can even support itself, up to some ill-defined point. But it also bodes huge risks.

Are you wound up yet? I hope so. We take money far too much for granted. But before you panic, let me confess to exaggeration. No money is normally devoid of intrinsic value. The Appendix provides more nuance.

Historically, money arose out of barter, the direct exchange of goods. Barter is inefficient because it requires a double coincidence: each must want what the other offers. When wants don't match, traders quickly realize the merits of extending the circuit. But it's hard to juggle a simultaneous multilateral exchange.

To simplify, find a useful good that is easy to transport, store, measure, and divvy up. Call this the money-good M. If ten people all sell their surplus goods for M and buy their wanted goods with M, the eleventh has an incentive to join in. In this way the orbit of M naturally grows.

Consider the savings. If there are n goods, and if we are looking to trade them without getting ripped off, we don't need to remember the fair exchange rates of all $\frac{n(n-1)}{2}$ pairs. The $n-1$ prices of every other good against M will suffice.

The division also helps distinguish two concepts: the direct usefulness (also known as worth, utility, intrinsic value, or use-value) of a good and its opportunity cost (also known as fair price, economic value, or exchange-value). Usefulness breeds individual satisfaction. Opportunity cost measures the sacrifice entailed. Money enshrines the latter.

As trade expands and the underlying division of labor deepens, goods and services become commodities, produced more for sale than for direct use. Common exchange for M tends to iron out divergences and to create a measure of social costs. M can also be used to hoard claims on future goods or to repay old debts. This helps gauge trade-offs between investment and current consumption.

In the process, M gains a new kind of usefulness, based on its ease of resale. Ease of resale means that new buyers are easily found and that the bid-ask spread—the gap between proposed buy and sell prices for immediate trade—is low. When money is easy to resell, market participants can convert economic value from one commodity form to another quickly, at low risk, and with minimal transaction cost. Trade works like a good engine, with minimal friction and wasted energy.

To the extent that we have any other aim than resale, money isn't really money. It's just a commodity, like gold bought to make jewelry. Conversely, insofar as a good serves as money, any other use is mostly wasted, like gold jewelry melted down into bullion. That's why fiat money appeals, provided confidence can be maintained.

Ease of resale has a shorter name: liquidity. In economic terms liquidity reflects a positive network externality. Whoever enters a market makes it easier for someone else to exit. The more we trade with money, the more liquid it becomes.

Liquidity in turn buoys money. In the early nineteenth century, Britain switched from a silver monetary standard to gold, mostly to reduce the size of large-value coins. This should have cheapened silver. It didn't. As Friedman (1992) explains, the proximate cause was French and U.S. bimetallism. The two countries tended to coin whichever metal was overvalued at a fixed rate of 15 or 16 to one. Moreover, the French demanded a lot of precious-metal coin, reflecting the lingering memory of hyperinflation during the Revolution. While silver lost ground in Britain, it gained ground in France and the United States.

In the 1870s, that dramatically changed. Defeated by Prussia in 1871, France was forced to pay large reparations convertible into gold. Silver plunged, and to avoid high inflation France demonetized silver in 1873–1874. Over the next few years most of continental Europe followed suit. So did the United States, in one line of an 1873 bill that attracted little attention at the time but later would be denounced as the crime of the century.

Official demonetization broke the long-standing parity. It took 16.4 ounces of silver in 1873 to buy an ounce of gold, and 18.4 in 1879. As silver's confidence network weakened, gold appreciated even more, transmitting deflationary pressures throughout Europe and the United States. The exchange rate was 30 in 1896, when a populist backlash in the United States failed to roll back the gold standard.

Liquidity as Perpetual Put

To probe the value of liquidity, it is helpful to define it more crisply. Here is my best stab:

> Money is a perpetual American put.

More precisely, money embeds a perpetual American put on itself, priced at its strike.

Let's walk through this definition. A put is the right to sell a security at a given price, known as the exercise price or strike. An American put adds the right to sell at any time before expiry, as opposed to a European put that can be exercised only at expiry. A perpetual put never expires. Hence money gives you the right to sell it whenever you want, for the price of the money. Beck and Stockman (2005) take a similar approach, except that they express this as money's call on other goods and services.

Like other options, the value of money's put depends on the current price of the underlying asset, its volatility, and the opportunity costs of waiting. It just can't depend on time to expiry, which is infinite. The optimal strategy is to wait for money to get dear enough and then sell. Equivalently, one can buy other goods when they become sufficient bargains.

In the base case, price is already enough of a bargain for something we want to consume. We resell our money as soon as we find it. Keynes (1936) called this the transactions demand for money.

Some money we hoard, in case a change of circumstances raises the effective returns from a particular good or service. A sudden thunderstorm or illness strikes, so we sell some money for an umbrella or medicine. We lose our job, so we sell money for food. Keynes called this the precautionary demand for money.

Sometimes we bet on the option value itself. If we expect others to be desperate for liquidity tomorrow, we might buy money today to resell to them. Perhaps the market will realize that money has been underpriced, allowing us to resell it against foreign exchange or gold. Keynes called this the speculative demand for money.

Thus, viewing money as a put embraces all of the demands famously categorized by Keynes. But does it embrace them enough? Keynes emphasized speculative demand because he was impressed and appalled by the strength of its fluctuations. Another renowned observer of financial crisis, Karl Marx (1887: chap. 3), commented even more passionately:

> On the eve of the crisis, the bourgeois, with the self-sufficiency that springs from intoxicating prosperity, declares money to be a vain imagination. Commodities alone are money. But now the cry is everywhere: money alone is a commodity! As the hart pants after fresh water, so pants his soul after money, the only wealth.

Absent crisis, precautionary and transaction demands should be relatively stable for the economy as a whole, while speculative demand should be limited. Under these conditions, money velocity, as measured by the gross value of transactions divided by the money supply, should be relatively stable. When it is, the inflation rate should move one-to-one with the growth rate of money supply.

However, if risk surges, precautionary demand will surge with it. This raises the value of money relative to goods and excites a speculative demand betting on the trend. If baseline inflation is modest, the extra demand for money may induce outright deflation, a fall in the price level. As long as this is expected to persist, cash promises a positive real return.

Puts that Fail

To best appreciate the merits of money, study societies that tried to do without it. There aren't many, outside those tied together by family or tribe.

During the civil war that followed the Soviet revolution, Soviet leaders tried to run the entire economy by commands only. The experiment was so disastrous that the Soviet leaders never banned money again, and indeed reintroduced a ruble tied to gold.

However, when the command economy regathered strength, it restricted cash rubles to retail trade. The core circuit involved wage payments from state enterprises spent on goods from other state enterprises. The state fixed prices, often at levels far from their opportunity costs, and taxed away all profits. This created huge inefficiencies. Nevertheless, for the next 50 years the Soviet leadership kept money in rough macroeconomic balance, by keeping wages low and letting high-priced alcohol and durable goods sales soak up excess savings.

Gorbachev's reforms worsened the balance in two ways. First, to reduce drunkenness they curbed state alcohol sales. Second, to promote efficiency they allowed state enterprises to invest or disburse some of their cash ruble profits. Neither reform achieved its aims: moonshine production swelled, and state enterprises continued to produce goods worth less than the resources they consumed. But they did inflate nominal take-home pay while curbing redemptions in retail trade. Nominal savings soared, and the ruble tanked on the black market, while labor incentives soured further (Osband 1992).

Excess saving meant the puts embedded in the ruble were failing. To revive them, price controls had to be abandoned. When they were, the huge surge in nominal inflation, hitting people accustomed to fixed prices, further undermined confidence. In reaction, the various Soviet republics clamoring for independence issued their own currencies or proxies.

The collapse of the Soviet ruble caused tremendous hardship. There were people who had worked for years in the frigid Arctic, living in primitive camps, in return for exceptional wages that would one day buy them an apartment in Moscow and a car. Suddenly they lost everything.

Ironically, the tiniest republic, Estonia, was the first to reestablish monetary confidence. It tied its money to the deutsche mark in a currency board arrangement, backing cash 100% by mark reserves. Currency boards piggyback on the confidence in the reserve currency, asking only the marginal faith that the issuer will keep its pledge.

The rest of the republics were too proud or confused to try anything so mechanical. They stumbled in monetary wilderness for years before they re-stabilized. In the meantime their people transferred confidence to a former archrival. For much of the 1990s the demand in the former Soviet

Union for cash U.S. dollars rivaled the demand for cash in the United States itself.

Money in Crisis

As noted, money in crisis can easily become a superior investment. It offers a positive or only mildly negative real return when most investments are crashing and tends to be negatively correlated with crash intensity. Demand for money soars.

While the shift is rational for each investor, it is dysfunctional for the economy as a whole. When investors hoard money, goods pile up unsold and production sputters. Without sales, debtors cannot repay their debts, so risk premia rise on credit and strengthen money's attraction as a countercyclical safe haven.

If strong enough, this yields the "debt deflation" cycle at the heart of Fisher's (1933) theory of great depressions. Keynesians speak of a "liquidity trap." It is monetary authorities' second biggest concern after spiraling inflation. The chief economist at the International Monetary Fund (IMF) has recently suggested raising inflation targets to counter the cyclical risks (Blanchard, Dell'Arricia, and Mauro 2010).

Resisting the contraction has dangers as well. If money jumped immediately to a high crisis price, it would trigger a tremendous transfer of wealth, hugely painful to the losers. But it wouldn't necessarily trigger expectations of deflation going forward. Indeed, expectations of deflation are tantamount to belief that the adjustment hasn't gone far enough. This is the essence of the Austrian critique of intervention—e.g., von Mises (1940). Defenders of intervention, like Orphanides (2004), counter that it is simply necessary to infuse liquidity more consistently, until deflation expectations are extinguished.

Regardless of policy response, the problem itself amazes. Money gains value through the confidence game that it enables and the social division of labor it facilitates. When that division of labor falters, one might expect money to crumble. Instead it gains even more importance as a driver. Why?

The core reason is that a money-driven economy is organized more from below than from above. Individual agents take the context of relative prices and wealth as given and adjust to it. If that context is upset, they will cling even harder to options in the new context. Confidence has to be rebuilt to get the real economy back on track.

The U.S. dollar gave a vivid illustration in the second half of 2008. For most of the previous two years, the dollar had been sinking relative to other major currencies, gold, and oil. Investors were concerned at the growing cracks in the U.S. economy and the Federal Reserve's apparent bias toward easing. Lehman Brothers's crash in September confirmed that problems were even worse than imagined; the Fed responded with its most dramatic loosening ever.

Instead of tanking on the vindication, the dollar soared. It soared even against gold and silver, tradition's favored stores of value in crisis. Gold plunged 20% in two weeks.

The core reason was disruption of the payments system. Through accident, apathy, and avarice, monies needed to settle short-term trading debts were mingled with longer-term investments. Demand depositors rushed to withdraw, triggering bank runs around the world and more disruption. But the payments still needed to be made, so that raised the premium on the world's most widely accepted, easiest-to-use payments medium—the U.S. dollar.

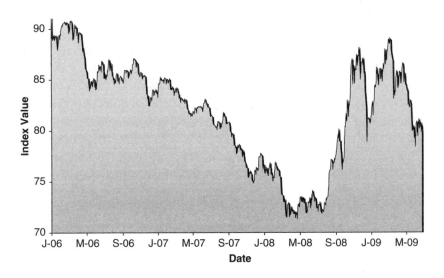

Figure 2.1
Dollar Index (DXY)

Granted, we cannot verify that linkage in the way a physicist would, for many factors determine market price and we cannot run a well-controlled experiment. Nevertheless, most economists now believe that the dollar's resurgence in the second half of 2008 was driven by thirst for liquidity. That is largely because of what happened after. Once liquidity reappeared, the dollar resumed its downward trend. Figure 2.1 charts DXY, an index of the dollar's value versus a basket of other currencies.

Mahserg's Law

The sticking power of money is so great that money often seems a free lunch for the issuer. Still, over time, good money drives out bad. Good money means money that—

- Is easy to identify, certify as genuine, and measure.
- Is guaranteed acceptance as legal tender for payment.
- Is not threatened with much loss through expropriation, inflation, devaluation, physical decay, or sacrifice of direct use.
- Is easy to store and transfer through banks, preferably at interest rates that approach the risk-free rate.

Gresham's Law claims the opposite: bad money drives out good. By that it means that under bimetallism, with two currencies having the same legal tender, the currency with less intrinsic value will circulate. As we have already observed, a low intrinsic value is a good quality for money, not a bad one. When we use gold for transactions that we could do with paper, we're wasting precious metal and sacrificing portability to boot.

Hence, Gresham's Law doesn't actually prove what it purports. Note too that Gresham's Law distinctly fails when the two currencies are legal tender in different countries. Otherwise Manhattan taxi drivers would carry around wads of Mexican pesos, and the euro would have built around the Greek drachma rather than the German mark.

I call the historical tendency for good money to drive out bad Mahserg's Law. Mahserg spells Gresham in reverse. Gresham's Law is just a special case of Mahserg's Law.

The troubling part of Mahserg's Law is how slow-acting it often is. That stems from the network externality involved in money. Once established, the standard gains a lot of inertia. Indeed, as we have seen, it can appreciate in the crises that expose its weakness.

Inertia prompts abuse. At first the dominant issuers retain the discipline that made the currency top dog. But when they do falter, the market's acquiescence tempts a repeat, until eventually the exception becomes the rule. This triggers the emergence of alternative global monies and standard-setters. These cycles are the most prominent international expression of Mahserg's Law.

The last 150 years have witnessed three major cycles of monetary standardization. The first—and in many ways grandest—cycle is known as the classical gold standard. It might be better called a pound sterling standard, as most countries held their reserves in sterling, while the Bank of England managed the price of gold. In its colonies, Britain introduced currency boards tied to the pound. World capital markets were arguably freer in the early twentieth century than they have ever been since.

However, the gold standard cracked during World War I, when Britain and other European powers resorted to massive deficit financing. Afterward, Britain had trouble restoring old parities without triggering a major recession. The gold standard was abandoned during the Great Depression.

The Bretton Woods agreement of 1944 jump-started the second cycle of standardization. Chastened by the competitive devaluations and isolationism of the 1930s, Western policymakers resolved to establish a stable pro-market environment under U.S. hegemony. The dollar, whose exchange rate against gold was set at $35 per ounce, became the main reserve standard, with most other currencies tied directly or indirectly to it. Extraordinary recovery and new growth ensued.

The dollar standard began to unravel in the 1960s on the back of declining U.S. competitiveness and growing fiscal profligacy. The loss of competitiveness resulted less from what the United States was doing wrong than from what postwar Europe and Japan were doing right. The fiscal profligacy, however, was self-made. Borrowing for "guns and butter," the United States financed both an expensive war in Vietnam and growing social entitlements. Gold prices had to be floated in 1971, and major currencies broke free of the dollar. The 1970s and early 1980s saw high inflation and slower growth with very volatile exchange rates.

The United States maintained world economic leadership, however, and gradually put its macro house in order. By the late 1980s, a third cycle of standardization took shape. The dollar reigned, but not on its own. An autonomous mark and yen provided both competition and support.

Standardization accelerated after the Soviet bloc collapsed. Western European currencies tied themselves more closely to the mark, while German monetary policy took on a more pan-European perspective. This led to the formation of a unified euro. The euro convincingly outperformed the dollar in value retention and stability and gradually built up capital market support. Most other countries tied their currencies to the dollar or euro or managed an exchange-rate band versus a mixture.

Now this cycle is drawing to an end. The main culprits, once again, are the declining competitiveness and growing fiscal profligacy of the old standard setters. The loss of competitiveness is a tribute mainly to China, the new manufacturing center of the world. The profligacy once again is self-made, consisting of expanded health and retirement benefits that must be financed either through crippling taxes or spiraling debt.

Money Watching

To better appreciate the scale of uncertain risk, consider foreign exchange reserves at central banks and monetary authorities. These holdings, consisting mostly of short-term, low-interest bills from U.S. or European governments, are kept mostly as precaution against crisis. They have mounted by over $5 trillion in the past decade and now constitute a significant share of a year's global GDP. See Figure 2.2.

The holders naturally view their reserves as part of their national wealth, and could, if they wanted, sell them for goods and services from the United States or Europe. If they did, the inflationary impact on the United States and Europe would be severe; transfer would significantly affect consumption and perceived wealth. It would also likely accelerate the adoption of a Chinese yuan-based monetary standard, fulfilling Mahserg's Law.

However, Americans and Europeans rarely count foreign reserve claims as deductions from their wealth. They rarely think how they can work harder, export more, and consume less to satisfy the mostly poorer foreigners lending for their health care and retirement. Nor do they consider that a sounder monetary standard, with a greater foundation in Asia, would likely slash foreign holdings of U.S. and European IOUs. In that sense, one side's confidence is the other side's disbelief.

The confidence game supporting the world economy succeeds or stumbles in ways that no authority can completely control. Usually it is extraordinarily resilient. Occasionally it is shockingly fragile.

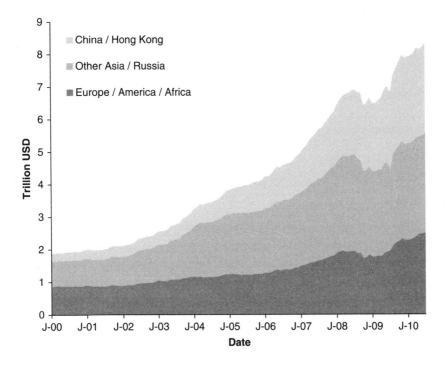

Figure 2.2
FX Reserves in Trillion USD

The importance breeds two types of monetary oversight. One type, typically calm and high-minded, is conducted at central banks and monetary authorities. It aims to bolster overall confidence by smoothing fluctuations in liquidity. The other type, typically frenetic and avaricious, is devoted to monetary market speculation. It aims to profit off fluctuations in confidence and differentials in liquidity.

To do their jobs, each side has to keep close watch over the other. Monetary authorities continually try to track market confidence and manage expectations. Speculators continually try to anticipate the news monetary authorities are looking for and how they are likely to respond. Tiny clues on sentiment or policy can be enormously telling.

Curiously, even when monetary authorities telegraph their intentions as publicly as possible and try to minimize the potential for surprise, arbitrage may aggravate systemic risks. For many years the Fed excluded asset price inflation from the price indices it tried to contain, with one notable exception: it cut rates when asset markets tanked. Traders called this the Greenspan put, after the Fed chairman who promoted it. Moreover, from 2003 to 2006 the Fed raised interest rates only gradually despite evidence of overheating. The combination helped feed a housing bubble, although it is far from the only contributor.

This book will keep returning to issues of boom and bust, exploring them from different angles. None of these explorations yield a cure. However, the weight of the evidence suggests that occasional jolts might be useful in building resistance to larger crashes.

Forest fire management provides a useful analogy. For decades it aimed to prevent all fires. Modern foresters appreciate the usefulness of small fires in clearing brush.

Financial risk analysis can stay agnostic on these issues. But it can't ignore them. The potential instability of money is one of the main risks markets face.

~

"I don't get it," said Prometheus. "Is fiat money intrinsically worthless or not?"

"That's an ill-posed question," said Pandora. "But the basic answer is yes. It's worthless because the sovereign has no intention of redeeming it in full and likely can't. It's worthy because people can pay taxes with it and trade it to others needing to pay taxes."

"That would seem to make it more worthy than unworthy, as long as the sovereign makes taxes onerous enough. People don't have to like an institution for it to be effective."

"Osband suggests that fiat currency can stick even without high taxes. People just need shreds of doubt about imminent collapse and a small willingness to trust others."

"He suggests a lot more than he proves. Where are those neat results he promised? He needs to model beliefs directly."

"He's just getting started, Prometheus. Give him a chance. Besides, I liked his discussion of Mahserg's Law. Good moneys turning bad, sometimes overnight. Better moneys battling inertia, sometimes for decades. And he's right to view liquidity as a network externality."

"He needs to set his sights higher. Trade of current goods and services for money can't explain more than a fraction of the mysteries. And while precautionary and speculative demands point to the future, they don't point far enough."

"Humans are creatures of the present. They can't help it. That's why money hangs together. So much evidence of money working gushes forth that it quenches doubt. I think that's what Osband is driving at."

"You call that driving? Without more mathematical horsepower, all he can do is putter. Besides, most financial wealth consists of claims that won't be realized for years. How do people gauge what they're worth? He needs to address that."

3

Great Expectations

Most financial wealth aggregates future earnings that we can't directly sample. We have to look backward into the future. In practice we discount heavily for tiny fears of disaster and prize perceived safety. It gives economies a tremendous incentive to boost confidence—sometimes beyond the capacity to deliver.

Money symbolizes wealth at hand. However, most wealth isn't at hand, and we couldn't consume it now if we tried. It is a claim on future value. We can never measure future value. We can measure only past value, current trends, and expectations for the future.

Expectations can't be consistently right, because no one can predict the future. Expectations won't be consistently wrong, because markets part fools from their money. We scramble between error and error correction. It's called learning.

Learning rocks and rolls our wealth. Between 2003 and 2006, most Americans stopped saving out of income, because their houses and equities saved for them. In 2008 $10 trillion of their wealth—and $50 trillion worldwide—vaporized, without war, hellfire, or alien invasion. The adjustment was only on paper and electronic chits. Yet the material and psychic tolls have been enormous.

Given the dangers, wouldn't it be better to stop forming half-baked expectations and wait to invest until we know? No, it wouldn't. We can't know until we try. Besides, asset markets force us to choose. Whether we buy, sell, or pass, we implicitly compare the price to fair value and reveal something about our expectations. That revelation in turn influences others and helps shift the consensus view.

This chapter explores the transformation of expectations into asset value. I will start simply, assuming a constant rate of growth. I will then introduce various layers of risk and uncertainty and sketch the implications for pricing.

Remarkably, asset prices suggest we're cowards, while investment behavior suggests we're not. This puzzle has had the economics profession scratching its head for decades. The most plausible explanation is that asset prices respond more to fears of rare disasters and fears of others' fears than long-term investment does.

Discounting the Future

Imagine an asset that pays a dividend of 1 every future period, from now to eternity. While the sum of all future returns is infinite, no one will pay infinity for them. Let P denote the asset price today. If we pay it, we collect 1 next period plus a residual asset that pays 1 from the second period on. By symmetry, the price of the residual asset will be P in the next period, provided the market environment stays the same.

Hence the market implicitly values $P + 1$ next period as worth P today. The implicit interest rate r is given by the dividend ratio $1/P$. Usually we flip this around, regard r as given, and value the risk-free stream as $P = 1/r$.

Next imagine an asset whose dividends start at 1 and grow at a constant proportional rate g. By symmetry, the asset price must also grow at that rate. In equilibrium, the dividend ratio plus the capital gains rate must match the risk-free rate r. Hence, the dividend ratio must be $r - g$.

In practice this relation gets muddied by differential taxation on dividends and capital gains. Let's ignore this, or assume that r and g are given in post-tax terms. Let's also ignore inflation, or assume that dividends are measured in constant real prices.

Typically, r won't exceed g by more than a few percentage points. People aren't that impatient, and growth tends to be positive. Hence the price-to-dividend ratio $P = \dfrac{1}{r - g}$ will be a few dozen or more.

No wonder, then, that wealth greatly exceeds current returns. It also follows that wealth will be very sensitive to g, holding r fixed. A shift of half a percentage point may change asset value by a quarter, half, or more.

Indeed, if g consistently exceeds r and dividends are positive, price should be infinite. That's not a sustainable equilibrium. Instead of paying out dividends, asset managers will reinvest them. Asset claimants will borrow against future wealth. To bring demand back in line with supply, interest rates must rise or forecast growth must fall. Now for the mysterious part: how do we forecast g? Ideally we would like to peer into the future and measure growth until the average settles down. Because of discounting, nearer years count for more than far. So let's try to make it easy on ourselves and peer only far enough to capture, say, 95% of the present value. How short a foresight will suffice?

Let's think about it. Every year we extract $1/P$ of asset value in dividends. After T years, residual value shrinks to $\left(1 - 1/P\right)^T \cong e^{-T/P}$. To reach $0.05 \cong e^{-3}$, T must be approximately $3P$.

Hence, we'll need to look ahead a century or so to capture 95% of value. Think how hard that is. It is hard even if we ignore the particularities of the asset and think only about the economy as a whole.

Imagine gathering the world's wisest seers in 1900 and asking them to forecast economic growth over the next century. Would they predict assembly-line manufacture, two world wars, highways clogged with cars and trucks, mass expansion of university education, computers on semiconductor chips, and the Internet? Would they predict the improvements in life expectancy and health, the impact of women's emancipation and retirement benefits on the workforce, and a population explosion that flattens out? Would they predict the retreat of global markets in favor of capital controls and central planning—and its rebound decades later?

Let us help them. Let's stuff a bottle with all that information, douse it with a charm potion that makes all who read believe, and smuggle it back in time. Our enlightened seers would still likely misestimate the impact on productivity and the rate of growth of wealth, unless our message explained that too.

To make forecasting easier, let us settle for capturing half of present value. That will chop our foresight needs down to a quarter-century or so. It will still be extremely difficult to predict the impact on economic growth.

Technological Progress

To better grasp change, science seeks to identify invariants—for instance, properties that stay constant in change. One wannabe invariant in economic growth is technological progress. In war or peace, by car or foot, under capitalism or socialism, humanity seeks to innovate. Innovation helps produce more and better for less.

However, no natural or social law dictates the pace of innovation. For most of history it seems to have been slow. For the past two centuries it appears to be accelerating but we can't be sure the exception is the new rule. The uncertainty reflects an age-old struggle between know-how and resource depletion.

DeLong (2001: chap. 5) provides some summary statistics, drawing on various sources. From 1000 B.C. to 1800 A.D., for the world as a whole, GDP per capita is estimated to have grown to $250 from $160, as measured in year-2000 dollars. Over the same period, world population is estimated to have grown to 900 million from 50 million. Combining the two estimates, real GDP grew 31-fold in 2,800 years. That works out to 0.12% real GDP growth per year and less than 0.02% per capita per year. If GDP actually grew twice as fast, the average growth rate edges up to 0.14% per year.

Granted, we don't know the relevant resource constraints. It is harder to support the billionth person than the fifty millionth. Still, innovation was sluggish by modern standards and mostly absorbed by population growth. People lived and died with little sense of overall enrichment.

Growth accelerated in the Industrial Revolution. From 1800 to 1900, per capita GDP more than tripled to $850 while population nearly doubled to 1.63 billion. That works out to 1.2% per year per capita and 1.8% for real GDP.

Growth accelerated again from 1900 to 1950: 1.8% per year per capita and 2.6% for real GDP. The second half of the twentieth century saw even faster growth: 2.8% per year per capita and 4.7% for real GDP. See Figure 3.1.

It is tempting to extrapolate this to the skies. The information revolution provides a plausible mechanism for acceleration, namely the ease of information sharing and new learning. Even if growth merely stabilizes at late-twentieth-century rates, discount rates may have to rise substantially to keep us from feeding off future nirvana.

Heady optimism ten years ago—see Kurzweil (1998) for an imaginative depiction of the coming century—helped propel the dot-com bubble in asset markets. Perhaps it will come back in vogue. However, there are numerous grounds for caution:

- Recent and current growth may embed a one-time catch-up factor as know-how spreads to laggards.
- We are gorging on a subsurface bounty that preindustrial technology couldn't reach. We are rapidly depleting fuel reserves, mineral

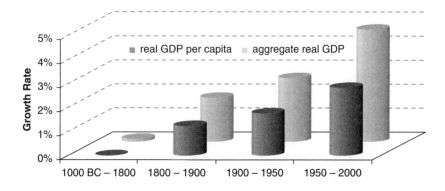

Figure 3.1
Average Annual Global Real GDP Growth

deposits, and underground aquifers accumulated over hundreds of millions of years. If scientists and engineers don't find cheap alternatives, standards of living could stagnate or even decline.

- Rapid growth tends to be socially destabilizing. While China and India are catching up to the developed world, most of Africa, the Middle East, and central Asia are not. Radical Islam is feeding on the backwardness it nourishes, and demographics are working in its favor. Meanwhile the developed West has hamstrung itself through entitlement pledges it cannot keep. In the struggle for spoils a lot of wealth will get spoiled.

- Human pressure on the environment might reach a tipping point, where growth is curbed either through disaster or preemptive regulation. In some ways it already has. We know neither the rate of escalation nor the costs of deferred action.

Looking Backward into the Future

Clearly, the available evidence on growth is open to widely diverging interpretation. Given the implications, why doesn't the market agonize about it more? The short answer is that it doesn't pay enough to care.

A longer answer distinguishes three causes: price offset, immediacy, and herding. The price offset stems from the positive correlation between average growth and the discount rate. Higher growth makes future goods and services more plentiful. The anticipated bounty makes us want to consume more even today. With current goods just as scarce as before, the discount-rate premium on them rises.

Indeed, depending on the structure of consumer preferences, the equilibrium r may move more than the equilibrium g, so that rapid overall growth cuts the present value of long-term assets. Many economic models inadvertently exaggerate these effects. Still, the evidence for a substantial price offset seems strong.

Immediacy refers to the time needed to wait for vindication. Nobody will know tomorrow whether today's guesses about the long term are right. Hard evidence trickles in slowly. All the market will tell us is which guesses gain popularity.

Speculators seeking a marginal edge are likely better off studying popularity than principle. Will carbon cap-and-trade keep oceans from rising in 2030? Investors can hardly be bothered. Will carbon cap-and-trade make it through Congress? Now there's something to trade on. Blaming traders for fad ideas is like blaming music executives for fad music. They're not looking for soundness; they're looking for what will sell.

Investors who do want to bet on real growth are best off focusing on differentials between countries, industries, and specific companies. The narrower focus makes it easier to build and maintain an edge. The growth itself is less vulnerable to a price offset.

Herding stems from the inherent inscrutability of long-term growth. Most of us shade our views toward the consensus, figuring that others know something we don't. This makes the consensus even more inertial than the trickle of evidence would suggest. Growth estimates change slowly.

That's not wholly bad. Convictions that oscillate widely tend to paralyze. We do nothing, or waste a lot of effort undoing what we did before. Critics who fault the market for error largely miss the point. It's like criticizing a dog for singing off pitch. The marvel is it sings.

But we shouldn't idolize the market either. Weighting opinions by moneyed convictions doesn't make the average right. It is especially likely to err when the forecast is far-reaching and the evidence thin.

The market knows this and adjusts by using proxies. The closest proxy for the future growth we can't see is the growth we just saw. That doesn't mean the two will match, or even that they will run parallel. But there should be some relation. On that basis we can test our forecasts against the evidence and modify our hypotheses about the future.

Each small modification sculpts our view of the future. It chips away here and adds there. It corrects old mistakes and makes new ones. Once in a while a great shock persuades us to toss out our old views and start over. Even then we look backward at some other history that seems more relevant. We're forever looking backward into the future.

Granted, we don't always look backward. We glance sideways; we scan the ground for clues; we peer into the sky. Piecing together the evidence as best we can, we close our eyes and imagine peering into the future. It is a wonderful proxy, except when it isn't.

One lesson for policymakers is not to abdicate their long-term responsibilities. No, the market won't punish them for it. Even when it recognizes what can't help but happen, it discounts heavily for not knowing when or how. But the future will punish a society for continually deferring what needs doing. When nobody saw it coming, it usually means nobody was looking.

Rates on Equities and Bonds

The risk and uncertainty of future growth shatter one discount rate into many. The less certain a future return, the less we'll pay for it unless its risk neutralizes other risks. As a first approximation, we can distinguish a risk-free rate for safe bonds and a risky rate for an economy-wide equity index. The difference is known as the risk premium.

Empirically, these rates are hard to measure. Actual bonds carry inflation, devaluation, and default risks, while equity returns are prone to long swings. Also, data are concentrated in the second half of the twentieth century, when a long market boom exceeded most expectations and so did inflation. This made bonds look richer and equities cheaper than they were likely intended to be.

Nevertheless, the evidence seems overwhelming that the risk-free rate is less than 3% while the risk premium exceeds 2%. In the late 1970s and 1980s, economists began calibrating their models to match this behavior. To their surprise, they couldn't. Indeed, standard models had trouble generating either a low risk-free rate or a high risk premium.

Over the past quarter-century, the rate puzzles have attracted more attention than any other controversy in finance theory. To this day there's no completely satisfying answer, or at least economists don't agree what it is (Mehra 2008). That already tells us something. If the ideal calculation of asset pricing baffles experts, we can hardly blame real asset markets for being erratic.

On balance, three answers resonate most with theorists. The first is that the risk premium reflects an aversion to occasional severe losses. The second is that people value future consumption for more than its direct thrills; the anticipation provides peace of mind or social stature. The third roots the risk premium in market uncertainty itself. The Appendix reviews the controversy and relates the answers to the puzzles.

If any of these explanations hold, discount rates on equities and bonds will depend critically on what we believe about the future. These beliefs are inherently wobbly, as new evidence continually rolls in and triggers reassessment. Hence, learning make asset valuations chronically unstable.

Granted, we could infer chronic instability just from the historical evidence. However, any specific experience can always be attributed to exceptional conditions or bad judgment. Theory reveals that markets upset our plans even when they act the way they're supposed to.

Because of this instability, long-dated bonds carry considerable mark-to-market risk even if payment is guaranteed. The obvious antidote is to trade long-dated bonds for short-dated bills. As Chapter 5 will show, bank regulators ignore this at society's peril.

The usefulness of short-dated bills in offsetting other kinds of risk can drive the risk-free rate well below the rate of time preference. In the aftermath of crises, when confidence has tanked, the real risk-free rate can be negative. Central banks' prime motive for targeting positive inflation rather than zero inflation is to discourage hoarding of risk-free cash and bills.

Yet if money is never allowed to be a safe haven, Mahserg's Law will favor other moneys. Hence central banks wobble between shoring up liquidity and taxing it. This wobble adds another layer of risk to asset valuation.

Regime Change

One of the biggest risks in markets is that the risks themselves vary. Markets can be calm for months or years on end, only to become extraordinary volatile and stay volatile for a while. Prices can trend upward for years, soar to new peaks, and then crash and slide. While a stable distribution of risks could in principle generate these shifts, the odds defy imagination. Instead we view one set of risk parameters—mean return, volatility, and so on—as giving way to another. This is called regime change.

Regime change can be needlessly confusing. For example, a classic random walk moves left or right one unit each period with probability $\frac{1}{2}$. We could redefine this as two completely stable trends, one moving left and the other right, with a 50% chance each period of a regime switch. But that's silly. Regime switching is best reserved for changes that can't be modeled more simply and have a large cumulative effect.

Many regime changes are rooted in real shifts in growth. As David and Wright (1999) explain, innovation comes in waves. Some major discovery or invention, like railroads or electricity or personal computers, captures popular imagination. Initial results usually disappoint, as other work practices need to change to make full use of the innovation. Eventually the infrastructure becomes more supportive, while people figure out new ways to tap the innovation. Productivity surges until the innovation becomes the new norm.

For example, while electric power was commercially available in the United States before 1900, it did not become a vital driver of production until electrical machinery and assembly-line production were invented. The main associated productivity boost occurred between 1919 and 1929 as factories reorganized. Peace and reengineering provided a bullish foundation for the Roaring Twenties.

The potential for regime change opens a Pandora's Box of interpretation. Once we allow risk parameters to shift we can never identify them precisely. Even the way we update our estimates is inherently fragile, as we shall see.

This fragility has immense significance for markets. If we knew the risks we were dealing with, asset prices would behave a lot less strangely than they do. They wouldn't bounce around so much or in such irregular ways. Markets wouldn't trade so frequently, or shake out so brutally.

Noisy growth and possible change in trend make for a potent combination. Sentiment swings between excess optimism and excess pessimism. Herding can aggravate the swings, as it encourages people to invest on momentum.

In other words, bad crises can start with things that are genuinely good. The good makes people feel better, which makes the real economy better and people feel better still. Eventually things become too good to stay true.

The Actuary Approach

Financiers handling other people's money tend to belittle regime change. The Canadian insurance industry offers a welcome exception. At one time, it provisioned for losses on long-term equity investment as if they were in-dependent deviations around a long-term mean. Thanks to work by Hardy (1999) and a responsive regulatory culture, it now takes regime switching into account.

Intuitively, extended runs of good years or bad years raise the odds of extreme outcomes. Like Moses's forecast of seven fat years followed by seven lean years, a regime-switching approach warns to lean against the current trend. It increases provisions in good years, reduces them in bad years, and penalizes products that aren't robust.

Figure 3.2 charts the impact of regime switching on index returns for the Toronto Stock Exchange (TSE), using parameter estimates from Hardy (1999). The horizontal axis represents the pretax percentage gain after five years from investing in TSE. Gross returns are spaced logarithmically to offer a clearer view. The vertical axis marks the probability density associated with each gain.

Compared to an ordinary lognormal density, the regime-switching density is squashed in the middle and fatter in the tails. It is also skewed downward. That's because bad news, while rarer than good news, is far more likely to repeat itself with regime switching than without.

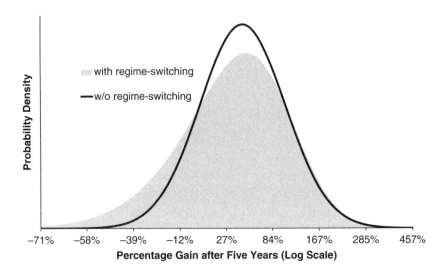

Figure 3.2
Estimated Risks of Five-Year TSE Investment

According to Hardy (*Wilmott* 2009), a strong actuary profession facilitated these reforms. Unlike most finance, where anyone who can say "yes, sir" and "nobody saw it coming" can legally sign off on risk, insurance risk requires certification by licensed actuaries. Actuaries must pass rigorous exams, pledge a fiduciary responsibility to the public, and answer to an independent professional board. Canadian actuaries were actively involved in discussions of the new methodology, in regulatory redesign, and in implementation.

Actuaries still answer to their employers, who expect them to help devise profitable products. Since the employers pay them, that loyalty normally carries higher weight. But the fiduciary responsibility matters too. It offers protection and authority when an actuary feels a risk is fudged.

Senior insurance executives wouldn't dare override an actuary's principled objections, unless an actuary board backed them up. In most banks or investment funds, by contrast, senior executives swat down risk managers at their discretion. It makes for a huge difference in risk culture.

The actuary approach discourages a cat-and-mouse game between regulators and risk takers. Instead, it trains intermediaries to high standards. It prizes respectful consultations.

For bang prevented per buck, few reforms would be more cost effective than extending the actuary approach to banks and investment companies. Granted, this can't be done overnight. Most financial risk managers need much better training in finance, economics, and statistics, to achieve at least master's-level proficiency in each. It will be even harder to change the cat-and-mouse culture.

～

"I love history," said Pandora. "The long fallow years, the sudden explosion of growth or conflict. No seer can foresee all of this.

"No market can either," said Prometheus. "Why should people expect otherwise?"

"Investments don't require getting the future right. They require welding a consensus to undertake them, and correcting big errors along the way. That's where asset markets shine. The tarnish comes after, when people look back and realize what they missed."

"I see. They blame markets for failures of social imagination. How human."

"I thought Osband conveyed that reasonably well. Are you satisfied now?"

"He writes loosely. This is bound to confuse."

"Getting lost in caveats is bound to confuse as well. Discount rates are huge drivers of asset prices. People need to realize how mysterious they are."

"That's not enough. Look how much effort equity analysts invest projecting revenue streams a decade or more ahead. Then they pull a discount factor out of a hat, with an impact that rivals the earnings projections. Saying it's a mystery won't help them do better."

"The Appendix provides more detail for those who want it."

"Well, I want it and don't get enough. He writes down the discounting equations as if they're easy to solve. Where does he recognize the dependence on hard-to-verify beliefs? Where does he acknowledge turbulence?"

"Prometheus, those are standard omissions for finance texts."

"His is supposed to be different. When he started talking about cumulants and the importance of small doubts, I thought he was getting warm. But he didn't follow through."

"You mean he hasn't yet followed through. Give him time."

"I'm not sure he's up to it. Tell him to start with the simplest case: debt that either pays in full or defaults completely."

4

Sustainable Debt

Debt trades current money for future money with interest. If wealth grows faster than the rate of interest, debt can potentially be repaid indefinitely out of rollover. This tempts self-financing bubbles of debt, which historically have ended badly. But hope springs eternal, buoyed by real prospects for growth or belt-tightening. The current era is the most hopeful yet.

Mammon, the false god of finance, is justly derided for avarice and injustice. Still, one has to admire his sense of humor. At one extreme he helps scrip pass for real wealth. At the other he buffets real wealth as if it were scrip.

Debt falls in between. As a deferred claim, it sacrifices the immediacy of cash. As a claim on money rather than profit, it insulates from many business hazards. Servicing should be semiautomatic, except when wealth falls short and forces default. Salvage after default should follow clear rules.

Nevertheless, Mammon manages to turn a square deal into a circle. A huge share of debt gets paid through refinancing. Lenders in effect lend to each other, with the borrower merely greasing the wheels. Borrowers' merit pales next to lenders' beliefs about their merit and their beliefs about other lenders' beliefs.

How sustainable is this circle? Can it twirl forever on its own anticipation? Or is it like a toy gyroscope pulled by a string, which eventually wobbles to a halt? The answer turns out to be the latter, but with a caveat on "eventually." The spin can outlast the spinners.

Let me caution that there's very little learning in this chapter, apart from ex post regrets. Borrowers promise to repay fixed amounts, lenders know what the promises are worth, and payment circuits continue until they break. That's not very satisfying.

Still, we need this chapter as foundation for the rest. When we estimate the likelihood of default, we're not just interested in the borrower's capacity to pay on its own. We're interested in the capacity to pay out a combination of its own resources and rollover. With a finite horizon and full information, the two versions are essentially the same. In the open-ended, uncertain real world, it's not. This chapter focuses on the open-endedness.

Worthy Debt

Let us begin our analysis with worthy debt, which the borrower always repays out of its own resources. Imagine the debt is an ordinary bond, paying some riskless rB in interest every period it is outstanding and the face value B of the principal at the end. At redemption, the borrower can presumably issue another bond of equal size and duration to cover the principal repayment. In that case, the debt is said to be rolled over.

Apart from the principal changing form midway, the issuer might as well issue a single bond for twice as long. Repeat this ad infinitum and we create a perpetuity, a debt paying interest forever with no obligation to repay principal. Economic theory registers no objections, because the net present value over all interest payments matches the principal.

In practice, nothing is perfectly riskless, so the lender will demand a premium to cover the risk. However, if default is considered remote enough, the premium will be modest. Britain issued the first perpetuity in 1752. Called a consol, it paid 3.5% interest in silver, or more precisely in a pound tied to silver. Lender comfort allowed the interest rate to be reduced to 3% in 1757.

Now let us consider a twist. Suppose that when the first interest installment of rB comes due, a second perpetuity of principal rB is issued. As long as the debt remains worthy, holders of the first perpetuity shouldn't feel cheated. The issuer has simply reduced the net payment to zero in the first period, in return for paying $(1 + r)rB$ in all subsequent periods.

To repay interest in the second period, issue yet another perpetuity. Repeating this process creates a net repayment stream that is zero for the first T periods and $(1 + r)^T rB$ for every period thereafter. Since there is no limit to T, the borrower can defer net repayment forever. Voilà: something for nothing!

Clearly, something is wrong. We are banking too much on the never-redeemed principal: an infinite payment discounted infinitely to yield a present value of 1. Most theory treats that as taboo. Practice should be averse as well. If a borrower repays purely via rollover, lenders should be wary of locking in forever at zero risk premium.

To restore sanity, let us invoke the finite service capacity of the borrower. Suppose that the issuer is a sovereign country and cannot pay more than a fraction d of GDP each year for debt servicing. The maximum value of the bond stock is then d/r times GDP.

Even at this upper limit, the bond stock can still grow as fast as GDP without increasing the debt-to-GDP ratio. At a growth rate of g, the allowable increment in debt is $\dfrac{gd}{r}$ times GDP. Moreover, if debt-servicing capacity d grows, say through more efficient tax collection and public acclimation to transfers, the sustainable debt stock can grow with it. The combination helps explain why poor countries tend to default at lower debt-to-GDP ratios than rich countries.

As explained in the notes to the previous chapter, risk-free bonds often sell at a substantial premium, because they help hedge against disasters. This offers a kind of seigniorage to a worthy sovereign. Since average growth in a modern economy exceeds the risk-free rate, the sovereign can potentially earn even more seigniorage by letting the perpetuities or bond rollovers finance themselves. For example, if $r = 1\%$ and $g = 3\%$, then for every $100 the government issues this year via one-year bonds, it can issue $103 in one-year bonds the next, use $101 for servicing, and pocket the remaining $2 without worsening the servicing ratio.

If issuance stays within limits, no one need feel poorer for this. Although cash and bond holders will never on aggregate recover the assets they have lent forever, they feel reassured by the ability to redeem on demand (with money) or with interest for deferral (with bonds). They don't realize they are just lending to each other.

Hence, a state that borrows from Peter to pay Paul can look richer for its debt. Its people will feel wealthier, because their bonds and cash outweigh the marginal taxes the issuance necessitates. They will spend more, invest more, and pay more taxes. Moreover, because bond seigniorage potentially outweighs cash seigniorage, the sovereign is encouraged to keep inflation stable and bond servicing reliable. The circle of confidence that money sustains gains longer-term backing.

Keeping Faith

Harvesting bond seigniorage is a lot harder than it appears. Lenders are skittish because nominally risk-free lending is rarely free of risk. Imagine someone 2,500 years ago had lent the equivalent of $100 risk free at a 1% real interest rate, re-lent all the proceeds similarly, and persuaded all descendants to do the same. The bond portfolio would currently be worth over $6 trillion. Between default, debasement, and expropriation, financial wealth is much less secure than it appears.

On top of that, borrowing needs are strongest when the sovereign is weakest. A natural catastrophe or economic downturn crimps tax revenues when relief spending is greatest. A war destroys productive capital while demanding more support of the army. A sovereign that wants to tap cushions during crisis should pad cushions during calm.

The best way for a sovereign to reinforce lender faith is to occasionally wind down large debts, if not absolutely then at least in proportion to revenue-generating capacity. The greatest example ever came from the United Kingdom in its imperial heyday. The Napoleonic Wars left Britain with a public debt of over 250% of GDP in 1820. By the eve of World War I, nearly a century later, public debt was around 25% of GDP. This reduction was accomplished without either outright default or de facto partial default through unexpected inflation or devaluation. The pound was fixed at 113 grains of gold (7.3 grams) despite appreciation of gold relative to most other commodities. In return, British debt inspired enormous confidence around the world and helped underwrite British expansion.

In general, public debt to GDP surges in a war and retreats after. Figure 4.1 charts the gross U.S. federal debt as a percent of GDP, using data from Chantrill (2010). It shows the fiscal impact of the War of 1812, the Civil War, World War I, and World War II. The largest spike by far came in World War II. The sharp retreat after was driven in part by unexpected inflation, which can be viewed as partial default.

I have clipped the chart in 1974, when the U.S. federal debt share of GDP had fallen below previous wartime highs. Historical experience would have suggested continued retreat. Instead, debt shares headed up again on the back of entitlements expansion, tax cuts, and disinflation. The recent crisis has brought yet another spike.

Most other developed countries also show peacetime bloat, although the timing and scale differ. Figure 4.2 lists Organisation for Economic Co-operation and Development (OECD) members by gross central government

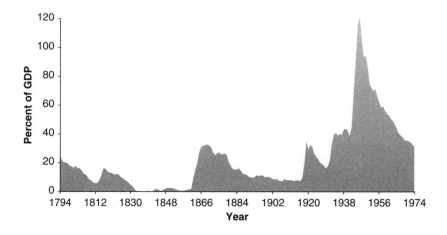

Figure 4.1
Gross U.S. Federal Debt as Percent of GDP

debt as a share of GDP, using data from OECD (2010). For clearer viewing the chart clips Japan, whose debt-to-GDP ratio exceeds 180%.

Will this debt prove worthy? We don't know. On the one hand, no fatal threshold has been crossed that guarantees default. Tax collection captures a much larger share of GDP than it used to, allowing sovereigns to whittle down big debts quickly if they make it a priority. On the other hand, few of the leading governments have made it a priority. They are relying on the public to roll over debt without reinforcing credibility through peacetime retrenchment.

Historical Perspective

The Anglo-American experience of the last two centuries is atypical. As Hoffman, Postel-Vinay, and Rosenthal (2007) note, sovereigns usually manage their fiscal affairs either much better or much worse. For example, the Ming Emperors of China often transferred huge quantities of grain from one region to another to address famine. But they did so without debt. They just seized the stockpiles, sent them where they wanted, and replenished the stockpiles through extra taxes.

Queen Elizabeth in England also managed her realm without big debts. She worked mainly with whatever Parliament provided, including when

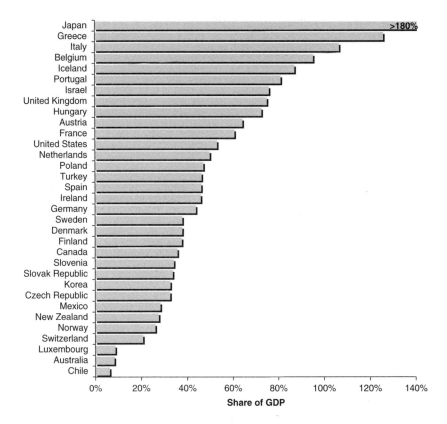

Figure 4.2
Central Government Debt in 2009 as Percent of GDP for OECD Members

battling the Spanish Armada. Granted, beating the Armada was largely luck, and she also cheated the system through grants of monopoly privileges to courtiers.

Debts remained minor until the Glorious Revolution of 1688–1689 cemented Parliamentary authority. The lender-dominated Whig Party helped keep Parliament prudent in authorizing debt and fastidious in repayment. Rates stayed low despite occasional sharp surges in debt issuance followed by long contractions while it was repaid. In war emergencies England would float short-term bills and later convert them to longer-term instruments, like the consols mentioned earlier. Without that foundation of trust, Britain's Napoleonic War debts would have been far more destabilizing.

French kings in the eighteenth century paid interest rates at least two percentage points higher than their English rivals paid, and frequently defaulted. Default reflected their chronic difficulty in covering military and court expenditures out of tax revenue. In 1788 Louis XVI convened the long dormant Estates General of elites, hoping they would vote a tax increase. Instead they insisted on constitutional reforms and hamstrung tax collection. The ensuing revolution financed itself through *assignats*, paper money that depreciated by a factor of 100 in five years. This ruined old lenders and crippled long-term French credit markets until the 1850s.

English and French experiences suggest that debt is more a symptom of a fiscal problem than a cause. Nevertheless, it can have a huge impact on the timing of a crisis, its intensity, its duration, and the eventual outcomes. The consequences can take decades to reveal themselves.

The revelations took even longer in sixteenth- and seventeenth-century Spain because of chronic uncertainty about the state's real means. Spain's unification had come at the price of restricted domestic tax authority, so Spanish kings financed their wars with bank loans and repaid them out of silver from Mexican and Peruvian mines. Unfortunately for both kings and creditors, the mines disappointed in output, while silver ships fell prey to storms, freelance pirates, or enemy fleets. Ten times between 1557 and 1662, the kings suspended payments and forced creditors to take long-term bonds called *juros* in partial compensation.

Curiously, these forced conversions did not ruin the debt market. They just injected a credit spread into short-term debt to cover the risks. The *juros* stayed relatively liquid and secure. Eventually, however, the decline in revenues forced Spanish kings to default on the *juros*. This wrecked Spanish financial markets and associated institutions like trade fairs.

Is this Time Different?

In an extensive empirical study of financial markets around the world, Reinhart and Rogoff (2009) conclude that—

- Financial crises are far more common than most people realize. The institutions we regard as sound grew out of many stumbles before and might stumble again.
- The most common trigger is domestic government debt. The devaluation, inflation, or defaults that typically ensue after a crisis slash

the government's real obligations and often are driven with that intent.

- Financial overoptimism often prolongs a reckoning, only to make the reckoning worse. Market participants don't see the huge credit imbalance, attribute it to superior productivity of the debtor, or find some other reason to believe that "this time is different."

- The latest crisis is huge by historical standards and will likely take years to fully play out. While equities often bounce back quickly, currency crashes and debt defaults have much longer time fuses.

One ominous sign in developed countries is the growth of quasi-sovereign debt. Quasi-sovereign debt is debt that the sovereign officially denies responsibility for but unofficially protects. It comes in three main types: sovereign-owned lenders and guarantors (like Fannie Mae and Freddie Mac, which subsidize housing mortgages in the United States), private banks deemed too big to fail (increasingly redefined to mean every large private bank), and major sub-federal governments (like the various European Union members or state governments within the United States).

How much the sovereign protects quasi-sovereign debt isn't clear, even to the sovereign itself. Typically it hints of enough support to encourage rollover at low rates while insisting that debt issuers ensure solvency on their own. The outcome depends on the force of external shocks, on the internal controls of the issuers, and on the politics within the sovereign.

The crisis in 2008 exposed weak links in the banking system, which we will examine in the next few chapters. Attention is now shifting to over-extended governments. The stronger sovereigns will have to either bail out the weaker or bear the fallout of default.

In Europe, commitment to the euro allowed weaker countries to piggyback on the credibility that Germany and several other European governments had built up over the decades. They borrowed at German rates without emulating German prudence. Debt-financed booms and deceptive accounting helped conceal the imbalances; crisis brought them to light.

The biggest offenders are Portugal, Italy, Ireland, Greece and Spain. Collectively they are known by the acronym PIIGS. A partial default through devaluation, followed by fiscal tightening and rejoining the euro zone at a more sustainable parity, appears the lesser evil economically but a last resort politically.

Turning to the United States, the states and leading municipalities of California, New York, and Illinois have mostly lost their fiscal bearings, with many others vying for dishonor. Ironically these tend to be rich states priding themselves on business talent and sophistication. Decades of political pressure from public-sector unions, optimism about revenues from capital gains taxes, and excessive discounting of future pension obligations encouraged profligacy.

By law U.S. states and localities are supposed to balance their operating accounts (which exclude interest payments on outstanding debt), and for most of their history they came close. However, the U.S. Government Accountability Office (GAO 2010a) estimates current state and local operating deficits at 0.8% of GDP absent federal stopgap relief, and worsening by 0.1% a year absent major policy change.

Ultimately such deficits will overwhelm the relatively modest tax take of state and local governments. And while the federal government might assume them, this compounds an already bleak outlook (GAO 2010b), summarized in Figure 4.3. Yet the bond market acts as if timely change is assured. Or does it?

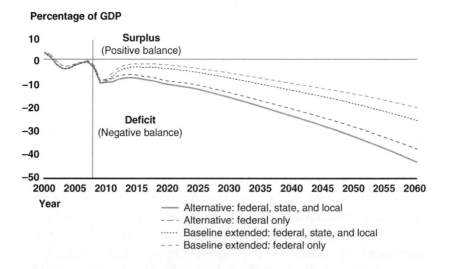

Figure 4.3
U.S. Budgetary Outlook (from GAO 2001b)

Worthless Debt

Our quick survey offers two visions of the future. In one, the world's sovereign mega-debtors keep repaying old debt with new debt and trim enough excess to retain confidence. In the other, debt eventually collapses on war, civil upheaval, or panic. Time will tell.

Given the history, financial markets seem remarkably confident in repayment. Perhaps lenders are projecting from recent decades. Perhaps they equate rollover with final repayment. Perhaps they believe that if no one else is worrying they shouldn't worry either.

To illustrate the forces at play, let us briefly examine the polar opposite of worthy debt. Worthless debt, as I will define it, cannot be repaid out of one's own resources and is not guaranteed rollover. The following model suggests that even worthless debt can be rolled over for a while, and possibly a long while, without making the debt sustainable in the long term.

To keep this simple, I will assume away every complication other than rollover. The operating budget, the risk-free interest rate, and growth will all be set at zero. The only challenge is to refinance one unit of outstanding debt.

In a full-confidence equilibrium, the sovereign pledges to reissue bonds forever. Creditors accept that pledge and refinance at the going interest rate of zero. The debt stays worthy.

Unfortunately, our economy is tinged with fear. The sovereign fears that creditors might one day redeem bonds without rollover, spend the cash on goods, and stoke a destabilizing inflation. Creditors fear that the sovereign might default and pay nothing. These fears are mutually reinforcing. The less assured creditors are of servicing, the more tempted they are to switch to goods. The less assured the sovereign is of rollover, the more tempted it is to default preemptively.

Let's assume some fear equilibrium is reached, where everyone agrees on the instantaneous default rate $\theta(t)$ at time t. That is, if the debt hasn't defaulted by time t, the chance of defaulting over the next short period dt is approximately $\theta(t)dt$. To counter the fear, the bonds offer a continuous interest rate premium $c(t)$, also known as a credit spread. Bondholders expect to lose everything under default, so their expected rate of return is $c(t) - \theta(t)$. As they are risk neutral, in equilibrium this must equal the risk-free rate, so that

$$c(t) = \theta(t). \tag{4.1}$$

Both principal and interest are paid by issuing new bonds. If $B(t)$ denotes the bond stock at time t, the growth before default can be expressed as

$$B'(t) = c(t)B(t). \tag{4.2}$$

where the $'$ denotes the first derivative.

To complete the specification of the model, let us assume the default rate is an increasing function of the bond stock. Specifically, I will model it as a power function. For some initial default rate θ_0 and positive constant m,

$$\theta(t) = \theta_0 B^m(t). \tag{4.3}$$

These equations have a unique solution. The survival rate $F(t)$, or probability of servicing without default until time t, is $(1 - m\theta_0 t)^{1/m}$, while

$$B(t) = \frac{1}{F(t)} = (1 - m\theta_0 t)^{-1/m} \tag{4.4}$$

and

$$c(t) = \theta(t) = \frac{\theta_0}{1 - m\theta_0 t}. \tag{4.5}$$

Initially, the bond stock grows so little that $\theta(t)$ stays close to θ_0. This phase may last a long time. For example, with $\theta_0 = 1\%$ and $m = 2$, it takes 25 years for θ to reach 2% and 40 years to reach 5%. See Figure 4.4.

Eventually, however, the bond stock resonates so strongly with default fears that survival rates plunge to zero. In the previous example, no debt can be refinanced for more than 50 years. More generally, the maximum rollover time is $\frac{1}{m\theta_0}$.

Hence, low interest rates don't imply that the market considers the debt worthy. They could just mean that debt hasn't yet mounted to levels that significantly jeopardize rollover. Conversely, surging interest rates and difficulties in rolling over long-term debt don't imply that creditors are trying to pressure the debtor. They could just mean that the debt has reached a tipping point.

The Appendix spices up the model to allow for economic growth, a positive risk-free rate, and a nonzero primary fiscal balance. While the expres-

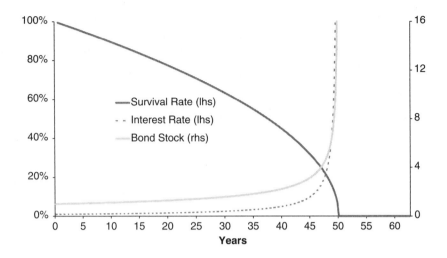

Figure 4.4
Worthless Debt for $\theta_0 = 1\%$ and $m = 2$

sions get messier, the main qualitative results stay the same. Beyond some threshold, debt becomes only temporarily sustainable. Yet for many years the market may not seem to mind.

The Appendix also explores some serious flaws in the model. Wholly worthless debt is no more viable than wholly worthless money. Nevertheless, I respect the model for clearly distinguishing between rollover risk and fundamental repayment risk, without divorcing the two completely. Models that assume either full congruence or permanent difference will face an even harder challenge in describing reality.

Prometheus was not impressed. "His debt bubble examples are too tame. Why not refer to the Trovidians, who built government debt to 30 times GDP before defaulting on every last farthing? The repercussions echoed through the galaxy."

"Not Earth's galaxy," said Pandora. "They can learn only from the disasters they know."

"Well, they're doing a great job of stoking a new one. Half of the world focuses on creating real wealth. The other half focuses on creating nominal wealth. This can't possibly end well."

"Many of Earth's leaders agree. That's why they keep feeding the debt bubble and enlisting more reputable funders to back it. They are trying to perfect the perpetually deferred perpetuity."

"That's terrible policy. Sure, sometimes a generation will borrow for rapid growth or to tide through a crisis. But don't spin profligacy into emergencies by indulging it for decades. Zeus knows how many kingdoms have crumbled over debt."

"Prometheus, the biggest debtors aren't kingdoms. They're democracies. The debt helps a lot of people live longer and better with less work, by drafting others to work for them."

"It's so unnecessary. The very advances that let people live longer and better will also let them defer retirement and pay their own medical bills. Why do they have to loot their progeny?"

"They don't see it that way. They see the payers as someone else's progeny, who might manage to defer the burden as well."

"Whoever their grandparents are, most of them can't vote yet. Wasn't it the Americans who revolted against taxation without representation? What if a real crisis comes and doubles their burdens? As for the European Union, what makes it so confident that Germans will keep footing others' bills?

"Their assurances of safety are very risky," said Pandora. "And no one who calls herself a financial risk analyst should forget it."

5

The Midas Touch

Banking arose as a means to facilitate payments. That remains its vital function. However, most banks focus more on borrowing short to lend long. This exacerbates the fluctuations of credit spreads and debt, which we can view as a kind of predator-prey game. Regulators have exacerbated systemic risks by prizing nominal safety over liquidity.

A grateful Bacchus, the god of intoxication, offered King Midas a reward of his choosing. Midas, likely intoxicated himself, asked that everything he touched turn to gold. It was a tragic error. What makes gold money is the ease of transforming it back into commodities. What Midas thought he gained he really lost.

Ever since, finance has sought to perfect the Midas touch. Imbue everything with "moneyness" simply by easing resale. Then extract a broker's fee for these services, or trade on speculation about future moneyness.

This intermediary role is both useful and suspect. Making assets more liquid gives more options to asset owners. They feel wealthier and will likely invest more. Yet liquidity can't do more than swap one material form for another. Brokers appear to leech on the interactions they foster.

At its best, finance cultivates confidence. It encourages people to trust the social division of labor and tap into it. At its worst, finance cultivates too much confidence, which then implodes into despair. Ironically, the financial regulations intended to tame booms and busts often serve to aggravate them.

This chapter explores the trade-offs. We will see how payment needs give rise to banking and how banking multiplies credit. Credit inflows reduce current default risks and bid up wealth in ways that are hard to distinguish from improvements in economic fundamentals. Conversely, credit outflows are hard to distinguish from fundamental economic deterioration.

Payment Systems

The usefulness of finance is most evident in large or remote payments. If we had to cart around all our money with us, protect it from theft, prove its legitimacy, and deliver it personally to vendors, the extra care would quickly wear us out. Banks arose to facilitate payments. Deposit money at one location and have the bank deliver the payment somewhere else.

The first bankers were money changers, who charged commissions for payments as they would for other exchanges. Measured as interest rates over time, the commissions generally exceeded 2% a month. It was more the liquidity the customers paid for than the deferral. The payments could be secured by either deposits or by goods in transit. Islam, which prohibits all outright interest on debt, has long been tolerant of trade finance.

Payment efficiency can be enhanced through aggregation and netting. If the goods shipping from London to Paris roughly balance in value the goods shipping from Paris to London, relatively modest inventories of money or liquid commodities can secure payments in both directions. With crisp accounting and reliable servicing, liquidity extends in time and space.

However, netting mingles credit risks. In a long chain of transactions, a single payment failure can put all at risk. It would be safer to insist that all accounts cover contracted payments and confirm that through immediate debit. Modern information technology makes that feasible at low marginal cost via giro accounts, direct debit, debit cards, and real-time settlement.

For most of banking history, debit clearing wasn't feasible, so the payment system evolved other methods of insurance. An early innovation, dating back to Roman times and still widely used in the United States, is the check. While a check is a promise to pay rather than payment itself, it acknowledges an obligation independent of other claims. This facilitates enforcement and invites third parties to add insurance. Notably, the bank that handles the payer's accounts might offer its own check, or a letter of credit that guarantees trade payments subject to proof of shipping.

Banks insure payments out of their own capital or the capital lent by others. As bank capital is hard to verify, banks cultivate reputations for caution and probity. Regulatory oversight and backing helps reassure customers. Still, bank capital remains the primary guarantor of credit risk. The ratio of debt outstanding to capital is known as the leverage ratio.

Nowadays many banks treat payments as mundane. Lending is where the action is. Sometimes banks will handle payments for free, just to get hold of money for loans. However, if an economy had to choose between two poisons, suspension of loans wreaks far less havoc than breakdown of the payments system.

One reason the former Soviet Union suffered so much in the early 1990s is that its payment system was geared to a slow ex post accounting among thousands of state enterprises. It couldn't handle millions of people suddenly seeking direct access to payments. As parts of the economy reverted to barter and other parts switched to dollars, the ruble lost value. This aggravated the cost of payment system delays and compounded the downward spiral.

While payment systems in developed market economies are far more technologically sophisticated, they can be sloppy in handling credit risk. Lehman's giant London-based brokerage provided a ruinous example when the parent firm failed in September 2008. While clients regarded the brokerage as the custodian of their assets (as it would have been under domestic U.S. rules), U.K. bankruptcy law treated the accounts as unsecured loans to Lehman. Panicked by the seizure, many investors closed out other securities accounts for safety, while lending against securities collateral temporarily dried up. This exacerbated the plunge in stocks, triggering margin calls that further strained liquidity.

Duration Mismatch

The safest payment systems require each payer to hold a positive money balance at all times, sufficient to settle any obligation coming due. For banks to provide similar guarantees to their customers, they must hold all demand deposits in short-term assets or cash reserves. Financial institutions that want to make longer-term loans will then have to secure longer-term funding.

Policies restricting banks in this way are known as narrow banking. Narrow banking has some illustrious proponents, including Simons (1934), Fisher (1935), Allais (1948), Friedman (1959), and Black (1985). Every great financial crisis tends to revive discussion; see Bossone (2002) for a thoughtful review. Clearinghouses and postal savings systems can be viewed as narrow banks. There are also analogues in Islamic banking (Al-Jahri 2004).

Banks rarely choose this path on their own. It is easy to see why not. Most bank customers maintain adequate liquidity for most transactions, without being forced. Since most calls for liquidity are effectively random, the individual reserves usually sum to excess reserves on aggregate.

Most of the time banks can lend out excess reserves without depositors feeling a pinch. Indeed, depositors may welcome this. The banks' profit on the loans and investments may subsidize payment services or boost interest paid on deposits.

"Duration," in financial parlance, refers to the weighted-average time of payment, with weights proportional to net present value (NPV). Deposits average much shorter duration than loans. Duration mismatch allows banks to create money. Banks prize that ability so much that many people think the prime function of banking is to "borrow short and lend long."

Like fiat money or debt repaid through rollover, duration mismatch adds to perceived wealth. Whether it adds to real wealth or simply inflates a bubble depends on context. Individual bank customers can rarely tell the difference. Flows from different sources are typically so interwoven that even experts find it hard to distinguish real wealth from masquerade.

To better appreciate the difficulty, consider the following thought experiment. A small volcanic island forecasts prodigious future wealth through high productivity growth, savvy entrepreneurship, and geothermal reserves. Borrowing in anticipation, it accumulates the highest per capita debt in world history and distributes the proceeds generously among the islanders. Within a decade the island's net debt is over six times GDP. However, domestic growth and islanders' holdings abroad are soaring, so perhaps current GDP is not a good benchmark. How truly sustainable is its debt?

If the government accumulates all the debt, it will be immediately suspect. The forecasts will seem too self-serving and other lenders' confidence too fragile. Realistically, most lenders will already have backed off, capping debt at much lower levels.

Suppose instead that most of the debt is accumulated by three government-owned banks on the island and by households who borrow from the banks. Thanks to rapid domestic growth and markups on foreign acquisitions, the banks report huge profits and a swelling capital base. This will likely instill more confidence in rollover. At least it should until analysts aggregate the accounts and form the same consolidated balance sheet as before.

To obscure this, let us restructure the island's banks so that they are private rather than state owned. Have them fund themselves mainly through deposits from households abroad, which they attract through Internet-based payment systems and premium interest rates. Keep banks' earnings margins positive by betting on the government's successful defense of a reputedly overvalued domestic currency, on a domestic housing and equities boom, and on an economic boom abroad. Keep the accounting sufficiently murky that analysts have to focus on the bottom line. Now the debt burden will look more sustainable.

Doubters should study Iceland. A country of barely 300,000 people, well integrated into the OECD and briefly one of its richest, would not appear difficult to monitor. Its economy underwent profound liberalization and reaped years of heady growth. In 2006, when financial markets started getting nervous about Iceland's huge current account deficits and bubble-like growth, a close colleague of Fed chair Ben Bernanke reviewed its finances and pronounced them sound (Mishkin and Herbertsson 2006).

Yet in 2008 Iceland's banking system—basically the central bank and three private ones—defaulted on the most debt per capita in history. The victims included nearly half a million retail depositors in the European Union and some of the world's leading investment banks. The Iceland stock market index, which had sextupled from 2003 to 2007, was essentially wiped out (Figure 5.1).

Too Good to Stay True

Like all crises, Iceland's was exceptional. Better luck, wiser oversight, or swifter response might have contained it. Nevertheless, it fits a broader pattern. The biggest crises start with things that are genuinely good and keep getting better, until eventually things become too good to stay true. Swings in financial leverage aggravate the boom and bust.

The core problem is our usual one. No market can pierce the veil of the present and measure output that has not yet been produced. It can only assess what was, what is, and what is believed will be. Good news makes the market more optimistic. Optimism raises valuations and lowers risk premia, adding more good news. While there are negative feedback loops as well, they don't operate as quickly and smoothly as we would like. The bolder and more justified the consensus shift appears, the more likely it is to overshoot.

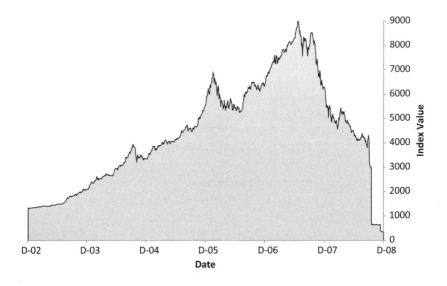

Figure 5.1
Iceland Stock Index (OMX 15)

In the late 1860s, the North's victory in the U.S. Civil War, the formation of the Austro-Hungarian Empire, and Bismarck's unification of Germany gave big boosts to capitalist development. The United States extended
railroads west, brought new lands under cultivation, and flooded central
Europe with cheap grain. Speculative railroad bonds sucked in British capital, encouraging rapid expansion. In central Europe, mortgage lending
triggered a real estate boom, which encouraged more borrowing despite
the erosion of competitiveness relative to the United States. After shrug-
ging off several financial scares, markets were overwhelmed in the Panic
of 1873. A severe depression engulfed the United States and Europe, with
profound economic and political consequences (Nelson 2008).

An even bigger boom started in 1922 in the United States. Reviving
after an unprecedented world war, upheaval across Europe, and sharp domestic contraction, the U.S. boom seemed to put the past behind. As David
(1991) emphasizes, electrification and the internal combustion engine rev-
olutionized industrial production and demand. Allowing machines to de-
tach from large fuel reserves enabled assembly-line manufacturing and
massive shifts in settlement and transportation patterns. Factor productivity in U.S. manufacturing grew faster than ever before.

Meanwhile, easy money and the spread of installment financing sparked a credit boom. Between installment loans, mortgages, and stock purchases on margin, total private credit in the United States was 410% of GDP, versus 240% in 1913. The corresponding expansion in the United Kingdom was even greater. Eichengreen and Mitchener (2003) call the Great Depression a "credit boom gone wrong."

Today the world is grappling with an even bigger boom gone wrong. The boom was founded on Pax Americana, a strong market orientation, the information revolution, resource abundance, and disinflation. A generation of strong growth naturally bred expectations of continuation. This drove up asset values worldwide and encouraged leverage. However, the dynamics varied considerably with the emphasis on investment or consumption. Conceptually we can distinguish a "Saveland" and a "Spendland":

- Saveland is fearfully diligent. It continually socks away surpluses for rainy days, rainy years, epoch-making floods, and influence over potential rivals. To keep its workers working and savers saving, it holds down its currency and lends to buyers of its goods.
- Spendland is fearlessly indulgent. It continually finds ways to monetize its wealth and borrow from it. To keep its consumers consuming, it lets its currency appreciate and seeks ever-expanding credit lines.

Debt-financed booms in Spendland gave it staying power. Housing prices spiraled up, padding household wealth and encouraging more financial innovation to tap it. Government spending rose faster than taxes, padding growth and price-to-dividend ratios. In effect, Saveland swapped current consumption for stakes in Spendland's housing appreciation.

With some oversimplification, we can use the United States, United Kingdom, and the PIIGS as a proxy for Spendland. Similarly, we can use Asia, the rest of Europe, and the oil-producing Middle East as a proxy for Saveland. In 2007, the two regions were close to each other in GDP, equity market capitalization and fixed income assets (IMF 2008). However, the trends were very different. Bank assets to GDP halved in Saveland while growing by over half in Spendland. Nearly all the extra banking leverage was tied to the housing market.

Over the previous decade, Spendland's gain in housing capitalization from new construction and appreciation exceeded 2007 GDP and roughly matched total equity market capitalization. Housing markets in Saveland were sideshows in comparison. In Japan and Germany, real housing prices declined by 20% to 30%, with little new construction. In emerging Asia, housing booms started from too low a base to have a dominant impact.

Housing booms in Spendland have since gone bust, taking down equities and GDP. Economic recovery has begun. But the banking systems remain fragile, and governments have overextended themselves in their defense. Lagging productivity growth, the implicit tax burden of high social benefits, and depletion of energy and groundwater reserves argue for substantial belt tightening. Yet the socialization of debt continues to defer a reckoning. Future generations will marvel at both the genius of rollover and its long-term costs.

Credit Orbits

In the model of worthless debt from the previous chapter, government fiscal policy is fixed, while default risk is a known increasing function of the debt stock. The debt burden stabilizes or spins out of control without provoking a change of policy, even though everyone anticipates what will happen. Let us now posit debtors and creditors as more adaptive and less anticipatory.

For simplicity, I will drop explicit references to time from the notation. Let r denote the current interest rate paid on the debt stock B. Suppose the debt stock B grows geometrically at rate $r + h(r)$, where the primary deficit h is a decreasing function of the interest rate r. That is, debtors try harder to wind down debt when interest rates are high. For more simplicity, imagine that h is linear with intercept a and slope $-b$. We can then write

$$B' = (r + a - br)B = (a - (b - 1)r)B. \tag{5.1}$$

For debt not to get infinitely high or infinitesimally low, both a and $b - 1$ must be positive.

All else being equal, r should rise with the aggregate servicing burden rB, since that raises incentives for default and investors' demands for insurance. However, a higher r helps reassure creditors that the debtor is trying to pay and that the risks are being compensated. Again assuming scalar coefficients, we write

$$r' = (Bd - c)r. \tag{5.2}$$

With full information and foresight, we ought to specify a default process and check that the risk premium fairly compensates for it. By ignoring this, our model implicitly assumes that creditors can't check to nearly the degree needed and just go with the flow. Should we believe that? Not fully, but our previous discussion suggests some elements are true, and many critics assert that they dominate. Let us briefly suspend our disbelief and work through the implications.

The system (5.1)–(5.2) is mathematically identical to the famed Lotka-Volterra equation, a stylized description of predator-prey interactions. In this case debt is prey and credit spread is predator. Any debt and credit spread combination we observe is bound to recur and hence can be viewed as a kind of equilibrium. Yet it will hardly ever feel like equilibrium. If we graph debt on the horizontal axis and credit spread on the vertical axis, the coordinates move counterclockwise in oblong orbits. Although there is a stable center, they never reach it.

An example is charted in Figure 5.2. A static equilibrium sets debt as 50% of GDP with a credit spread of 2%. Every other allocation orbits around it; arrows indicate the direction of motion. For small deviations

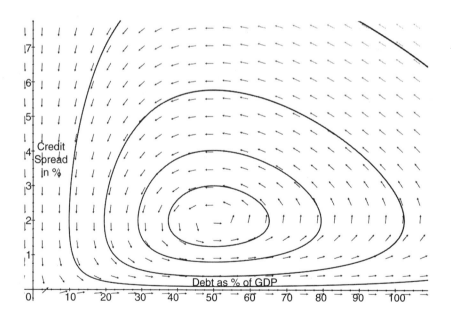

Figure 5.2
Examples of Credit Orbits

from equilibrium the orbit is nearly elliptical. For large deviations the orbit swings so wide that observers will fear the economy has entered a high debt/high credit spread trap.

Compounding the anguish, credit spreads will widen as debt shrinks, reaching their maximum at the equilibrium level of debt. Yet that same level of debt can recur later with minimum credit spread. The markets continually lag or overshoot.

The Appendix folds in two enhancements. The first makes fiscal tightening more than linear in the servicing burden, to allow for bolder response in crisis. The second makes the risk premium a decreasing function of debt growth, on the grounds that debt growth fuels near-term economic growth and eases rollover.

Under the first enhancement, credit orbits spiral inward. Under the second enhancement, credit orbits spiral outward. Combining them tends to create a stable limit cycle, with all orbits converging toward it. All these limit cycles swing out at extremes, giving the impression of a debt trap.

While no deterministic model can do justice to the credit system, it is hard to escape the impression that prudence pays. Economies that issue whatever debt the market will accommodate seem inherently prone to boom-bust cycles. Credit spreads can easily warn too little before crisis and too much after.

Breakdown and Regulation

A perceived debt trap wrenches a financial system. It tempts debtors to default, creditors to pull their funding, and political overseers to intervene. Even if a wide debt orbit is stable in theory, it will likely be unstable in practice.

The best-known breakdown is a bank run, where customers rush to withdraw their deposits. The key trigger for a bank run is fear of fear. If I fear that enough other investors will withdraw their deposits to exhaust the bank's reserves, I may withdraw my money first and spread contagion.

At heart, the doubt game undermining banks is no more peculiar than the confidence game boosting money. However, the confidence game makes people feel richer, while the doubt game makes people feel poorer. Hence policymakers and the public are far more disposed to quell a panic than a mania.

Time after time, a heady boom ensues, with little care to rein it in. When boom turns to bust, regulators rush to save investors from the consequences. Nowadays most deposits in developed countries are regarded as completely insured, regardless of the lending strategy of the bank. Even regulators who deny that feel compelled to provide insurance when crisis breaks. The realization has helped drive financial leverage to previously unimagined heights.

Recall the Fed's loosening bias under Alan Greenspan, known as the Greenspan put. Borio and Lowe (2002) warned of destabilization, to little avail. The Securities and Exchange Commission (SEC) exacerbated the risks by allowing U.S. investment banks virtually unlimited leverage in their financing of large customers. It took the subprime mortgage crisis to expose the costs.

The European Central Bank (ECB) ostensibly exerts more discipline. However, the refinancing facilities it offers to eurozone banks basically treat any eurozone government bond as riskless. This encourages banks to buy the highest-yielding bonds in the zone, put them to the ECB as collateral, and pocket the differential credit spread. Naturally those are the bonds from the fiscally challenged PIIGS. Technically the banks remain liable to the ECB if the PIIGS default, but between bankruptcy and upheaval few will manage. In this way PIIGS bonds have come to dominate the euro's reserves, although the public little realizes it. It is Gresham's Law applied to sovereign debt.

In defense of the Fed and ECB, a refusal to provide liquidity in emergencies threatens far more immediate damage than a rollover of bank debt. Other regulations and bankers' self-interest are supposed to promote longer-term banking system health. The Basel Committee on Banking Supervision, which links together various national regulators, has sought to raise international standards. In 1988 it published a set of minimal capital requirements for banks, known as the Basel Accord, which the Group of Ten countries officially adopted in 1992. Various shortcomings, many of them exposed in the crises of 1997 and 1998, led to promulgation of new standards in 2004, known as Basel II.

Basel II focused on clear measurement and labeling of default risks. Each asset's exposure would be multiplied by its estimated risk weight. Banks would have to keep a capital buffer of at least 8% of total risk-weighted assets. The apparent aim was to cover all risk 99.9% of the time.

The formulas for measuring risk were complex. Basel II's banner document (Basel Committee on Banking Supervision 2004) ran to 239 pages.

Nevertheless, the formulas ignored most fluctuations stemming from observer uncertainty, market herding, and overshooting. It is as if orchard owners decided heating and irrigation needs based on average yearly temperatures and rainfall, rather than on how cold or dry it can get.

Consider, for example, Basel II's main precaution against bank runs: total capital adjusted for default risk. Bank capital can stop a run only if it can be converted quickly to cash. While real estate, ownership stakes in enterprises, and long-term bonds may remain creditworthy, they can generate cash only by selling a stake or borrowing against it. A bank run is the worst time to generate this cash, because the mad dash for liquidity it reflects likely pervades the financial system as a whole.

Long duration aggravates bank difficulties in crisis. The closer investments are to delivering cash in hand, the more nearly liquid they are. They will command a premium in crisis, or at least sell with less discount. Also, risky credits that come due in crisis can be reissued at higher spreads, helping to offset losses.

Yet Basel II hardly looked at duration mismatch, market volatility, bid-ask spreads, and other signs of potential illiquidity. Indeed, by allowing unlimited leverage for notionally safe credits, Basel II removed a traditional stabilizer. It is one of several ways in which Basel II aggravated the economic cycle.

A popular view of the recent crisis is that an unregulated financial sector ran amok. The reality is even more disturbing. Curbs were in place but inadvertently steered in the wrong direction. See Persaud (2000, 2008), Kashyap and Stein (2004), and Financial Stability Forum (2009) for more discussion.

∽

"It looks like credit cycles are inevitable," said Pandora. "Market participants can't distinguish well enough between changes in liquidity and changes in fundamentals. Their seemingly rational reactions to current conditions make markets overshoot."

"It's interesting how well veiled the cycle is," said Prometheus. "The boom can last enough to seem the natural state. The bust can be sharp enough to look like an aberration. No wonder so much policy is geared to stimulus rather than to stability."

"Yes, policymakers are much warier of high inflation when it involves current goods and services than when it involves asset prices. It's understandable. Who wants to criticize the confidence boost it represents, and which might be justified? But a credit boom begs a bust.""

"Duration mismatch makes the cycle worse. Why don't bankers focus on the payments business?"

"Because borrowing short to lend long is more fun and profitable. At least it is until it isn't."

"And when it isn't, governments or central bankers usually bail them out."

"Of course. They don't want financial confidence collapsing. And they want to help short-term depositors, who couldn't reasonably have seen it coming. Sure, sometimes they go to extremes. That's inevitable in panic."

"I'm not faulting them for panic," said Prometheus. "But when calm returns they ought to think more about the laws of cause and effect. If the government insures short-term deposits, let it insist they fund short-term assets. Problems will come quicker to the surface that way, with less risk of inflating a credit bubble."

"Many economists think that governments should subsidize long-term investment. Channeling short-term deposits toward long-term loans helps do that."

"Many of those same economists worry about current demand being too low or a global savings glut. They're not consistent."

"Surely you're not proposing to ban long-term loans."

"Of course not. I just want them backed by long-term funding."

6

Safety in Numbers

Many credit markets behave as if they are inferring from only a few dozen years of relevant observations and fractional evidence of default. Their beliefs are modeled most plausibly as highly dispersed distributions, where the consensus might be wildly wrong. The uncertainty calls for much larger contingent reserves on top-rated credits than standard regulatory calculations recommend.

Modern bond markets are highly sensitive to perceived default risk. Credit spreads are normally measured in basis points (bps), which are one-hundredth of percentage points. While default might not trigger complete loss, the residual or salvage value of a defaulted claim is often less than half the nominal value. Ideally the market wants a 1 or 2 bps accuracy in its estimates of default risk per annum.

There is no way to achieve that degree of accuracy for the debtors we care most about. Knowledge is always rooted in directly relevant observation, and we don't have nearly enough. So analysts branch into indirectly relevant or possibly relevant observation and draw on their imaginations. They are lucky to obtain one-in-one-hundred part accuracy.

This problem is fundamental to financial risk analysis. Yet it receives scant attention. To redress the balance, let's start with a real-life example.

Real-Life Ignorance

The Soviet bloc imploded around 1990, give or take a few years. The countries that emerged from the wreckage were a motley crew. Some had strong resources and human capital bases; some did not. Some had thriving market sectors before the collapse; some strangled markets down to the end. Some were committed to democracy and the rule of law; some stonewalled. Some had serviced foreign debts faithfully, some hadn't, and some hadn't borrowed at all.

Despite these differences, nearly all of the new authorities were desperate for cash. Their economies were plummeting, tax collection was in tatters, and needs for reconstruction were immense. Western governments and international agencies provided tens of billions of dollars in debt forgiveness and new lending. It wasn't enough, and much was squandered or stolen.

As the post-Soviet successor states found their footing, they reached out to private Western lenders. Many of the latter were amenable—indeed eager—toward winning new clients. But they did want to cover the default risks. How much were those?

Even big investment banks had to admit they did not know. They had few contacts in the area and were hesitant to project from other experiences. So they looked for new hires to assist them and clients. I was one.

For an economist, getting hired by an investment bank was a bit like Scarecrow receiving a diploma from the Wizard of Oz. However, Scarecrow rose to the occasion better than I did. I didn't know the relevant default risks. I didn't claim to know.

How I envied my colleagues focusing on Latin America. They tapped better data sets with more clearly relevant histories. They consulted with seasoned technocrats at treasuries and central banks. Analysts weighed in confidently not only on default but also on related risks like currency devaluation.

As the year unfolded, the markets grew increasingly anxious about Mexico's ability and will to maintain the peso's targeted exchange-rate band versus the dollar. However, most Wall Street analysts remained confident that the target band would hold. Sure enough, the band held—until it didn't. In just a few days in late December the peso lost one-third of its dollar value.

Only then did I realize that my fog of ignorance wasn't just mine. It permeates the market as a whole. That was my first taste of real market knowledge.

Default Uncertainty

Would that market data were as abundant and easy to categorize as sub-atomic particles. Every spoonful of matter offers a trillion trillion potentially relevant observations. Contrast that to a couple of dozen countries emerging from the Soviet bloc. Even if we understood precisely every economic, political, or ideological factor relevant to debt servicing, we would not know how they hang together. What objective basis does that give us for knowing default risk?

Imagine, for example, that we could find 100 years of debt-servicing experience exactly analogous to Slovakia's debt servicing in 1994 but independent of it. Suppose that three defaults occurred. The single most likely default risk is 300 bps. But wait, the bond market wants us to gauge basis points, and our experiment rules out fractional defaults. Hence it would seem fairer to infer a most likely default risk ranging from 250 to 350 bps. The uncertainty would span 100 bps. And that is just for a single year of default risk. The price of a Slovak bond maturing in ten years could wobble by several percentage points without making a fair-value analyst cry foul.

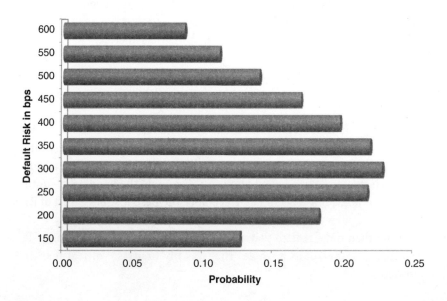

Figure 6.1
Default Risk Versus Probability of Three Defaults in a Century

Indeed, the uncertainty extends wider. A 450 bps default risk has a 20% chance of defaulting three times in a century. A 200 bps default risk has an 18% chance of defaulting three times in a century. So we shouldn't rule them out on the basis of this evidence alone. Indeed, any default risk between 150 and 540 bps is at least half as likely to trigger three defaults in a century as a 300 bps default risk is. See Figure 6.1.

Let us turn the question around. How many independent observations would we need to confidently identify a narrow range for default risk? The answer in most cases turns out to be hugely more than we have.

Suppose we want 99.9% assurance that our estimate lies within 10 bps of the underlying yearly default risk. If the true risk is 1%, we will need 100,000 independent yearly observations. If the true risk is 10%, we will need nearly ten times more. While credit cards and mortgages can generate those volumes of observations, only a fraction will share the same risk category and environment.

Is 99.9% confidence too stringent? Let's trim it to 95%. That demands barely one-third as many observations. Still the numbers are huge.

In sovereign debt, these thresholds are completely out of reach. If a few dozen countries experienced similar risks over a few dozen years, that yields only about a thousand yearly observations. A thousand yearly observations are unlikely to squeeze the confidence interval to less than 150 bps.

Hardly Any Defaults

Since we can't extinguish uncertainty, let's find ways to live with it. The simplest is to assemble T years of relevant independent observations, count how many D indicate default, and use the frequency D/T as an estimate of default risk. Since reasonable people will disagree over relevance and independence, both D and T will be fuzzy. But the market price will reflect a consensus weighted by wealth and conviction, so we can use that as a wobbly proxy.

Even without wobble, the estimate will move as new evidence comes in. Each step will look like this:

$$\frac{D}{T} \begin{array}{l} \nearrow \dfrac{D+1}{T+1} \text{ if default,} \\[2mm] \searrow \dfrac{D}{T+1} \text{ if payment.} \end{array} \tag{6.1}$$

Let's suppose we gather T more years of evidence and it's all good: not a single indication of default. This will halve the estimated default risk. Hence, minimal halving time should provide a reasonable estimate of T.

In practice, it took only a few years for the best ex-Soviet performers to halve their initial credit spreads. If we generously accord each of them up to ten identical-but-independent comparators, T is at most a few dozen. In that case, the baseline D even for a relatively weak credit must be less than 3.

One might object that spread tightening reflected improvements in the economies and fiscal governance. This would make some reference defaults irrelevant. However, it would likely make many other observations irrelevant as well, shrinking T.

Even before the Soviet bloc collapsed, Hungary kept spreads tight despite many similarities to Poland, which defaulted. Evidently it persuaded markets that Polish default was barely relevant. Why then should subsequent Polish servicing be much more relevant? In general, while sovereign default often is contagious to spreads abroad, the impact usually fades within a year if others keep servicing. In effect, observations from other countries and periods get only fractional weight. Again, this shrinks the relevant T.

Even at fractional weight, enough related experience might trickle in to swell T overall. To estimate how much, let us consider what happens when a sub-100 bps credit risk suddenly defaults. It is hard to imagine its credit spreads not surging by 300 bps or more. Yet D is only 1 higher than before. Hence T must be only a few dozen, in which case the baseline D must have been much less than 1.

Bond markets' traditional emphasis on trust supports this interpretation. Good borrowers portray themselves as completely reliable, in hopes of issuing at minimal spreads. Any default is treated as disgrace. Yet if creditors completely believed borrowers, spreads would be zero. Only fractional evidence of default can reconcile trust with caution.

Consider too the difficulty in finding high-risk comparators. Leo Tolstoy wryly observed in *Anna Karenina* that while all happy families are alike, each unhappy family is unhappy in its own way. Trustworthy debtors are like happy families: they borrow cheaply, they repay promptly, both sides win, and the simple story repeats itself. Each defaulter, by contrast, has its own tale of why past failure should not be held against it now, as well as its uniqueness relative to others who have pledged the same and failed again.

Rational Updating

Fractional evidence of default is strange. Let's see if we can avoid it. Instead of positing a simple counting process for risk estimation, let us allow for varied beliefs and update them optimally given new evidence.

Bayes' Rule can accommodate a wide variety of behavior. At one extreme it can justify dogmatism. If I am 100% convinced default risk takes one particular value, applying Bayes' Rule won't change my mind. At the other extreme, it can justify a giant leap to conclusion. If I assign 50% probability of certain default and 50% probability of certain servicing, then the very first observation catapults me from maximum uncertainty to maximum conviction.

Still, Bayes' Rule implies some regularity in change. The most striking regularity concerns the mean default risk given beliefs. If we define *news* as the unexpected component of an observation, the following relationship always applies:

$$\Delta \operatorname{mean}(\textit{beliefs}) = \operatorname{var}(\textit{beliefs}) \cdot \frac{\textit{news}}{\operatorname{var}(\textit{news})}, \qquad (6.2)$$

where Δ denotes the change induced by observation and var denotes variance. If we denote the mean belief by E and the variance by V, the preceding simplifies to

$$\Delta E = \begin{cases} +V\!/\!E & \text{if default,} \\ -\dfrac{V}{1-E} & \text{if payment.} \end{cases} \qquad (6.3)$$

For example, if beliefs are roughly normal around the mean with a 50 bps standard deviation, then a century of reliable servicing will shave the mean by barely 25 bps, while three defaults in a row will boost the mean by less than 100 bps. Investors are a lot more skittish than that. Hence, market beliefs must be widely dispersed.

As long as E is small, the exceptional default will be far more newsworthy than servicing. The mean will jump when default occurs and slowly decay when it doesn't. The expected shift remains zero, which makes sense. If we observe what we expect, it shouldn't change our minds.

Initially we used equation (6.1) to model the updates on risk. Equation (6.3) will match this if $E = \frac{D}{T}$ and $V = \dfrac{E(1-E)}{T+1}$. Is there any probability distribution that has this property?

Indeed there is: a beta distribution with defining parameters D and $T - D$. The beta distribution is the most widely used probability model for variables spanning the continuum from 0 to 1. And its parameters don't need to be integers, just positive numbers. So our simple model with low T and fractional D looks more plausible than ever.

Figure 6.2 presents some charts of beta distributions with mean 1% and D ranging from 0.2 to 2. Even at $D = 2$, convictions are dispersed widely relative to the mean. Shrinking D increases the dispersion. For $D = 1$, convictions dampen exponentially as default risks rise. For $D < 1$, the mean is an uneasy compromise: most likely the true default risk is much lower or much higher.

As time between observations gets shorter, it is more convenient to work with the continuous-time counterparts known as gamma distributions. The relevant formulas are nearly the same. The Appendix provides details.

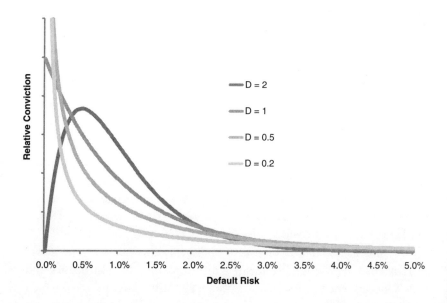

Figure 6.2
Beta Distributions with Mean of 1%

Contingent Reserves

Suppose a lender owns a basket of n credits considered identical in odds of default and independent in outcomes. Those qualities make them ideal for risk estimation. We pool them and similar credits to count D and T and form the same belief distribution for each. How should we estimate default risks for the portfolio as a whole?

The expected number of defaults is just n times the expected default risk E for each credit. Multiply by the average loss per default to estimate the expected losses out of nominal proceeds. Typically accountants will book a reserve to cover this, so as not to overstate lenders' anticipated profit.

Excess losses will chip away lenders' capital. To help stay out of trouble, prudent lenders will set aside an additional buffer, known as a contingent reserve. Ideally, the buffer should equate the marginal cost of excess reserves to the marginal cost of falling short.

If losses are distributed normally, a three standard deviation buffer provides 99.87% certainty of protection, while a four standard deviation buffer provides 99.997% certainty. For a small fixed default risk, the variance will roughly match the mean nE. Therefore contingency reserves are often judged adequate if they cover three or four times the square root of expected losses.

That judgment glosses over several problems:

- The risk environment might change, altering E. This is so important that the next chapter is devoted to regime change.
- Low D and low nE widen the standard deviation multiple needed for a given degree of protection. Intuitively, the fewer the expected number of defaults, the more scrunched most of the distribution will be against the origin and the fatter the tail risk of outliers more than three to five standard deviations from the mean.
- Lower D also fattens the tail, as defaults will be expected to cluster in high-risk scenarios. To take an extreme example, if we believe the joint default risk is either zero or 100%, then we expect to observe no defaults until everything defaults.
- Learning can change E substantially even if actual risks stay the same. This follows from equations (6.1) and (6.3). New evidence of default will boost E by a fraction $\dfrac{V}{E^2} = \dfrac{1-E}{D+E} \cong \dfrac{1}{D}$. For D small this will imply a huge percentage change in reserves.

Hence, a bank that leverages itself to the hilt can have more to fear from its low-risk assets than its high-risk ones. Low-risk assets reassessed at, say, 40 bps rather than 10 bps could double the standard reserves required for unexpected losses, and hence halve maximum leverage for a bank that relied on those assets to meet capital requirements. Longer-maturity assets are especially vulnerable, as they leave more time before redemption for observers to change their views.

This realization seems to have escaped the designers of the Basel Accords. Their differential capital requirements strongly favored nominally sound sovereign debt and mortgages. Lenders would naturally concentrate there, aggravating the credit cycle. Moreover, the regulations favored taking credit with the highest spread to nominal risk rating—the very credits the markets considered most overrated.

The extreme was the zero risk-rating for top-rated sovereign debt. In a way it's touching. Having lost the *droit de seigneur* and in some cases the *droit de seigniorage*, eminent sovereigns sought to assure the *droit de prêt*: the right to rollover debt indefinitely without a premium.

Many consider this a good idea, on the grounds that it builds trust and defers debt repayment to a richer future. They rarely stop to consider its costs. To begin with, most of these sovereign borrowers would deserve more respect if they pared down their debts. The last half-century has blessed most of these countries with peace, growth, and an enormous wealth and productivity advantage over the rest of the world. Their future looks comparatively tougher, even if peace prevails, because of demographic slowdown, resource depletion, and catch-up elsewhere. More structural fear would do them good, by encouraging them to save more and borrow less.

A second cost is abuse of some sovereigns by others. Many sovereigns, including Europe's PIIGS and several state governments in the United States, keep their top rating only because other sovereigns implicitly protect them. Helping the protected stuff their debt to banks doesn't reduce the protector's burden; it just obscures the connection. Eventually crisis forces the protector to choose between bank bailout and chaos.

A third cost is discouragement of bank lending to small- and medium-sized business enterprises and lower-rated large business. Their default rates are relatively high, so Basel rules require high contingent reserves. However, businesses are numerous and relatively diverse. This increases the relevant T in estimation and reduces the variance in aggregate performance.

In broad baskets of business loans, most unexpected risk comes from the credit cycle itself. Regulators should try to dampen this by encouraging a smooth flow of credit to business. Pegging contingent reserves to recently observed default rates does the opposite.

Banks have a comparative advantage over bond markets in lending to smaller or weaker business, since they are better poised to get inside knowledge and better able to recoup costs of learning. Discouraging this in favor of sovereign lending or the origination of loans sold to third parties dampens real investment and reduces employment. While specialty finance companies step into the gap, their high returns suggest they tackle only the worst inefficiencies.

A fourth cost is concealment of risks through regulatory arbitrage. Regulatory arbitrage refers to repackaging that shrinks capital requirements without trimming actual risks. If capital requirements are set too high, regulatory arbitrage can benefit society. However, its very uniformity encourages concealment of the same kinds of risks in the same kinds of ways, until the very concentration poses huge systemic risks.

For example, under Basel I, a bank with a standard corporate loan would bear a capital charge of 8%. If it bought credit protection for this exposure from another bank via a traded derivative, the capital charge would sink to 1.6% (Servigny and Renault 2004). Basel II partially plugged that loophole by tying the capital charge to the insurer's credit rating. In doing so it opened a lucrative opportunity for top-rated insurance companies to offer credit guarantees that allowed banks to multiply their leverage.

The American International Group (AIG) was one of the few insurance companies that felt comfortable in this area, possessed a top rating, and faced little scrutiny from its external regulators or actuaries on derivatives exposure. So much banking system risk piled up at AIG that when it stumbled after Lehman's collapse, the U.S. government funneled $180 billion through it to bail out the banks AIG insured.

In fairness, the AIG episode points more to the dangers of high leverage and concealment than to the dangers of the particular forms that Basel II fostered. The main beneficiaries of AIG's bailout included some U.S. investment banks like Goldman Sachs that were subject neither to Basel II regulations nor the "Basel I plus leverage cap" applied to U.S. commercial banks. Also, some of the fallout could have been avoided by forcing more transparency into the credit derivatives market and requiring participants to post collateral for obligations likely due.

Rethinking Regulation

Financial risk regulation has created a kind of parallel universe. It aims to measure market risks better than the market does, with more objectivity and stability. It feels as though it works, except when it doesn't. When it doesn't, regulators invent new measures, which once again work until they don't.

Unlike Soviet-style planners, the masters of the parallel universe aren't antimarket. However, they share with Soviet-style planners an obtuseness to unintended incentives. Uniform rules for contingent reserve formation encourage uniform failings. Rigid risk pricing encourages imbalance and wasteful arbitrage. Decades of rewarding form over content have bred a culture of cynicism and irresponsibility.

This parallel universe desperately needs to be brought back to ours. The most important priority is to rethink the central aim of financial regulation. Is it to make everyone agree on risk? No, because that's impossible. Is it to help sovereigns and banks roll over their debt? No, unless one places them above the societies they are supposed to serve. Is it to decide what other lending is appropriate? No, because that's the job of lenders and credit markets.

Regulators should aim instead to dampen large fluctuations in aggregate credit. Market participants too easily confuse these with real changes in wealth and lose their bearings as a result. Regulators won't be perfectly clear themselves. But they are better placed than individuals to monitor credit markets and adjust policy accordingly. In spirit it's like adjusting money supply to stabilize inflation.

Some restraints on duration mismatch and leverage will be essential. Fixed caps are a lesser evil than no caps. In principle these caps ought to be related to aggregate credit growth, so that booms tighten leverage constraints while busts relax them.

Leverage caps would automatically assure some contingent reserves. As for the rest, lenders deserve more leeway to design their own policies. The basic mark-to-market test would be solvency, measured as an excess of assets over liabilities when valued at a moving average of market prices. Lenders having long-dated liabilities could average over much longer windows than lenders funding themselves via demand deposits.

The ultimate penalty for failing these tests would be "living death." Living death refers to prespecified procedures for addressing insolvency without the disruption or delays of ordinary bankruptcy. It would tap private and public backup financing immediately and transfer ownership to the financiers. In some ways the U.S. government's Troubled Asset Relief Program did that by funneling credit quickly in return for equity stakes. It has been more effective and less costly than critics feared.

To supplement market valuations, and also to help markets appraise the lenders more reasonably, lenders would publish regular risk accounts. Risk accounts would look broadly like risk reports do now but with less pettifogging detail and with every important risk forecast accompanied by an estimate of its uncertainty. Risk accounting methodologies would require approval from professional associations and regulators.

One report that definitely has too much influence is perceived safety. Safety is usually highly uncertain, for statistical reasons regulators can't wish away. High uncertainty increases the reserve requirements for all assets but especially for the perceived safest. Tarashev (2009) makes a similar point.

Where the risk is well known, current regulations create perverse incentives to exploit it. Suppose a bank knows it's safe except for once in a blue moon, and that regulators don't fret blue moons. Then the bank is free to write a host of insurance contracts that capture premium every day and pay out in blue moons. Alternatively, if blue moons come too often for comfort, the bank can get back into regulatory grace with contracts that insure a fraction of failures but make the remainder far worse.

Some of the brightest minds in banking and structured finance are devoted to dubious estimation of unknown risks and intentional worsening of known risks. It is a huge disservice to society. When crises bring this into the open, the public is outraged and demands more regulation. Little does it realize how previous remedies worsened the problem. Better fewer regulations but wiser.

$\sim$

"Fractional evidence of default is odd," said Pandora. "But now that Osband explains it, I don't see any other way to reconcile empirical evidence with theory."

"I see it as a reduced form," said Prometheus. "If we take a mixture of beliefs, each with single default over different sample periods, the aggregate can resemble a beta distribution with fractional default."

"I prefer the simpler model. But I'll let him know; perhaps he can weave it into a later chapter. Do you have any other messages for him?"

"There's a new set of global banking regulations being drafted," said Prometheus. "Basel III. Ask him why he doesn't mention it."

"I already did. He said he doesn't know the details, and that key practical tweaks are still to come."

"They're introducing a leverage cap. They're raising capital requirements. They're demanding more backing for counterparty credit risk. They're demanding more liquidity coverage. Those are all good things."

"How about reducing procyclicality, improving risk models, and discouraging regulatory arbitrage?"

"They emphasize that as well. Only I'm not sure how. I do get a sense the Basel Committee is genuinely seeking new ideas. Plus there's some positive experience to draw on. Canada, for example, weathered the financial crisis a lot better than the United States or Europe did, thanks in part to better regulation."

"Do you think the reforms will turn the corner?"

"I'm not sure. It's going to be years before the new provisions are in place. A lot of big banks remain sorely overextended, particularly in Europe, and a PIIGS default would send them reeling."

"There will be huge political pressure to treat PIIGS debt as risk free."

"There already is. Likewise for the debt of California, New York, Illinois, and several other U.S. states that have borrowed well beyond their means."

7

When God Changes Dice

Risks often change with little notice, rendering past observations obsolete. We can use dynamic mixtures of simple models to track change robustly. Still, tiny doubts about big outliers can make a huge impact on forecasts. We can't fully predict this impact and will frequently disagree with each other on best approximations. That is why markets trade so much.

For all his genius, Albert Einstein never accepted the randomness inherent in quantum theory. He repeatedly denied that God would play dice with the universe (Born 2005). Modern physicists find these denials endearing, because it gives them an opportunity to feel cleverer than Einstein. Few doubt that chance is central.

Standard finance theory thinks it is clever because it allows for risk. But it tends to ignore the uncertainty enveloping risk, which is often the chance that most matters. Rarely does it note the dearth of relevant observations, much less the implications for pricing and risk management.

This chapter addresses an even deeper problem, namely that observations may cease to be relevant. In finance God doesn't simply throw dice. Sometimes He changes His dice without telling us.

By dice I mean the regime that defines the relevant risks. With default risk the core die is a biased coin with chance θ of heads. Changing the die means changing θ. We can introduce new parameters to describe the probabilities of regime change, and then let those probabilities change too.

Some regime changes are clear-cut. A coup brings to power a ruler who vows to repudiate the nation's debt. Presto, credit spreads soar before a single new payment comes due. More likely there will be doubts. Sometimes regime changes are purposely obscured. How many companies heading for bankruptcy advertise the fact beforehand?

Indeed regimes may change without emitting any immediate signal. The evidence accumulates only later, in outcomes that strain previous interpretations. These are the regime changes we will focus on here.

Unfittingly Fit

The counting game described in Chapter 6 has a fatal weakness. Neither D nor T ever decline. Hence, every time a particular $E = \frac{D}{T}$ frequency recurs, the variance $V \cong \frac{E}{T}$ must have shrunk. In the limit, V vanishes, making updates irrelevant.

As long as the underlying risk stays fixed, the observed frequency should eventually fit it extremely well. The tiny variance will reflect enough justified confidence that Bayesian statistics call the inverse of an estimator's variance its precision. However, high precision is hard to reconcile with financial practice. Empirically, market behavior binds most T to a few decades or less. And if the risk ever does materially change, we might need centuries to restore a close fit.

In other words, the model in the previous chapter doesn't truly solve the problems it identified. It just defers them until D and T age. We need some potion to keep them young.

Could this problem be peculiar to beta or gamma distributions? Let's check. Equation (6.2) relates ΔE to V and unexpected news. The corresponding relation for ΔV works out to

$$\Delta V = \kappa_3 \cdot \frac{news}{\mathrm{var}(news)} - (\Delta E)^2, \tag{7.1}$$

where κ_3 denotes the third-order cumulant of beliefs, or skewness times the standard deviation cubed. Since *news* by definition is expected to be zero, V must be expected to decline. Indeed, if default risk stays constant, the following relation will hold:

$$\Delta \langle \text{precision}\,(estimator) \rangle \cong \text{precision}\,(news). \tag{7.2}$$

Hence, the problem isn't the choice of distribution; it's our Bayesian updating method. The precision of the estimator ideally grows with the precision of the latest news, regardless of the distribution or current conviction. It works great when default risk stays nearly constant and terribly when it doesn't.

Evolutionary biology has long noted a similar dilemma. Darwin's theory preached survival of the fittest. But if the environment changes, fit can become unfit. Fisher (1930) derived an equation analogous to (A6.2) (see the Appendix), showing that the mean genetic fitness should increase in proportion to genetic variance. He called it the fundamental theorem of natural selection.

High variance means that many genes, and the organisms expressing them, aren't best suited to the current environment. Yet variance promotes more fitness in the long run. Optimal specialization depends on robustness, yet conflicts with it.

Mother Nature long ago devised an ingenious way to reconcile improvement with variation. It is known as sex. By mixing genes and keeping a recessive one in reserve, sexual reproduction maintains more variance than asexual reproduction. Indeed, if mutation and selection are slow enough the variance will stay approximately constant, a result known as the Hardy-Weinberg Principle after Godfrey Hardy (Hardy 1908) and Wilhelm Weinberg (Weinberg 1908).

Financial selection is far more destabilizing than sexual selection. But there must be some way to restore variance longer term. The only plausible explanation is mindfulness. Observers realize that past information may have lost relevance, and old inferences fade.

Updating can thus be viewed as a two-stage process. The first phase is standard Bayesian updating of beliefs given new evidence, assuming the risk regime θ stays the same. The second phase factors in beliefs about likely changes in θ and their impact.

Disturbingly Tiny Doubts

To illustrate the difference the second phase of updating can make, let us consider a situation we've all encountered: the suspicion that the game we're playing isn't fair. If outcomes revert to the mean we'll feel reassured. What if they don't?

To make this concrete, suppose we're relatively confident a coin is fair, based on 500 heads in 1,000 observations, when new evidence arrives of 30 flips that all came up heads. If we model our uncertainty as a beta distribution with parameters (500, 500), the new information raises our consensus estimate E to $\frac{530}{1030} \cong 0.515$. That is less than one standard deviation away from 0.5, which hardly seems to merit concern.

Or does it? Given a fair coin, the chance of no tails in 30 flips is one in a billion. Something doesn't smell right.

As an alternative, let us posit a small ε chance, say one in a million, that the coin was switched before the latest sample. Suppose we're also highly unsure what a switch might entail. To convey that, let us model the conditional risk as a beta distribution with fractional parameters, say (0.1, 0.1).

These tiny allowances suffice to raise E to 99.5% after 30 heads. Why the huge difference? Intuitively, 30 heads in a row make us highly confident a switch occurred to a heads-biased coin.

Hence tiny doubts can restore variance. However, they do so in a highly irregular way. If we tracked the evolution of beliefs in this example one toss at a time, our tiny ε would initially make little impact. After 15 heads in a row, E for the next round would be only 50 bps higher than if we ignored possible switches. But after ten more heads E would surge to nearly 0.95, or 4,300 bps above the baseline.

Naïve observers might think we had flipped out. Here are 25 heads, each with the same probability, but we get excited only about the last ten. We seem to have started out too complacent, scrambled to catch up, and possibly overreacted.

Strangely, our more suspicious neighbors, with an initial ε of one in a thousand, appear to have suffered similar mood swings. However, they reacted about ten heads sooner than we did. After 15 heads in a row they would lay 20 to 1 odds that the next round is heads, but they won't need to because we think 2 to 1 odds are ample for betting tails. They will part us fools from our money, unless the fair coin really was fair and our caution turns out to have been justified. In that case our neighbors will look foolish for reading spurious patterns into randomness. See Figure 7.1.

This example is extreme. However, the qualitative features resonate throughout finance. They explain why financial views evolve much more quickly than nature does and with more spasms. Specifically,

- Doubts introduce new beliefs with high dispersion and new means.
- This increases the aggregate variance, which equals the mean variance of its components plus the variance of its means.

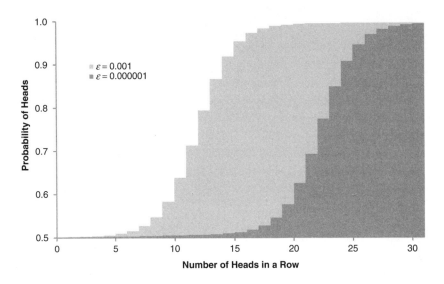

Figure 7.1
Reactions to Tiny Doubts

- If the regime has indeed changed, the realization will come slowly at first, quicken substantially, and then slow again near certainty.
- The combination can make the transition very steep, as in the curves in Figure 7.1. It is as if people ignore evidence until they hit a tipping point and abhor the uncertainty between.

Complexity Through Simplicity

Now we see how important it is to incorporate regime change into our models. But it is far from clear how. There are countless possible regimes, at least one for each default risk, and "countless squared" switching propensities between them. We can't even write down the full set of equations, much less identify them, unless we impose major constraints. Since even small doubts about one parameter can have a big impact, our choice of constraints can easily deceive.

For example, suppose we identify two regimes, with λ_{ij} the conditional switching rate from state i to state j. The optimal updating equation for the conviction p on the first regime is approximately

$$\Delta p \cong p(\theta_1 - E)\frac{news}{\text{var}(news)} - p\lambda_{12} + (1-p)\lambda_{21}. \tag{7.3}$$

The first term provides the Bayesian updating. Since $P(\theta_1 - E) = p(1 - p)$ $(\theta_1 - \theta_2)$, it generates the S-curve effect of being slow at the edges and fast in the middle. The second and third terms give the regime-switching outflow and inflow, respectively.

The expected change will be zero at $p^* \equiv \dfrac{\lambda_{21}}{\lambda_{12} + \lambda_{21}}$, where outflow balances inflow. If regimes switch rapidly enough, p will tend to stick closely to p^*, in which case it's hardly worth monitoring outcomes. Conversely, if switching is rare, p will usually be close to 0 or 1. These traits are shared by more complicated models. However, the strict band confining risk is more assumption than result, as is the possibility of describing risk evolution with a single variable. Moreover, equation (7.3) implicitly assumes that we know the switching rates, when in reality they're very hard to identify precisely.

Returning to our simple counting game, let us figure out some simple adjustments for regime change. The easiest is to let past observations fade in relevance at a constant proportional rate λ. That is, in every short interval dt, old T shrinks by approximately $\lambda t dt$ while old D shrinks by approximately $\lambda D dt$.

If new observations enter at rate dt, the net impact drives the relevant observation time T toward a constant value $\frac{1}{\lambda}$, where rates of new evidence and fading relevance match. Near that value, each λ implies an estimator of the following form:

$$dE \cong \lambda \cdot news = \lambda(dx - E dt), \tag{7.4}$$

where dx equals 1 with default and 0 otherwise. The long-run average E should match the average default rate, regardless of λ. But E at any given time will hardly ever be right. Higher λ exacerbates the swings. Shortening the average information lag or effective observation period makes E less precise when risk is stable and more responsive when risk changes.

Another name for "estimator" is "filter," because it screens information for presumed relevance. If the filter above runs infinitely long, it will form an exponentially weighted moving average rate of default. Let us call it an exponential moving average (EMA) filter for short. It is widely used

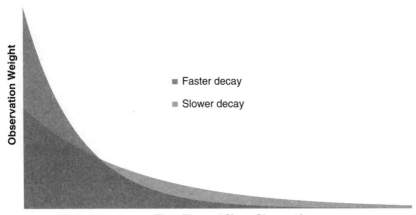

Time Elapsed Since Observation

Figure 7.2
Weights for Exponential Moving Averages (EMAs)

in practical financial modeling; the preceding reasoning helps to justify it. Figure 7.2 depicts two sets of EMA weights.

The average information lag or duration for an EMA filter is $\frac{1}{\lambda}$. Long-duration filters will behave quite differently from short-duration filters, and in practice we will rarely know which is best. So let us take as our aggregate filter a weighted average of different EMA filters and use Bayes' Rule to update the weights. A small weight on EMAs of less than a few years' duration corresponds to a dispersion of tiny doubts. An EMA with centuries-long duration implies much tighter confidence bands. Identifying an ultrasafe asset implicitly requires a duration of millennia.

To update the convictions p across different EMA filters, treat each filter i as if all beliefs were concentrated at its current mean E_i, and apply equation (7.3) without any switching. That is, substitute E_i for θ_1 and set $\lambda_{12} = \lambda_{21} = 0$. Remarkably, dividing a complex aggregate update into combinations of simpler equations (7.3) and (7.4) does not distort the results. It is similar to how statistical mechanics divides the internal flux of various ensembles from the motion of centers of mass.

An example is charted in Figure 7.3. Four simple EMAs and a dynamic mixture respond to a stream of servicing interrupted by two defaults. For each simple EMA, the estimated E decays exponentially until default and

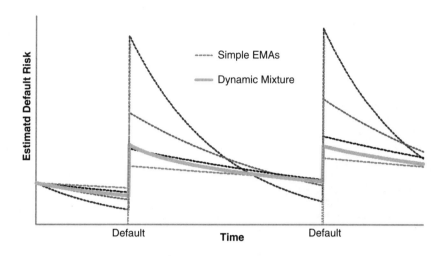

Figure 7.3
Estimators for Default Risk

jumps at default in proportion to the decay rate. The dynamic mixture also alternates between continuous decays and jumps, but without fixed proportionality. If we rescaled the vertical axis in logarithms, the decay paths would be straight lines for simple EMA filters but curves for the dynamic mixtures.

Inferences from Markets

The aggregate filter behaves like an EMA with unsteady λ, whose values we can infer by fitting equation (7.4) to market data on E. When debt is being serviced, the effective λ will change gradually, and usually downward as if a gamma-distributed belief were collecting new observations. On default the effective λ will jump, and usually upward as if some past observations were suddenly rendered irrelevant. However, if we're fairly confident default risk is high, λ will start rising after extended servicing without default and jump down after default. Figure 7.4 provides a few examples.

More shapes are possible. The degree of confidence can vary in more ways than E itself. It reflects centuries of history, yet also incorporates myriad beliefs about the future.

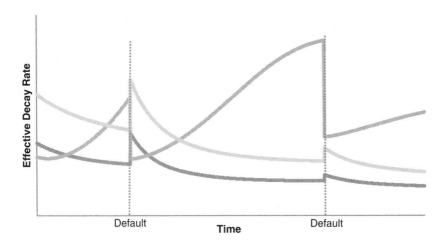

Figure 7.4
Examples of Decay Rate Evolution

In all cases, the effective λ is greater than the confidence-weighted average over individual λ, as the variance across different E values also contributes. The discrepancy is even greater between the effective observation time (the inverse of the effective λ) and a confidence-weighted average of the observation times. These effects will make observers appear more myopic than they really are.

Dynamic mixtures of EMAs help justify the approximations used in the previous chapter. In the short term, beliefs behave as if they are gamma distributed with fractional D and T of a few dozen years or less. In the long term, dispersed beliefs about regime change offset the ratchet effects on D and T. We can even account for default "discarding" more prior history than servicing does, without needing to posit emotional reactions to shocks.

Dynamic mixtures of EMAs also help explain the glue-like character of monetary expectations. Suppose we treat fiat money as debt that is repayable only through others' voluntary rollover for material goods and services. Despite this dubious support, millions of exchanges every day testify to reliable servicing. Not only does E drop for every individual EMA, but also confidence shifts toward shorter-duration filters. Within a few years, the aggregate E can sink to seemingly infinitesimal levels. Yet if confidence is very short-term, evidence of monetary breakdown (or payments failure, if mediated through banks) might easily trigger panic.

Again this supports the notion that high-grade debt is inherently fragile. We're highly confident in servicing, yet suspicious about our confidence. Neither borrowers nor regulators should take market confidence for granted.

Given the high uncertainty, it is tempting to make the market's belief distribution our own. We can try to infer the structure from credit spreads at various maturities and options on those spreads, or simply by tracking current spreads very closely. We can then decide to believe those inferences, on the grounds that the market knows best.

No speculators fully believe this, as otherwise they will never find cause to trade. But they must believe it in part, both because the market's view frequently triumphs over theirs and because it's stressful to disagree. Hence nearly every speculator bends his views toward the market consensus. This shrinks the variance of beliefs and makes the consensus more stable, in line with equation (6.2).

Proponents call this deferring to the wisdom of the hive. That's a bit misleading. The true wisdom of the hive comes from assimilating the foraging efforts of all its member bees. The variety and span of foraging is the hive's variance. It presumes error, as few bees will be foraging in the best place. But variance is what the hive needs to adjust quickly to new information. If all bees cleave to consensus, the hive is doomed.

However, some cleaving to consensus is useful. Uncertainty can be debilitating. By helping stabilize prices, herding reassures that the future is manageable.

Unpredictability

The very complexity of the world saves us from forever believing alike. It makes it impossible for any observer to know exactly what the market believes now, much less how those beliefs will change tomorrow. Our predictors are bound to falter because of tiny doubts or errors that mount over time.

This follows mathematically from an extension of equations (6.2) and (7.1). Just as the change in mean is proportional to the variance, and the change in variance is proportional to the skewness, so too the change in skewness is proportional to the kurtosis. All these measures are known as cumulants. In general, each cumulant changes proportionally to the cumulant of next higher order, which gets progressively harder to identify and control.

I call this relationship Pandora's Equation. It explains why market risk can never be tamed. Most puzzles in finance trace back to it.

The only remedy is to continually come back to the market, look for discrepancies between the behavior we predict and the behavior we observe, and readjust our beliefs about the market's beliefs. In effect that's what traders do when they study pricing charts. It's not the useless exercise Samuelson (1965) and many other distinguished economists have claimed it to be. On the contrary, for short-term prediction it's nearly always more important to study the market than to study economic fundamentals.

In that respect markets are like the weather. Whatever the forecast says, it's a good idea to look outside and check. Almost surely the forecast will need some revision.

This isn't just a question of timing, say, when a rainstorm will begin. Our best supercomputers can't predict the weather more than a few weeks in advance, and even inside that horizon they occasionally make gross errors. Forecasters used to hope that better computers would muscle through. Lorenz (1963) discovered that miniscule errors in weather forecasting equations mushroomed into huge discrepancies. The discovery was seminal to what is known today as chaos theory.

Chaos theory shows that nonlinear deterministic equations can generate what seem like random results. Some invoke chaos theory, wrongly, to deny randomness in markets. However, our beliefs do have elements of chaos in that even perfect foresight of all future defaults won't suffice to predict their evolution. They're inherently turbulent.

This has huge implications for trading. Since each forecast bears the birthmarks of private beliefs and estimation errors, it frequently will disagree with other forecasts. That's why financial markets trade so much.

Bear in mind too that expectations can affect real risks. If lenders think my default risk is high, I can't borrow. But if I can't borrow, I can't readily change their minds. Conversely, if no one expects me to default, I can roll over my debts and defer default.

Turbulence makes financial markets harsh and unfair. Like the ocean or the winds, or the fickle Greek gods, financial markets can rage with tempest on little notice. When they do, they can wreck us or speed us to our destination. No wonder man fears them and tries to bring them under control.

However, we can't confine financial markets to rigid boxes and shouldn't try. Financial markets represent social imagination. They distill what we believe about the future, and what we believe others believe. We need to respect them and give them room to play.

Oddly, the world's most famous critic of markets understood the power of imagination better than most market apostles:

> A spider conducts operations that resemble those of a weaver, and a bee puts to shame many an architect in the construction of her cells. But what distinguishes the worst architect from the best of bees is this, that the architect raises his structure in imagination before he erects it in reality. (Marx 1887: chap. 7)

As usual, Marx overstated the case. In some ways that proves the point. No other species stretches imagination the way humans do, and then strives to make it real. That path can never be smooth.

◠

"At last Osband is getting to the point," said Prometheus. "Regime change under uncertainty is central to finance."

"How does that distinguish finance from other fields?" asked Pandora. "Heraclitus observed 2,500 years ago that change was universal, and quantum physics has shown that all matter embeds uncertainty."

"In finance the uncertainty is so big, and the relevant observations so few, that even the expectations can't be measured precisely. Markets measure the beliefs about risk rather than risk itself. And risk changes often enough that beliefs rarely have time to converge on the truth."

"Twentieth-century finance theory focused too much on risk, too little on changes in risk, and hardly at all on beliefs about changing risk."

"Yes, that's why it missed your equation. Each cumulant of beliefs gets updated according to the next higher-order cumulant. It makes for an endless ladder, except in the special case of perfect normality."

You give me too much credit, Prometheus. I barely understand what a cumulant hierarchy is."

"You understand what it means—that financial markets will never completely predict their own evolution. That a lot of what we call forecasting is just dynamic tracking. That risk stays outside the box."

"Will readers understand the connections?"

"I'm not sure. The cumulant hierarchy arises naturally from the Fokker-Planck equation. Physicists have known about it for generations. In fluid dynamics they call it the moment-closure problem, and consider it essential to understanding turbulence. But I have never seen scientists apply it to beliefs."

"You're seeing it now."

"He needs to elaborate. At the very least apply it to continuous random walks. There your equation takes an even neater form. The volatility of each cumulant of belief varies directly with the cumulant above."

"Give him time, Prometheus. Let him motivate the questions better before charging off to answer."

8

Credit-ability

Credit rating has spawned a huge industry, far more
complex than the simple counting game at its core. Still,
uncertainty pervades ratings and deserves more disclosure. This needn't make ratings gyrate wildly. In analogy
to magnetism, a mild preference for agreement on relative safety can induce remarkable stability. The flip side is
that a few defaults can trigger widespread ratings shifts.

The marvel is less that public confidence in Western finance occasionally
plummets than that so much persists and rebuilds. It's like a starfish growing back arms. One of the confidence boosters is credit rating.

Credit rating proper is associated with regulators and with major
credit rating agencies like Moody's and Standard & Poor's (S&P). By con-
vention, credits are assigned letter grades. Triple-A (Aaa for Moody's,
AAA for S&P) is the highest rating, followed by double-A, single-A, triple-
B (or Baa), and so on down to C. Grades below triple-A are subdivided by
number or plus-or-minus sign and sometimes attach warnings of imminent migration.

In general, any ranking of credit safety, including the ranking implicit
in trading, can be considered a credit rating. Nearly every major financial
institution has credit scoring departments or uses third-party scoring services. Some services, like Riskmetrics or CreditRisk+, provide a mixture
of scores and advice on scoring methodology.

This chapter will examine the ratings process in more depth. We
will find that the counting game isn't so simple after all, and warrants
respect. However, it pretends to more precision than it can deliver. Much
of the agreement we observe about risk is just a form of social bonding.

While useful in encouraging joint effort, it occasionally bodes huge misdirection.

Credit Grades

Credit rating is a valuable service. It takes time and expertise to identify relevant signals and estimate their implications. Having invested time and gained expertise, it makes sense to resell the estimates to others. Debtors appreciate knowing where they stand. Lenders appreciate the feedback on their own evaluations.

To some extent ratings are self-fulfilling, as high ratings help issuers roll over debt while low ratings hinder. Some institutions are restricted by charter to holding investment-grade debt, rated triple-B or higher. Sub-investment grades were once known mostly as "junk" and could hardly place bonds at all. Nowadays markets actively trade a broad spectrum of credit. Their feedback provides a check on ratings, with wide discrepancies encouraging reassessment.

Credit grades don't claim to indicate the absolute default risk. The latter fluctuates with economic cycles, technological change, and political shifts outside the scope of most rating exercises. Also, the rating agencies don't want to be held culpable for potential debt implosions. They emphasize that their grades are opinions on relative rankings within asset classes, with potentially limited relevance across asset classes or over time. Moody's (Moody's Investor Service 2009) reference on rating symbols and definitions doesn't mention a single quantitative benchmark.

Fortunately for the rating agencies, regulators don't believe their disavowals. They use the credit grades, or let the entities they regulate use the credit grades, as proxies for absolute default risk. To facilitate comparison, major rating agencies periodically report the empirical default rates for different credit grades over horizons ranging from one year to more than ten years.

Table 8.1 is a compilation from Moody's (Emery et al. 2009: exhibit 36) of average one-year U.S. corporate default rates between 1920 and 2008. They are grouped by Moody's credit grade at the beginning of the year in which default occurred. Next to it is similar data from S&P (Vazza, Aurora, and Kraemer 2010: table 25) covering 1980 through 2009.

The two lists are remarkably similar given the differences in agency and time period. The only major discrepancy occurs in the lowest categories,

Table 8.1
U.S. Corporate Default Rates in bps

Moody's Rating	Default Rate 1920–2006	S&P Rating	Default Rate 1980–2009
Aaa	0	AAA	0
Aa	6	AA	4
A	9	A	9
Baa	27	BBB	28
Ba	106	BB	104
B	340	B	486
Caa-C	1,325	CCC-C	2,892

where Moody's shows much fewer defaults. That discrepancy would largely vanish if Moody's averages were calculated from 1980 onward. Compilations from different asset classes, countries, and periods show more diversity. However, several regularities stand out:

- Default rates are generally low except in the lowest credit rungs or sharp recessions. To qualify as investment grade, default risk over the economic cycle should be less than 50 bps per annum, even before we factor in typical recovery rates of roughly half.
- Credit risks scale logarithmically, with a drop in letter grade roughly quadrupling the one-year default risk. Since estimation errors and intrayear regime switches muddy the actual results, the target gradient must be even steeper. Writing for Moody's, Yoshizawa (2003) describes the "idealized" default risks as roughly doubling per drop in alphanumeric notch and hence octupling per drop in primary letter grade.
- Macroeconomic fluctuations can swing the default risk a letter grade's worth in either direction. Hence, credit grades point to average default rates over a cycle.

Factor Analysis

For good credit analysis, it is crucial to identify a few common driving factors and to collect a lot of relatively independent observations on their impact. This makes U.S. corporate debt an inviting subject of study. There are thousands of different issuers, with tens of thousands of years of debt servicing experience under a relatively stable legal environment.

Using Fisher's (1936) discriminant analysis, Altman (1968) developed a famous credit score based on working capital, retained earnings, earnings before interest and taxes, and sales—all measured relative to assets—and net worth divided by liabilities. More refined models have been developed since. Servigny and Renault (2004) provide an excellent overview.

To keep scores from predicting a negative default risk, models typically estimate the log odds. In the range of most interest, log odds basically coincide with log risk. This helps justify the association of credit grades with a logarithmic scale of default risk.

Rating agencies combine quantitative scoring with discretionary judgments. They also take into account market information like prices, volatility, and credit spreads. Their primary focus, however, is economic drivers, since they aim to provide independent guidance on fair price.

From a counting game perspective, viewing different credits as bundles of a smaller set of primary factors raises the effective D and T. This makes estimates more reliable and trims uncertainty. Without these kinds of decompositions, formal or informal, credit rating would be a farce.

Even with a factor analysis approach, we don't get nearly as many plausibly independent-but-relevant observations as we would like. Look at the heavy clustering in Figure 8.1. Inspired by Giesecke et al. (2010), it depicts yearly default rates from 1866 through 2009 for bonds issued by U.S. non-financial corporations.

The default rates are strikingly uneven. They fluctuate in irregular cycles of varying intensity, with peaks about ten times neighboring troughs. Intensity has receded overall, though not in linear fashion. One can plausibly argue that regime changes occurred around 1900, 1940, and 1980.

The credit cycles do not coincide with standard macroeconomic cycles. Giesecke and colleagues find a correlation of 0.25. If we use the fluctuations themselves to define an explanatory factor, we are bound to overfit and have limited predictive power. If we ignore the fluctuations, our observations won't be conditionally independent. If we search for cycle proxies, we'll experience both problems, though it is hoped in smaller measure.

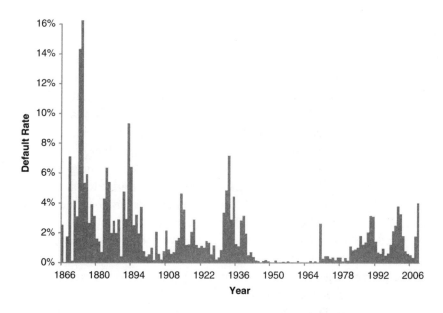

Figure 8.1
U.S. Corporate Bond Default Rates

Hence, even for the bond market as a whole it's hard to identify a long-term default rate within a factor of two. The similarities in Table 8.1 between 1920–2006 averages and 1980–2009 averages seem a well-chosen coincidence. Judging from Figure 8.1, any other long period would show different averages.

Even if we correctly identify the mean default rate, estimated default rates at extremes can be unreliable. If we fit a straight line through a cluster of data, errors in the slope affect the outer estimates much more than the inner. Nor can we be sure that the best fit is a straight line, and again the errors matter most in the extremes. It's always riskier to extrapolate than to interpolate.

This risk comes to the fore whenever safe assets meet severe crisis. We'll likely be uncertain about both safety and severity; the outcome will refine our views. The main reason U.S. mortgages retained such high ratings until the national housing bubble burst is that they had never previously experienced a bubble burst of that scale.

Grading Uncertainty

Credit ratings summarize decades of detailed analysis and the web of confidence they support. That doesn't mean any particular credit risk is graded correctly. The raters can't easily know, and we can't easily check.

For example, the post-1920 historical averages suggest that A-grade default risk should be less than16 bps. That's less than one default per 600 years of servicing. But a 20 bps risk could plausibly stay default-free that long. Indeed, a 20 bps risk has a 1% chance of servicing for 2,300 years straight.

Higher credit grades are even harder to distinguish. Suppose we think a credit has either no risk or 2 bps of risk and accordingly warrants a triple-A or double-A grade. Starting from even odds, we would need the equivalent of 20,000 years of unbroken servicing to become 99% confident in the triple-A label.

It's safe to say that no one has ever conclusively identified triple-A safety. Any risk that low would be overwhelmed by invasions, volcano eruptions, plagues, civil wars, fraud, terrorism, mass extinctions, or other disasters we can't yet imagine. I am tempted to call it "Who Knows What Can Happen" risk. A refined name is "force majeure."

The only plausible way to defend particular credit labels is to identify them as hopeful means of much broader confidence intervals. To assist that, rating agencies ought to report the confidence interval they think applies. Analytically this corresponds to reporting T as well as $E = D/T$. But expressing sample limitations and other uncertainties in terms of upper and lower grades will make them easier to digest.

Reporting confidence intervals will make it easier to compare risk across asset classes. Sovereign credit risk is a lot harder to identify than corporate credit risk, as there are many fewer observations and the mechanisms for enforcing claims are murkier. Broader confidence intervals can highlight this. Confidence intervals should also be wide for poorly documented securitizations or credits facing unprecedented stresses.

Confidence intervals will also assist in pricing longer-dated bonds. The more dispersed beliefs are around the mean, the more a long-dated payment tends to be worth. This may surprise those who expect risk-neutral investors not to care about uncertainty and risk-averse investors to loathe it. But technically it is analogous to the value of interest rate convexity, a concept well known in bond pricing. For an extreme example, compare these two scenarios:

- 99% chance of being riskless and a 1% chance of being worthless
- 100% chance of 1% annual default risk

A bond payment ten years forward needs be discounted only 1% for credit risk in the first case, versus nearly 10% in the second.

Change won't come easy. The current system is well ensconced. Rating agencies have been awarding single grades for generations. Regulators have grown accustomed to treating risk estimates as certain. Neither side has much expertise in analyzing uncertainty systematically. Neither side seems itching to gain it.

Nevertheless, high/low grading offers some advantages to both rating agencies and regulators. By allowing for mixed ratings, it can soften the uproar caused by sudden loss of investment-grade status. It encourages more timely adjustment of ratings, since agencies can visibly qualify their decisions. It can tidy up the credit watches and advisories that hint at uncertainty.

On the regulatory side, formal disclosures of uncertainty can aid in setting contingent reserves. While Basel II wanted banks to develop their own internal ratings system, the requirements were cumbersome. Many banks found it cheaper to purchase ratings from rating agencies, as Basel II allowed. In effect Basel II delegated a lot of regulatory authority to rating agencies, without demanding much from rating agencies in return. More disclosure of uncertainty is a wholly legitimate demand.

Some critics would go farther and remove rating agencies' special status as regulatory advisors. I disagree. Overall, the delegation breeds more competence and less corruption than wholly government-run ratings. We do, however, need to trim some ludicrous incentives to shade risk estimates down. Demanding more disclosure will help, though not as much as trimming the marginal leverage for higher credit grades.

A prominent example is the triple-A rating accorded U.S. and U.K. sovereign debt despite agency warnings about mounting servicing burdens. By rating agencies' own criteria, even a strong hint of problems should nix a triple-A grade. But of course sovereigns are special, both in their funding possibilities and in their ability to take away quasi-regulatory privileges. Even the recent downgrades of PIIGS, long overdue, triggered a huge outcry. High/low grading would provide a quieter middle ground.

Uncertainty grading is no panacea. The housing bubble had a constellation of other causes, ably surveyed in Ellis (2008). The overstretch of sovereign debt in the United States and Europe mostly stems from excessive benefits to pensioners and public employees. Deflating overconfidence in servicing won't make problems go away. But it will expose them better to public view. Finance needs to get away from the mindset that others' irresponsibility excuses one's own.

Credit Migration

Credit ratings are bound to migrate because of estimation noise or actual regime switches. The previously mentioned Moody's and S&P studies paint similar pictures of ratings migration:

- Averaging over the past quarter century, roughly 25% of corporate alphanumeric ratings change per year. Some 40% of these, or 10% of the total, change primary letter grades.
- Migrations are roughly 50% more frequent in subinvestment grades than in investment grades.
- Most migrations head to neighboring ratings. Occasionally there are big jumps, especially downgrades related to defaults.
- Downgrades are more frequent than upgrades for investment-grade credits. Credits below B tend to migrate up if they don't default. Credits between single-B and double-B migrate relatively equally in each direction.
- Migration rates are uneven. Downgrades surge around actual default surges. Upgrades surge when defaults recede. However, the fluctuations are not nearly as sharp for migration rates as for actual defaults.

Bayesian updating for evidence of default helps explain the jumps and irregularities. To model the gradual diffusion and mean reversion, let's step back a moment and think about default risks the way physicists think about gases or biologists think about populations. Some factors make them expand, some factors make them contract, and some just add noise. Expansion outweighs when default risks are low, because money is easy and borrowers get complacent. Contraction outweighs when default risks are high, because borrowers work down their burdens through fiscal tightening or restructuring.

To simplify calculations, imagine these forces operating continuously over time without jumps. Since default risk can't be negative, let's model noise as proportional to a positive power m of current risk θ. A tractable model that delivers this is

$$d\theta = a\theta^{2m-1}(1 - b\theta)dt + c\theta^m dz, \qquad (8.1)$$

where a, b, and σ are constants, $d\theta$ is the change in default risk over infinitesimal time dt, and dz represents standard Brownian motion with zero drift and unit rate of volatility. May (1973) used an equation like this with $m = 1$ to model a large population θ subject to a natural growth rate a, a stable carrying capacity $\frac{1}{b}$, and random influences c. He showed that it implied a long-term gamma distribution for θ.

Indeed, equation (8.1) implies θ is long-term gamma distributed for every m, unless there's no interior equilibrium at all. Examples include the famed Cox, Ingersoll, and Ross (1985) model of the spot interest rate, where $m = \frac{1}{2}$. Moreover, Dennis and Patil (1984) have shown that most growth and decay models with nonnegativity constraints imply a long-term gamma distribution or something close, even when (8.1) does not exactly apply.

Hence, gamma distributions arise naturally both in the long-term distribution of default risk and the short-term distribution of beliefs about default risk. However, let me emphasize that the two gamma distributions aren't nearly the same. The long-term shape parameter (i.e., the counterpart to D in the model of credit beliefs) must significantly exceed one to account for the concentration of ratings around double-B.

The Appendix analyzes equation (8.1) in more detail. The most curious finding concerns the power m. Faster migration among lower ratings appears to require $m > 1$. Yet most credit models assume $m \leq 1$.

Estimation error makes the discrepancy even more striking. As we have seen, high ratings are much harder to estimate than low ratings. All else being equal, we should expect to see more migration among higher grades than among lower grades.

In short, top grades seem unusually sticky. Why? Presumably rating agencies are reluctant to publicly change their minds. However, that can't be all there is it to it, since the frequency of ratings changes varies significantly over time, between credit grades, and across asset classes. Also, the market has plenty of participants who watch the credit watchers. Systematically blatant errors should incite systematic countertrading, which I would expect to leave noticeable tracks.

Deference to Consensus

The rest of this chapter will explain ratings stickiness in terms of a preference for consensus. This may sound like either a tautology or a slur on humanity. However, I'm not imputing a strong preference, just a mild deference to "the wisdom of the crowd" when highly uncertain. And I will apply it in an unusual way, namely to show why top ratings are stickier than others.

The model is inspired by Ising (1925). Ising-type models are widely used in physics to explain phase transitions in matter. While highly stylized, their core predictions often match the predictions of far more complex models.

Consider, for example, ferromagnetism. Place a cool block of iron in even a weak magnetic field and the atoms will tend to align in spin, creating a magnet. Shut off the field and the magnetism persists. Heat the iron enough and the magnetism disappears. How can we reconcile these behaviors?

The basic Ising explanation is that the iron atoms face two kinds of forces. One is ordinary random motion related to heat, which favors maximum disorganization. The other is the attraction of like spins, which encourages neighbors to align in the same direction. At low temperatures only a few atoms will have enough energy to flip spins against the alignment, and these will randomly flip back, so the core alignment perpetuates itself.

Similar phenomena occur when water cools to ice. A crystal formed randomly encourages neighbors to coalesce with it. Ising-type models help explain how the transitions can be sharp even though the temperature change is gradual.

In our model, many observers make many comparisons between two credits. Each comparison estimates a difference ω in perceived default risk, which might be any real number. However, all that gets reported is which credit is riskier. This is a stylized version of ordinal credit rankings, with very fine gradations.

Why don't the full ω values get reported? There are several plausible explanations, including:

- Spelling out the environmental assumptions underlying point estimates might require more attention than the estimates are worth.
- Since different ω likely assume different environments, comparing them would be difficult without conversion to coarser measures.
- Reporters might be embarrassed to report ω values way out of line with consensus.

We can view these reports as signals $S = \pm 1$, with rare exceptions where $S = 0$. A fully independent reporter should set S to the sign of ω. However, reporting usually involves some deference to consensus. This leads to a decision rule along the lines of

$$S(\omega) = \text{sgn} \, (\omega + \varepsilon \cdot consensus), \tag{8.2}$$

where sgn indicates the sign and ε is a tiny positive weight.

Clearly, there must be a threshold $\overline{\omega} \equiv -\varepsilon \cdot consensus$ where S vanishes. Below that threshold S is negative; above it S is positive. Denoting the cumulative distribution of ω by H, and assuming $\overline{\omega}$ is rare, $consensus$ should stabilize near $\left(1 - H(\overline{\omega})\right) \cdot 1 + H(\overline{\omega}) \cdot (-1) = 1 - 2H(\overline{\omega})$. In equilibrium,

$$H(\overline{\omega}) = \tfrac{1}{2}\left(1 + \overline{\omega}\big/\varepsilon\right). \tag{8.3}$$

By Ising model standards, this is an extraordinarily simple equilibrium condition. But it generates similar kinds of results.

Ratings Stickiness

To demonstrate Ising-type behavior with minimal clutter, I will assume that the two credits have identically distributed beliefs. In that case $H(0) = \tfrac{1}{2}$, so one equilibrium sets $\overline{\omega} = 0$ as expected. I will also assume that the mode or peak density h_{max} of H occurs at zero, which should be true unless beliefs are distributed very unnaturally.

To check for other equilibria, Figure 8.2 graphs both sides of equation (8.3) as functions of candidate $\overline{\omega}$ values. The right-hand side, which I call the control line, has a steep slope of $\tfrac{1}{2\varepsilon}$; the chart is stretched for clarity. If that slope exceeds h_{max}, the origin will be the only equilibrium.

Otherwise, there will be two additional equilibria. Where H is left of the control line, the candidate $\overline{\omega}$ will tend to increase—i.e., more reports will flip negative. Where H is to the right of the control line, the candidate ω_0 will tend to decrease. This makes the outer equilibria stable and the equilibrium at zero unstable.

Hence, when h_{max} is sufficiently high, one credit slides into favor and stays there absent a major upheaval. The biggest and stickiest distortions occur when most beliefs about ω are tightly concentrated

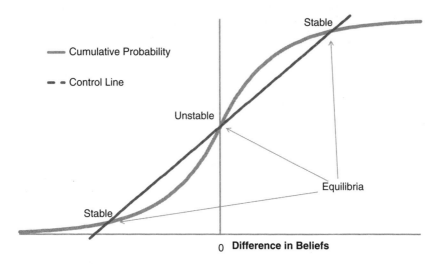

Figure 8.2
Equilibria for $\overline{\omega}$ with Symmetric Beliefs

around the origin. In that case H resembles a step function (nearly flat, nearly vertical and nearly flat again), and the stable equilibria are close to $\pm\varepsilon$.

This is most likely to occur with top-rated credits. As seen in Chapter 6, their beliefs tend to cluster tightly near zero, with infinite density at zero itself. If we compare two such beliefs chosen at random, or two mean beliefs calculated with random exclusions, the resulting h_{max} will be infinite as well. This will guarantee distortion.

While ε is tiny, it can be large relative to top-rated default risks. We thus have a clear explanation for the stickiness of top ratings. A taste for consensus creates a self-sustaining bias. The paucity of news for such credits—i.e., they tend to service just as expected—helps keep the bias in place. Most observers perceive both risks as so tiny that they're reluctant to challenge the accepted ranking.

The bias isn't permanent. When evidence of default does arrive for top-rated credits, even indirect and fractional evidence, it tends to come as a huge shock. This shakes up rankings the way that a furnace shakes up ferromagnetism. When the risk environment cools, new rankings will emerge. Some of them will incorporate genuinely new information. Some may reflect just another random consensus.

Our analysis also applies to stickiness of perceptions about fiat money, wealth, and debt sustainability. Between deference to consensus and the infrequency of payment crises, people can easily convince each other that the real risks are negligible. The network of trust can shave the real risks by facilitating rollover and encouraging investment. Nevertheless, the model here reminds us that our strongest beliefs can have weak foundations.

~

"What a disgrace this worship of credit ratings is," said Pandora. "Nothing good can come of idolatry."

"Pygmalion would beg to differ," said Prometheus. "The statue he worshipped became his wife."

"He had help from Aphrodite. Looking back she's sorry she did. All the gods have retreated from the idol worship they used to foster. When will regulators do the same?"

"They feel their banking system is safer when credits have top ratings—even though they lack the reserves to cover mistakes. The truth is closer to the opposite. When banking systems run low on reserves, even top-rated credits can become unsafe."

"Reserves should be geared to the scope for surprise, not to risk itself," said Pandora. "Most casinos take risky wagers all the time without harm. Their main concerns are attendance and the depth of pockets of those who attend. The analogous concern for banks is the phase of the credit cycle."

"Regulators presume that safer bets have much lower variance than risky bets. That's true when the risks are known. However, estimates of high safety tend to be highly uncertain. Additional buffers are needed to cover that."

"Making rating agencies formally indicate their uncertainty might help. At the very least it will remind regulators and the public how fine credit gradations are, and that no one really knows what grade is deserved."

"The rating agencies might not like that," said Prometheus. "They profit from the aura of certainty. The regulators might like it even less. A lot of highly rated but uncertain credits are sovereign or sovereign-backed. They want that debt rolled over cheaply."

"Acknowledging uncertainty needn't undermine all confidence. Indeed, it might better justify the confidence we have. As the Ising-type model shows, a little deference can breed an unduly rigid consensus. Smoother adjustment might help the system weather big shocks."

9

Insecuritization

Large portfolios are commonly rated for risk as if aggregate losses are bound to fall within a few standard deviations of the perceived mean. This can be wildly inappropriate, especially for senior debt tranches. Ignorance, greed, and bad regulatory incentives have driven gross misuse verging on fraud. We'll examine some healthier alternatives.

Readers who have been fretting the dearth of moneymaking advice in this book need look no further. This chapter will demonstrate how to rake in fortunes through creative statistical fraud. Granted, others have beaten us to much booty. Still, foolish regulations, negligent rating practices, and irresponsible fiduciaries invite more ill-gotten gains.

Here is a basic recipe:

- Take a big bunch of different credit risks, just like a normal bank does, only with far less supervision.
- Repackage the claims in tranches ranked by seniority, and give them impressive names like Collateralized Debt Obligations (CDOs).
- Let the lowest tranches shoulder the mean observed risks and the middle tranches the risks of three to four standard deviation outliers.
- Assume the risks are normally distributed to prove that the highest tranches are nearly risk free.
- Hire rating agencies to certify the calculations, and rely on regulators and major institutional investors to accept the certifications on faith.
- Offer the certified tranches for sale as tradable securities.

- Once a credit boom gathers steam, offer the highest tranches to anyone seeking something for nothing.

Like any sting, this recipe works best if the buyers don't realize they're being had. For awe and admiration, hire finance PhDs and MBAs with impressive qualifications, great networking skills, and little real understanding of what they're hawking. When in doubt, speak of Gaussian copulas. Faced with doubt, emphasize that securitization itself inspires trust by providing liquidity.

This chapter will expose the statistical underpinnings to these facades. It will also show how to analyze portfolio risks better. Hopefully it will encourage higher standards for portfolio risk analysis.

Exchangeability

The easiest way to understand dependence across risks is to conceive each individual risk as very simple and statistically exchangeable with other risks. Simple we already know: default risk. So let's take n credit assets and tag them in some order. The portfolio outcome is a string of zeros and ones indicating which pay and which default. Exchangeable means that if the tags get mixed up we can't detect any difference in the probabilities; all that matters is how many assets default or don't.

Given 100 default risks, there are 2^{100} distinct portfolio outcomes. If those risks are exchangeable, 100 probabilities completely define the rest. That is a colossal savings over the general case. We need something like that to make the analysis tractable.

However, even tracking 100 probabilities is a lot of trouble. So we look for summary statistics like mean and standard deviation. Unfortunately, means and standard deviations don't do a very good job of indicating tail risks, even in perfectly exchangeable portfolios.

Osband (2002) introduced a contraption that tries to make this intuitively clear. He called it Devlin's Triangle after a fictional character and hoped risk analysts would adopt it. They haven't, and since I hate to see an orphan, I will claim it for my own.

To build an Osband triangle, lay a bed of $m + 1$ nonnegative numbers on the bottom, with gaps in between. For the layer above, add neighboring numbers and fasten the sum over the gap. Keep adding layers until there's a single number. Then divide every element by the top number. Here is an example for $m = 3$.

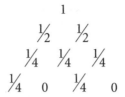

Every triangle constructed in this fashion turns out to represent a feasible set of exchangeable default risks. The kth entry on the $n + 1^{th}$ row denotes the probability that in any subset of n assets, the first k assets default and the rest do not.

To calculate the probability that k out of n assets default in any order, multiply these entries by the corresponding entries in a much better-known triangle. It is called Pascal's triangle in the West and Yang Hui's triangle in China, although Persian and Indian mathematicians invented it centuries before. That triangle also starts from one at the top but adds neighboring elements down rather than up. The kth entry on the $n + 1^{th}$ row indicates the number of distinct combinations of k hits and $n - k$ misses. Unlike in an Osband triangle, the numbers are always the same and look like this:

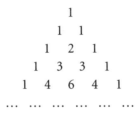

In the example above, multiplying the two triangles tells us level by level that—

1. The probability of the whole is 1.
2. Every asset is equally likely to default or service.
3. Pairs of assets have a 25% chance of both defaulting and a 25% of both servicing.
4. Three assets together have a 25% chance of no default and a 75% chance of two defaults.

At first glance it might seem impossible for exchangeable risks to take this form. The following example refutes this. Three companies are competing for a government contract to set a new networking standard. Securing a contract is life-and-death for the companies. The government considers four alternative awards: to the first, to the second, to the third, and to all three jointly. If each award is equally likely it generates the risk structure above.

This example starts out looking like a standard coin toss but isn't. Usually it's impossible to infer from any given row what an Osband triangle looks like below. The main exceptions can't be extended at all. In particular, there's no way to extend the row [¼ 0 ¼ 0] or any other row with an element more than twice the sum of its neighbors.

For more generic behavior, we might exclude Osband triangles that can't be extended indefinitely, even if they hit bedrock only after millions of layers. De Finetti (1931a) showed that only one class of default risks is infinitely exchangeable. This "mixed binomial" class denotes, in effect, that assets are conditionally independent given the default rates.

In general, most exchangeable random variables can be viewed as conditionally independent. This is known as de Finetti's Theorem. It is an extremely important result in probability theory. It carves a world of interdependent randomness into things that move completely in sync and things that move completely on their own.

Imagine that a physicist is measuring molecular motion inside a balloon when a child runs away with the balloon. It would be helpful to distinguish the random movements inside the balloon from the child's motion that shifts the balloon. It would be even more helpful to separate child from balloon. That creates a controlled experiment. Unfortunately, most financial analyses are so loosely controlled we have to settle for distinguishing things in our minds.

The mixing distribution corresponds to the child's motion. It determines which θ applies. Given θ, we assume the remaining risks are independent and identically distributed.

Creation of Correlation

It's a lot easier to think about mixing distributions for conditionally independent risks than to estimate separate probabilities for every joint outcome.

However, many risk analysts lack patience even for that. They prefer instead to think about summary statistics of the joint distribution, particularly the mean and the correlation.

As we've seen, the mean is hard to measure. The correlation is even harder to measure. But let's imagine we nail them both. Indeed, let's imagine that we can measure any moment we please, and eliminate any default risk triangle yielding a different value. What is left?

The answer is remarkably neat. The first n moments of the portfolio uniquely identify the first $n + 1$ rows and vice-versa. (The first row can be viewed as matching the 0th moment, which sums the probabilities to one.) In particular, the mean and correlation indicate the probabilities of zero, one, or two defaults in any pair of credits. That leaves a lot of wiggle room for rows further down.

Let's work though an example. Suppose we own 1,000 exchangeable default risks. We estimate a mean of 0.5% and a correlation of 2%. This implies a 0.9751% risk of one default in a pair and a 0.01245% risk of two defaults in a pair.

Now let us infer the risk of experiencing 50 or more defaults. That is at least ten times the mean and marks a 4.4 standard deviation outlier. Moreover, if we cheat and claim zero correlation, the standard deviation of defaults will collapse to 2.2 from 10.2, making this a 20 standard deviation event. Very few risk analysts—let alone their employers, clients, or regulators—knowingly worry about 20 standard deviation events. So it's tempting to round the number to zero and move on.

However, all our certainty technically implies is a 50 bps mean and 99.75 bps standard deviation on the mixing distribution. One mixing distribution meeting those criteria puts a 3.8% probability on a 550+ bps risk and all remaining probability on a 30 bps risk. In that case, there's over a 3% chance of 50 or more defaults. Another feasible mixing distribution attaches 25.1% probability to a 199 bps risk and the rest to zero risk, for a probability of 50+ defaults of barely one in 500 million.

In general, all the correlation ρ tells us is the ratio of two variances:

$$\rho = \frac{\text{var}(commonRisk)}{\text{var}(singleCredit)}. \tag{9.1}$$

Hence, from a mixing distribution perspective, correlation isn't causing anything. It's simply a measure induced by the variance of the common risk.

And since the variance can't describe the full tail of risks, correlation can't either. Neither can the skewness or kurtosis, which specify another one or two rows down the Osband triangle.

Consequently, when practitioners infer tail risks from estimates of moments, they fold in explicit or implicit assumptions about the forms of the mixing distribution. There's nothing wrong with that per se. The problem is rather that the most popular assumptions chronically understate the tail risks.

The biggest single error is to take recent history as representative of all likely regimes. If recent history is turbulent, people are reluctant to take the risk. Once bitten, twice shy. Conversely, if recent history is calm, people presume it will persist and tend to take on too much risk. However, the next few pages assume the correlation is correctly estimated.

Binomial and Normal Approximations

The simplest mixing distribution doesn't mix. It puts all its weight on a single default risk θ. That yields a standard binomial distribution for the portfolio. With n equally-weighted assets, the standard deviation of portfolio returns will be approximately $\sqrt{\theta/n}$. As n increases, risk gradually fades away.

With positive correlation ρ, the standard deviation of portfolio returns converges to $\sqrt{\rho\theta}$ rather than zero as n gets large. That can make a huge difference in regulatory capital. It's as if n were capped at $1/\rho$. Quadrupling ρ doubles the minimum standard deviation. So even though default correlations are generally low and might not appear significantly greater than zero, a lot rides on the value selected.

Adjusting n to make a binomial distribution generate the target standard deviation is the essence of Moody's Binomial Expansion Technique, or BET. First proposed by Cifuentes and O'Connor (1996), it improves on standard binomial models by allowing a wider dispersion. The adjusted n, called the diversity score, can be interpreted as the effective number of independent assets.

The diversity score typically ranges from five to a few dozen. With exchangeable assets, it can never exceed $1/\rho$. This makes risk estimates quite "lumpy" and ill-suited to calibration of high safety thresholds. As Fender and Kiff (2004) note, BET is particularly prone to understate the risk on senior tranches of portfolios with low diversity scores.

Gaussian (normal) approximations are far more popular. By allowing continuous returns and making all risks scale with standard deviation, they avoid the lumpiness of BET and make thresholds easier to calculate. Adding to the attraction, a multivariate normal distribution with a single correlation parameter ρ has a neat interpretation. For every unit of default risk, a common component contributes ρ and an independent component contributes $\sqrt{1 - \rho^2}$. That's a convenient way to think about risk.

However, the convenience comes at a steep price. It can't handle a crisis, when the common factor surges in intensity. This became glaringly evident when the mortgage bubble burst. Gaussian models denied that senior CDO tranches were seriously threatened, even as the market imploded.

The implausibility of normal distributions shouldn't surprise. They can't fit high odds of zero losses without also assigning high odds to negative losses. They presume symmetry around the mean. They tie all risk judgments to standard deviations.

Nevertheless, the normal distribution has abnormal appeal. It's the most widely used distribution in finance, often with good reason. Force of habit encourages using it even with bad reason. Few risk analysts grasp the central limitations of the Central Limit Theorem: how much it depends on independent components, and how slowly it converges in the tails.

Fat-Tailed Approximations

Single-parameter approximations needn't be thin-tailed approximations. The exponential distribution is the best-known example. Moody's Correlated Binomial (CorBin) distribution, developed by Witt (2004), provides another.

CorBin assumes that the conditional correlation when all other observed assets have defaulted equals the ordinary correlation. This provides a recursive formula for calculating the right edge of the Osband triangle, where everything defaults. While the probability of complete default shrinks as the portfolio expands, it stays bounded away from zero. The other entries get calculated through successive subtractions.

CorBin can match the first two moments of any BET distribution. Yet it is much fatter-tailed. To choose between CorBin and BET scientifically, one needs to consider higher moments or try to estimate the outer tail risk directly.

I have found no evidence that Moody's made such tests. Still, it shelved CorBin quickly. During the credit bubble, other rating agencies avoided fat-tailed distributions, too. While some of their quants warned, the business side overruled. Acknowledging fat tails would have made it harder to award lucrative top ratings.

Apart from money there was little excuse. The rating agencies knew from experience that portfolio risks tended to be fat-tailed. If they found CorBin too complex, they could have opted for the tractable CreditRisk + methodology, published by Credit Suisse First Boston (Wilde 1997).

CreditRisk + acknowledges the instability of default risk and the merit of mixed binomial models. It proceeds to approximate a low-mean binomial risk as Poisson and a low-mean beta mixing distribution as gamma. The resulting Poisson-gamma mixture is known as negative binomial (NegBin) and is very easy to work with.

NegBin tails decay at rates that converge to constant fractions. In contrast, binomial and normal tails decay at accelerating rates. Hence, NegBin distributions tend to be fatter-tailed than binomial or normal.

To make this more concrete, let's suppose we have a portfolio of 100 exchangeable credits with a mean default risk of 2% and correlation 5%.

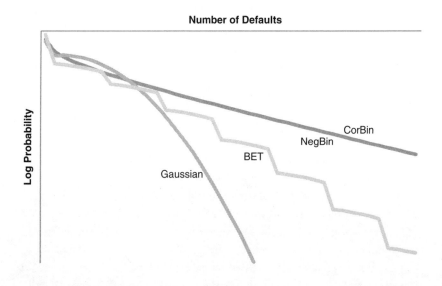

Figure 9.1
Default Risks for Correlated Debt Portfolios

Table 9.1
Maximum Defaults Expected for 100 Credits with 2% Mean Risk and
5% Correlation

Confidence	Gaussian	BET	CorBin	NegBin
95%	7	6	9	9
99%	9	11	16	16
99.9%	12	17	26	27
99.99%	14	21	36	38

Each of the four models generates probability distribution for defaults. I chart them all in Figure 9.1 in log terms. Only three lines are visible because NegBin and CorBin coincide on the scale shown. The jaggedness in BET reflects lumpiness that my linear interpolations couldn't smooth out.

Charts for other plausible examples look broadly similar. Apart from twists near the origin, the logarithm of probability decays quadratically for Gaussian and near-linearly for NegBin and CorBin. BET tails are fatter than Gaussian tails but thinner than NegBin or CorBin tails.

How much fatter or thinner? That depends on the part of the tail we're looking at, as well as the default risk and correlation it's attached to. In the range we're interested in, the differences are big even at the 95% confidence level and widen as confidence gets more demanding. Table 9.1 presents a table for the previous example.

Although CorBin tightened confidence standards, it was introduced during a credit boom, when assessments of mean risk were dropping. The correlation confused a journalist for Bloomberg (Smith 2008), who made CorBin a symbol of rating agency laxness. Spurred by the article, a Congressional hearing demanded that Moody's executives defend themselves on why they had used the CorBin model at all. Unfortunately, confusion pervades public discussion about the reform of financial risk analysis.

False Confidence

A negative binomial distribution is the best simple way to model risky debt portfolios. It is based on a gamma distribution for default risk, which provides both a natural way to model uncertainty in default risk and a long-term equilibrium for actual risk. A correlated binomial distribution offers similar predictions, although it is far less tractable The main BET and Gaussian alternatives are implausible and unduly rigid.

Shifting to NegBin or CorBin would expose much false confidence in our credit ratings. Imagine a portfolio derivative that pays 1 if k or fewer defaults occur and 0 otherwise. Let's call it a k-CDO and use the historical average default rates reported in Chapter 8 to assign it a credit grade.

In the example above, a 10-CDO would get rated as low triple-B by Gaussian, double-B by BET, and single-B by NegBin. A 12-CDO would get rated as double-A by Gaussian, a low triple-B by BET, and a low double-B by NegBin. A 14-CDO would get rated as triple-A by Gaussian, triple-B by BET, and double-B by NegBin.

These are huge differences. If rating agencies had applied stricter methodologies, a lot fewer claims on debt portfolios would have been rated investment grade, much less triple-A. It would have been much harder to gain leverage by arbitraging the loopholes in Basel II. With less leverage, housing prices wouldn't have bubbled up so much or come crashing down so hard. Never in world history have toxic statistics stirred more false hopes or rude awakenings.

NegBin models also have dramatic implications for bank regulation. Recall from Chapter 6 that Basel II tied bank capital to estimated buffers against excess losses. Since ordinary reserves are supposed to cover expected losses, and since 99.9% confidence is a fashionable definition of regulatory safety, the buffer calculation can be stylized as the "99.9% threshold less the mean."

For a Gaussian distribution, the buffer is always 3.09 standard deviations and will scale approximately with the square root of the mean risk. For NegBin, the buffer will be higher but scale less rapidly with the mean. We saw that in Chapter 5 with beta and gamma distributions: low means are associated with high uncertainty and a long tail. As NegBins are gamma-Poisson mixtures, the same reasoning extends to them.

Figure 9.2 compares the size of Gaussian and NegBin buffers at 99.9% confidence. As mean default rises from 2 bps to 512 bps, the Gaussian buffer increases from less than a quarter of the recommended NegBin buffer to more than half. While the chart below sticks with 100 assets and 5% correlation, experiments with other values generate similar pictures.

Whereas a Gaussian or binomial approach advises nearly ten times the buffer for a 500 bps risk as for a 5 bps risk, NegBin advises less than five

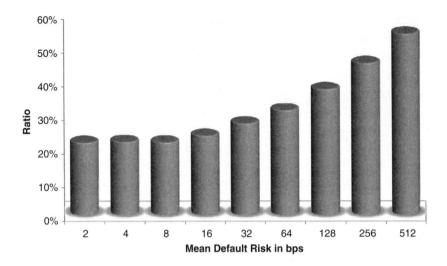

Figure 9.2
Gaussian Buffers as Percent of NegBin Buffers

times the buffer. Since most of Basel II presumes binomial or Gaussian dependence, one quick patch would halve the gradient between strong and weak credits. Granted, no quick patch can fix Basel II. Still, I want to emphasize that thoughtful uncertainty can generate regulatory advice that is at least as clear as the feigned certainty underlying Basel II.

Copulas

Over the past decade it has become fashionable to use copulas to model dependence. Copulas describe the joint distribution once each individual asset is transformed to a uniform random draw of real numbers between 0 and 1. That transformation is sufficiently unnatural for discrete default risk that it is hard to convey good intuition for copula application to CDOs. Ironically, that appears to be one of the main attractions of copulas.

Think of it this way. By distinguishing clearly between conditionally independent risks and common drivers, de Finetti's Theorem begs investigation into the form of the mixing distribution and the uncertainty of estimation. Copulas obscure that with complex formulation. Most critics feel too intimidated to poke around.

Li (2000) introduced the Gaussian copula to finance. It quickly became an industry standard thanks to its one-parameter depiction of common and independent components in default intensity. However, as we have seen, a fixed Gaussian distribution can't handle crisis.

This is now widely recognized. In an article that captured the public eye, Salmon (2009) described Li's model as "the formula that killed Wall Street." Patterson's (2010) best seller casts the blame more broadly on "a new breed of math whizzes."

Brigo, Pallavicini, and Torresetti (2010) defend the new breed and its tool kit. They cite numerous efforts to refine Li's model and make copulas more flexible. They present a tractable framework for pricing credit derivatives in line with market beliefs. They also note that models should not be held responsible for their misuse.

Both sets of arguments have merits. On the one hand, quants wittingly or unwittingly fed the exaggeration of credit derivatives safety. On the other hand, better modeling of credit derivatives would doubtless have warned sooner of crisis and thereby tempered some extremes. It will doubtless temper extremes going forward.

For a historical parallel, consider the product known as portfolio insurance. It is supposed to neutralize the overall market exposure or "beta" of a given basket of securities. Usually these securities are equities, and the market exposure is summarized in an index like the S&P 500.

The classic Black-Scholes (1973) model of options pricing presumes that any derivative's risk can be instantaneously measured and hedged out using a specified fraction or "delta" of the underlying asset. By equating delta with beta, it suggests a potentially automatic way to provide portfolio insurance. By the mid-1980s, few major trading houses were not using Black-Scholes models. Portfolio insurance became one of their most lucrative products.

Portfolio insurance worked well until it was most needed, during the 1987 crash. Prices plunged too fast for the hedging programs to keep up. Their attempt to keep up aggravated the crash, because the lower prices fell the more the programs sold in order to neutralize their net delta exposure.

After the crash, there were heated calls to ban program trading in options or to restrict derivatives trading more broadly. With time the heat faded. Soon program trading and derivatives had regrown even bigger than before, with even more sophisticated models.

However, two notions were discredited. One was that market prices followed steady Gaussian distributions as assumed by Black-Scholes. The other was that portfolio insurance could costlessly lock in returns.

As the mortgage wreckage clears, the credit derivatives market will likely regrow even bigger than before. Copulas or related techniques for analyzing portfolio dependence will become even more vital to modeling. Hopefully we'll pay more attention to common driving factors.

However, credit markets will need to abandon two illusions. One is that credit tails are thin enough to be analyzed using Gaussian or binomial distributions. The other is that quant chefs can easily convert risky debt portfolios into an abundance of nearly risk-free derivatives.

Securitization transforms the tips of sow's ears into silk purses. Insecuritization tries to smuggle in the rest of the sow. To better distinguish the two, we'll need better thinking, higher rating agency standards, and wiser regulation. For more insight on current deficiencies, see SEC (2008) and Witt (2010b).

Let me caution that there's no panacea. In practice, underestimation of the variance or correlation often dwarfs the choice of model. That was clearly the case in 2005/6. The low defaults and calm markets experienced in the previous few years cut nearly all models' estimates of tail risks. The main exceptions explicitly focused on identifying market bubbles—e.g., Zhou and Sornette (2006).

∼

"Portfolio risk is tricky," said Prometheus. "The aggregate tail risk often behaves far differently from the average of the individual tail risks. Almost anything can happen, given enough assets."

"Yes, and knowing the correlations won't suffice to pin the tail risks down," said Pandora. "It's shocking how many skilled risk analysts get this wrong."

"If they're getting it wrong, they've got the wrong skills. Too much normality drilled into their brains. They should study Osband's risk triangles."

"Perhaps the diversity of portfolio tails is too daunting. Risk analysts have to give practical guidance. They can't just shrug their shoulders. Normality is a convenient crutch."

"It's the wrong crutch," said Prometheus. "Normality in highly rated debt portfolios is highly abnormal. Better to choose a distribution with much slower-decaying tails. Negative binomial, correlated binomial, gamma, lognormal—take your pick. They all decay approximately exponentially where it matters. But not normal, and not standard binomial, either."

"I would urge more focus on common risk drivers. People lose sight of the iceberg for the ice cubes."

"Or their absence. When analysts looked back 60 years and couldn't find a U.S.-wide mortgage crisis, it was easy to assume there wouldn't be one."

"Strange, the price explosions were right under their noses," said Pandora. "They should have looked for the massive leverage supporting it,"

"Good point. But our approaches aren't contradictory. Fluctuations in common risk drivers help explain slow-decaying tails. In using normal and standard binomial distributions, regulators implicitly presume a fixed common risk."

"I see. With slower decaying tail risks, it becomes harder to portray senior claims on weak portfolios as strong. If uncertainty gets graded as well, obscure multilayered securitizations will lose most of their appeal. Securitizers will have less incentive to create them. Credit graders will have less incentive to turn a blind eye to them."

10

Risks in Value-at-Risk

Standard Value-at-Risk (VaR) methodology pretends to superior identification of the risks of large market losses. Instead, it indulges the common fallacy of extrapolating from small losses. It needlessly sacrifices precision in big-picture forecasts and reads too much into minor details. We can do much better by tracking short-tem volatility and allowing for uncertainty.

Most financial assets offer a much broader range of outcomes than pay-or-don't-pay. Estimating all the probabilities directly is cumbersome and imprecise. Instead we formulate summary statistics like mean and standard deviation.

Risk analysts worry a lot about big losses, so they often supplement mean and standard deviation with measures of (lower) tail risk. That is where Value at Risk (VaR) comes in. The name appeals, as it suggests a definite cap on losses.

In fact, VaR is closer to a floor than a cap. There's nothing definite about it. And if calculated in the standard way, it is grossly inferior to a host of other measures. Using standard VaR to tame financial risk is like using cigarette filters to tame cancer risk.

A Chance Encounter

'Twas a chance encounter that opened my eyes to VaR chance. I was walking down the street when a man called out of an alley, "Buddy, can you spare a million dollars?"

He was well dressed but had a dazed look in his eyes. "You must be a banker," I said.

"Correction. I was a banker. What kind of banker asks for only a million dollars?"

"Point taken. So what are you now?"

"A financial risk analyst."

"That's still expensive. Look, if you're selling magic beans, I'll give you a cow."

"Very funny. What I offer is far more valuable than giant bean stalks. I will tell your value at risk."

"I already know. If I give you a million dollars, I risk it all."

He shook his head. "No, you don't understand. I invest your money in liquid markets. Every day the value wobbles. By studying that wobble I can divine the most you will lose most of the time. That's the Value at Risk, or VaR for short."

"I can divine the most I will lose at any time. It's everything."

"That's the most most. VaR refers to the least most. It's the maximum loss in all but q% of cases."

"And the minimum loss in the rest?"

"Well, yes. . . . I rank observed losses for a year or two and find a threshold where approximately q% are worse."

"So if I'm a soldier in a VaR-rated vest facing a hail of bullets, I expect only about q% to get through. How comforting."

"Finance isn't war. If clients can't take a few hits they shouldn't invest. Besides, they can set q wherever they want. That's one of the beauties of VaR."

"And if clients don't know where to set it?"

"Then I set it at five. It is relatively more precise than most other VaR estimators."

"What's wrong with the rest?"

"Nearly all estimators are wrong. The observed averages will seldom match the expected values going forward. In finance, the average deviation is typically a significant fraction of what we're trying to estimate. But it's a lot less for 5% VaR than for, say, the 0.1% VaR."

"Really?"

"Sure. To begin with, I need about 1,000 observations to even calculate an empirical 0.1-percentile. Really I want at least two or three observations below to keep some extreme outlier from polluting the results. That's about eight to 12 years of daily data, and I don't know how much of the older stuff will stay relevant. But even if I had centuries of relevant data, the far tails are relatively harder to pin down than the near tails."

"Why is that?"

"Far tails focus on a small subset of outcomes. Also, VaR is crude. In a way it likens everything to default risk, with VaR the cutoff between default and servicing. Since the vast majority of observations exceed the VaR, most valuable information comes from the few that don't."

"Hmmm, reminds me of the problems in estimating tiny default rates. But even the 5-percentile you prefer will discard a lot of information. How does it compare with the ordinary standard deviation estimator?"

"It's usually two or three times as crude."

"So why not estimate the standard deviation and infer the tails from it?"

"That's a normal mindset. Markets don't have to be normal. Usually they're not."

"We don't have to assume normal tails. We can assume a fat-tailed distribution and infer the tails for it."

"Aha. Assumptions again. Empirical VaR doesn't make those assumptions. It just measures the tails and uses them as forecasts. If the 5-percentile doesn't give enough buffer, double it. That's what a lot of my best clients do."

"What if they triple or quadruple the empirical standard deviation instead?"

"They'd likely get better accuracy with less data. But that wouldn't be empirical VaR, would it?"

"No, I guess not. But given what you've just revealed, do you think I'm a likely buyer?"

"No, I guess not."

Fat Tails

When risks are normal, the chances are 5% that losses exceed 1.6 standard deviations, 1% that losses exceed 2.3 standard deviations, and 0.1% that losses exceed 3.1 standard deviations. Risks that exceed these levels are called fat-tailed. Most portfolio risks are fat-tailed.

Kurtosis, a measure of the standardized fourth moment, is the best single measure of tail fatness. It's zero for a normal distribution and typically positive for fat tails. Indeed, a positive kurtosis is usually taken as the rigorous definition of fat tails.

As we saw with exchangeable debt portfolios, kurtosis can't fully describe tail risks. That's the main reason we might want to estimate tail risks directly. However, a measure at one tail doesn't confine the conditional risk further out. In principle, the risk distribution can take any non-negative shape.

For benchmark analysis, it's helpful to posit a distributional form that inflates normal tails in a smooth way. The most favored form is "Student's t," also known as the t-distribution. In addition to mean and variance, it depends on a positive parameter known as the degree of freedom. However, to facilitate comparisons I will express everything in terms of kurtosis. This works as long as kurtosis is finite.

Student's t arises naturally in the estimation of confidence intervals. It amounts to a mixture of normal distributions of different variances, with the inverse variances following a gamma distribution. As is evident from Figure 10.1, Student's t densities decay log-quadratically near their peaks before slowing to log-linear or less. The only exception is the zero-kurtosis case, which corresponds to Gaussian normality and decays log-quadratically throughout.

To maintain the same standard deviation as a thin-tailed risk, a fat-tailed risk must have a taller head. That is, it must pile up more density near

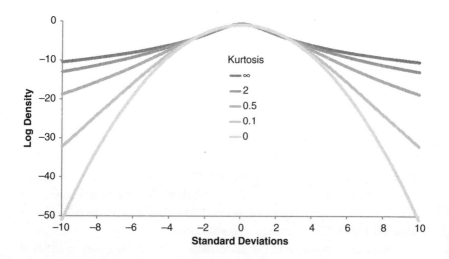

Figure 10.1
Log Densities of Student's t-Distributions

the center. The cumulative distributions must match somewhere in the shoulders. For *t*-distributions with finite kurtosis, that somewhere is around 2 standard deviations, near the 2.5-percentile. (This helps explain the widespread association of 95% confidence with a ±2 standard deviation confidence interval.)

The 5-percentiles and 1-percentiles aren't far apart, either. In standard deviation terms, the 5-percentile ranges from 1.5 to 1.6; the 1-percentile ranges from 2.3 to 2.6. The spans are around a tenth of the midpoint.

The differences widen farther out into the tails. The 0.1-percentile ranges from 3.2 to 5.1 standard deviations. The span is nearly half of the midpoint. If we know only the 5-percentile, converting it to a 0.1-percentile might require less than a doubling or more than a tripling.

Hence, even when tails scale smoothly, it's dangerous to infer the outer tail risks from either the standard deviation or the inner tails. Empirical VaR seeks to estimate the tail risks directly. If we take 999 observations and rank them from lowest to highest, we might reasonably assign the lowest to the 0.1-percentile, the next lowest to the 0.2-percentile, and so on. If we have more observations and their assignments skip over the percentile we're interested in, we interpolate.

Since empirical VaR makes no assumptions about distributional form, it might appear quite robust. It concentrates on what actually happened, without using theory as a filter. However, this is also its critical weakness. It reads too much into accident. As an estimator, it's far less precise than its name suggests.

Imprecision

Let's get more precise about imprecision. The simplest measure is the mean squared error. If on average the estimator gets the mean value right, the mean squared error will on average match the variance, making it the inverse of the Bayesian precision we met in Chapter 7. That's appealing.

However, if we rank risk estimators by mean squared error, estimators of tiny risk are bound to look better than estimators of huge risk. Usually we care far more about the percentage error. The standard relative error (SRE) is the square root of the mean squared percentage error. The SRE is never less than the percentage bias (the relative distortion of the true mean by the estimator) or the percentage standard deviation, and never more than their sum.

As the standard deviation scales inversely to the square root of the number T of independent observations, we'll always prefer nearly unbiased estimators in sufficiently large samples. However, in analyzing daily portfolio returns, we rarely have more than a few hundred observations we're confident are relevant and independent. This forces a trade-off between what we'd ideally like to estimate and what we can estimate best.

For example, suppose we estimate the standard deviation of a market portfolio as the square root of the mean squared daily return. This is a biased estimator since it ignores both the sample mean return and the distortion imposed by taking a square root. However, for most markets and at least 20 independent observations, the bias will be small. The imprecision works out to

$$\mathrm{SRE}(ordinary\ std\ dev) \cong \sqrt{\frac{2 + \mathrm{kurtosis}}{4T}}. \tag{10.1}$$

To achieve an SRE of 10%, we'll need roughly 50 observations when kurtosis is 0 and 200 when kurtosis is 6. For fat tails and moderate numbers of observations, other estimators of standard deviation work better. The simplest multiplies the mean absolute return by 1.3. While often biased by a few percentage points, it dampens sensitivity to extreme returns. Variants on this are good foundations for more complex estimators.

Turning to percentiles, Kendall and Stuart (1972) provide a large-T approximation that can be expressed as

$$\mathrm{SRE}(q\% - ile) \cong \frac{\sqrt{q\%(1 - q\%)/T}}{\mathrm{density}(threshold) \cdot |threshold|}. \tag{10.2}$$

To achieve an SRE of 10% with a 5-percentile and t-distributed risk, we'll need over 150 observations when kurtosis is 0 and nearly 300 observations when kurtosis is 6. That's a lot less efficient than the ordinary standard deviation, although the relative gap narrows as tails fatten. While the 5-percentile can achieve a better SRE than equation (10.1) for a kurtosis exceeding 12, even then it will tend to be much less efficient than a trimmed standard deviation.

The SRE at other percentiles is worse, and soars for extreme tails. To achieve an SRE of 10% with a 0.1-percentile and t-distributed risk, we'll need about 1,000 observations when kurtosis is 0 and 9,000 observations when kurtosis is 6. As a result, financial analysts rarely rely on direct estimation of the 0.1-percentile. Instead they infer it from data closer to the center. This belies the oft-made claims that VaR measures extreme risks without assumptions on the distribution.

In general, when the far tails are easy to estimate directly, we don't care that much about doing so. When we do care about them they're hard to estimate. Standard VaR promises something it can't deliver.

VaR's poor precision reflects its focus on a sliver of information. The vast majority of observations simply confirm the noncriticality we expected. For most of the rest, the estimator cares only about which side of a threshold they fall on. The distance from the threshold matters only if it's small enough for a change in threshold to flip sides. Contrast that with our standard deviation estimators, which incorporate every magnitude.

As Jorion (1997) notes, we're better off inferring VaR from the standard deviation than using the empirical VaR. Granted, we may need additional information, like an appropriate kurtosis range. Zumbach (2007) presents empirical evidence for modeling risk with t-distributions having kurtosis between 1.5 and 12. RiskMetrics, the best-known commercial provider of risk analysis tools, revised its methodology to incorporate this insight. Unfortunately, there is scant regulatory pressure to enforce high standards of analysis.

Worse, too few risk managers appreciate the difference. For example, it is widely believed that, whatever its other shortcomings, standard VaR better captures extreme tails than standard deviation does. This is untrue. For t-distributed risk, the 5-percentile gets smaller in standard deviation terms as the extreme percentiles grow. This reflects the crisscross we noted earlier between densities having the same mean and standard deviation.

A Practical Illustration

In practice, neither volatility nor kurtosis stays constant, and a single t-distribution underestimates the rockiness of risk. The very coarseness of empirical VaR can help it stay robust. However, practice brings another problem to the fore. The standard rolling window of observation is typically too long to stay relevant.

Many risk managers think the opposite. They believe that averaging over multiple years is bound to improve precision. They forget that what matters most for forecasting is the identification of the current regime and its likelihood of switching, not some average over past regimes.

This is true whether or not one is investing for the long haul. Suppose we own an orchard facing severe frost in January. Would we justify a failure to turn on heaters by noting that it's plenty hot in July and that we want the trees to last for years? Of course not. Then why use a thermometer measuring long-term averages, regardless of the evidence the weather has changed?

For a practical illustration, let's see how various VaR and standard deviation metrics would have forecast the risks of the S&P 500 Index (SPX). For each day from January 1954 through August 2010, I compared the actual log return with the risk threshold estimated for it. The estimation used the previous T daily returns as a rolling observation "window."

The first metric was a 0.1-percentile estimated on a four-year window. The limit was breached 44 times, versus an expected value of 15 if the indicator were accurate. The chance that occurred strictly through bad luck is one in a billion.

To check for overcautious risk limits, I reviewed every quarter of every year for losses that exceeded half their threshold. If none occurred, I rated the quarter unusually calm. Whenever two consecutive quarters were unusually calm, I scored this as one "under limit" event.

Half of a 0.1% threshold is typically between a 5% threshold and a 2.5% threshold, implying a 4% to 20% chance of unusual calm. With 225 quarters examined, fewer than 10 under-limit instances are expected, unless tails are unusually fat or the estimated threshold was too high. The actual number was 38.

I then proceeded to convert other estimators into a 0.1-percentile proxy and test their forecasts similarly. I multiplied the 0.1% estimator by 1.5, the 5% estimator by 2.5, and the standard deviation estimator by -4. These multipliers represent the averages for t-distributions of kurtosis 1 to 3, rounded to the nearest 0.5. I refrained from finer calibration to reduce over-fitting.

The results broadly confirmed the superiority both of standard VaR projections over direct estimation of small percentiles and of standard deviation over standard VaR. See Table 10.1. However, the differences using like windows were less than simple theory suggests. What most stands out is the superiority of short windows. One-year windows fed better predictions than two-year windows. Six-month windows fed better predictors than one-year windows. The best predictor of the lot was a rolling three-month standard deviation.

Table 10.1
Risk Outliers for Daily SPX Returns 1954–2010 under Alternative Methodologies

Type	Percentile	Multiplier	Window Length	No. Over Limit	No. Under Limit
VaR	0.1	1	4 years	44	38
VaR	1	1.5	2 years	46	16
VaR	1	1.5	1 year	42	8
VaR	1	1.5	6 months	48	1
VaR	5	2.5	2 years	41	34
VaR	5	2.5	1 year	33	13
VaR	5	2.5	6 months	36	2
VaR	5	2.5	3 months	39	0
Std Dev		−4	2 years	39	34
Std Dev		−4	1 year	31	13
Std Dev		−4	6 months	28	4
Std Dev		−4	3 months	27	2
Std Dev		−4	1 month	30	1

If risks are stable, the ordering should be reversed. So risks must be fluctuating on time scales of a few months.

Figure 10.2 confirms that. The dotted line is a proxy for realized SPX volatility from January 2000 to August 2010. I constructed it using a trimmed standard deviation on a window stretching one month forward from the date in question.

With a window that compressed, the SRE is at least 15%. That accounts for a jiggle over 0.5 logarithmic units wide. However, the jiggle can't explain the big secular changes. The total variation is 2.4 in log terms, or a factor of 12 in nominal terms. It took less than two years to go from trough in December 2006 to peak in October 2009, and most of that was reversed within a year.

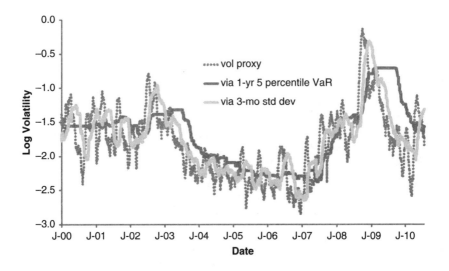

Figure 10.2
Volatility Proxy and Predictors

No indicator that equally weights a year or more of data can keep up with that pace of change. It will lag six months. An indicator that equally weights three months of data will lag only six and a half weeks. The difference is quite noticeable in the chart, which overlays volatility predictors based on 1-year 5-percentile VaR (I divided by 1.6 before annualizing) and three-month standard deviation.

Sharp fluctuations in realized volatility explain why the three-month 5-percentile (which basically takes the third lowest observation) outperforms the two-year standard deviation. The latter has a colossal advantage in static efficiency. Yet that becomes irrelevant when the risk regime changes so much so quickly.

Figure 10.2 also reveals one of the main attractions of standard VaR: it's relatively stable. Using a rolling window, over 90% of new evidence leaves the estimator unchanged. This naturally focuses VaR reports on the subset of changes. Other estimators hop around more; their reports require more work to filter out significant changes from noise.

The flip side is that VaR can get stuck in a rut. The chart displays an extreme example in 2009. For nine months the one-year 5-percentile held rock steady even though short-term volatility more than halved. During that period, standard VaR was useful only in predicting itself.

Scoring Rules

A short lag isn't always better. When risk is relatively stable with only a mild trend, as occurred between 2004 and 2006, a longer-term measure will track it with less noise. When risk oscillates, as it did between 2000 and 2002, a short-term measure can get out of phase.

For simpler updating rules and more plausible motivation in terms of regime switching, we can substitute EMAs for simple moving averages. However, EMAs will still respond fast or slowly depending on their weighted-average lag, with the same basic trade-off between reliability and relevance.

Since the optimal trade-off can change without warning, we'll usually get better results with a dynamic mixture of short-, medium-, and long-term measures. We can view the relative weights $\{p_i\}$ as probabilistic convictions that we update using Bayes' Rule. A simple approximation that generally works well is

$$\Delta p_i \cong \tfrac{1}{3} p_i (forecast_i - \text{mean}(forecast)) \frac{news}{\text{var}(news)}. \tag{10.3}$$

Elsewhere I have called this approach SAMURAI (Osband 2002–2005). That's short for Self-Adjusting Mixtures Using Recursive Artificial Intelligence. It slices through a lot of estimation knots.

Remarkably, SAMURAI can also be viewed as a market game, in which each forecaster has credibility capital w_i and bets near-optimally. "Near-optimal" means using the equivalent of a fractional Kelly criterion (Kelly 1956; Thorp 2000). Unlike much of finance, a fractional Kelly criterion is something both theorists and lauded practitioners tend to agree on. For an excellent popular account, see Poundstone (2005).

Other predictors draw on the prices of market options. They're usually superior to crude historical statistics. Some people say that's because markets look forward while statistics look backward. But that grossly overstates the difference. All predictions look backward into the future. The market's advantages lie in mixing different predictors and infusing human intuition. From a machine perspective, human brains' superb filters for relevance often outweigh their sloppy recall and crude calculation.

Whichever forecasting methods we choose, we should have ways of measuring their performance so that we learn what works best and don't encourage intentional misreporting (Osband and Reichelstein 1985). This is a classic problem in both weather forecasting and economic planning, and has stimulated much research on "proper" scoring rules. "Proper" means that the expected score is never higher for a dishonest forecast than for an honest one. See Gneiting (2010) or Gneiting and Raftery (2007) for recent surveys.

My heuristic comparison of SPX risk outliers doesn't qualify because it doesn't award a single aggregate score. An SRE doesn't qualify because it doesn't encourage unbiased estimation. However, proper scoring rules are easy to find for moments or percentiles, as Savage (1971) and Thomson (1979) showed. Here are two of the simplest:

1. If a forecaster reports a q-percentile of y, score the outcome x as $yq\%$ less any loss $y - x$ beyond the threshold.
2. If the forecaster reports an mth moment of y, score the outcome as $y(2x^m - y)$.

To test VaR more systematically, I assembled ten years of daily data for hundreds of different equity indices, commodities, foreign exchange swap spreads, and individual U.S. and Japanese stocks. I scored forecasts every day for predictors of standard deviation, 5-percentile and 1-percentile. To reduce noise and prevent a few outliers from dominating results, I aggregated daily results into hundreds of thousands of multimonth games, and aggregated the games into a couple hundred tournaments.

Standard VaR did not win a single tournament. It didn't win even on its 5-percentile home ground. Whatever we use to measure risk, let it not be standard VaR.

Even when VaR is right, it can be wrong. Imagine that VaR requires limiting the risk of $100 million trading loss to 5%, when the real risk is 9%. Imagine a contract that is equally likely to halve the loss or double it (or triple or quadruple it). From a VaR perspective that makes the trading book safe again, even though it's a bum deal for whoever underwrites it. While every risk measure can be gamed, VaR is particularly vulnerable because it cares only about the frequency of excess losses and not their intensity.

Regulators take note. If your charges claim to rely on standard VaR for risk control, they're either fooling you or fooling themselves. But you don't need to prescribe a particular non-VaR method. Just insist they keep tabs on their own methods and continually strive to improve.

~

"I feel sorry for the American cigarette companies," said Prometheus. "They got in so much trouble over exaggerated claims for filters. They should have introduced a Cancer-at-Risk standard. It would explain the worst cancer the healthiest 95% of smokers would develop in two years."

"That wouldn't have saved them," said Pandora. "The standards for peddling tobacco are much stricter than the standards for peddling financial carcinogens. In finance, let the sucker beware. Besides, you overlook the power of the name."

"A rose by any other name would smell as sweet. . . ."

"That's because a rose is directly material. Value is a perception."

"Markets make value material, by trading money for real goods and services."

"By that criterion VaR isn't even value. It's a threshold. Have financial institutions issue puts to cover the losses beyond their VaR. Now there would be value. But it could deviate a lot from the VaR."

"If VaR is such rubbish, why not ban its use?" asked Prometheus. "Or make users post big health warnings, like 'VaR is hazardous to your financial health.'"

Pandora smiled. "I like the health warning idea. But I fear it would get tucked into the long disclaimers that lawyers write to each other. Besides, every estimate of risk can be converted into a VaR measure given some auxiliary assumptions. There's nothing wrong with that."

"People think empirical VaR is better, because it doesn't need conversion."

"That's another big misconception. The only thing empirical VaR is great at predicting is itself. Most days it doesn't change at all."

"I like Osband's approach. Pick a measure of observed tail risk, set up a market contest to predict it, and use the market-clearing consensus as the predictor. But I'm not that impressed with the measures he uses. He would do much better looking at trading ranges."

11

Resizing Risks

Scanning price charts for channels has a bad reputation among economic theorists. Good traders do it anyway for the insight into uncertainty. It's a secret of their success that shouldn't stay secret. The extra information can warn of crisis and help all investors dynamically resize their portfolios. However, it will never completely tame market risk. Pandora's Equation won't let it.

While VaR lost every tournament described in Chapter 10, conventional standard deviation estimators didn't win. Estimators based on daily trading range walloped both. This chapter will explain how they work and show some useful things we can do with them.

Range estimators are a formalization of what good traders have done for generations. Uncertainty is center stage for traders, and their livelihoods depend on managing it right, unlike a host of other risk managers who just report measures to others. So it makes sense that traders would evolve useful, intuitively appealing techniques.

In saying that, I have violated one of the norms of finance. It says that theorists and discretionary traders should never take each other seriously. The very existence of this norm invites a closer look.

Traders as Chartists

Any big bookstore in a major financial district will have a large section on financial engineering. Some of the books there expound standard finance theory. Many more instruct in so-called technical analysis, also known as charting.

This is strange, very strange. No major university offers comprehensive professional instruction in market technical analysis. One never hears of tenure-track appointments for chartists, much less Nobel prizes awarded for their profound insight. Lo and Hasanhodzic (2009, 2010), two scholar-practitioners trying to bridge the gap, are welcome exceptions. Why do traders demand so much instruction in something academics rarely provide?

To some this just confirms traders' irrationality. Still, the scale and intensity amaze. Bookstores near pharmaceutical labs don't sell alchemy recipes. Bookstores near NASA don't sell incantations for magic carpets.

Traders' unusual reading predilections merit more scholarly attention. If some Amazon tribes were discovered to eat bat guano, ethnobiologists would leap to explore the benefits. But I have never seen a medical study of the therapeutic effects of charting.

If anthropologists study professional traders in their habitats, one thing they will immediately notice is the close quarters. Big trading outfits tend to cram desks and people back-to-back and side-to-side. The few offices tend to be walled in glass, the better to see out and look in. Traders also tend to cluster in compact financial districts, despite the ease of relocating somewhere cheaper and more serene. Everything is geared to maximize face-to-face communication.

Indeed, great discretionary traders tend to be first and foremost great networkers. They are far more interested in market beliefs than in economic fundamentals. Their knowledge is broad rather than deep, intuitive rather than analytic, and short on detail.

That doesn't mean they're stupid. Computers often have trouble recognizing faces that two-year-olds can distinguish at a glance. Why? Human brains are wired with millions of lateral connections, whereas computers are wired more serially. Great discretionary traders combine the intuitive pattern recognition of a child with a grasp of abstract market connections. In a sense they read the faces of the market.

Nowhere are those faces more visible than in the charts of market prices. Yes, the charts are backward-looking and noisy. Still, no other record better summarizes the hopes and disappointments that underlie current beliefs.

Readers schooled in orthodox finance may doubt whether that's necessary. The parameters describing drift and volatility ought to tell us everything of note. I agree. So let's go back to the bookstore and pick up the latest reference handbook on diffusion parameters of various assets.

Oh no, it isn't there. Amazon.com doesn't carry it either. Yet it is easy to find reference handbooks on diffusion parameters for basic industrial materials.

Perhaps financial diffusion coefficients are too valuable to publish. Perhaps they're stored in encrypted files at major banks and hedge funds. Then why hasn't some hacker found them and published them online? Why hasn't some disgruntled quant kissed and told? Moreover, if the true values are already known, why do quants spend so much of their time re-estimating them?

The only plausible answer is that the values aren't stable. We likely never knew them precisely and never will. Studying price charts is a search for relevant approximation.

Adjusted Trading Range

For a simple charting analysis, graph a time series of (log) prices, pick an interval without a glaring break in trend, and draw a straight line from the first point to the last. Then draw two parallel lines with the same slope, just touching the outliers on either side. All prices in that interval are confined to the channel in between.

Figure 11.1 presents a simulation. I generated random variables from a t-distribution of kurtosis of 6 and formed the cumulative sum to represent a log price series. Although there's no inherent drift, the observed trend slopes upward.

I will call the vertical distance between the two channel lines the adjusted range. It tends to scale directly with the cumulative volatility. (The cumulative volatility is the square root of the cumulative variance, which equals the average variance times the time interval.) Hence, we can use adjusted range to back out a point estimate for volatility. We can then combine these point estimates into a range-based estimator by taking moving averages or dynamic mixtures of moving averages.

In principle, range-based estimators of volatility are far more precise than ordinary standard deviation estimators. To confirm that, let's start with a little transformation. If we subtract the observed trend from the sample, prices will start and end at the same value. The adjusted trading

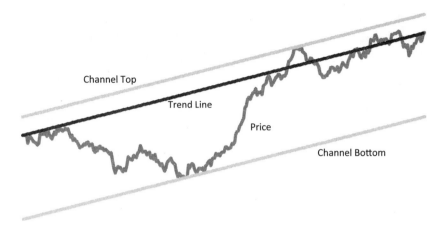

Figure 11.1
Slanted Trading Range

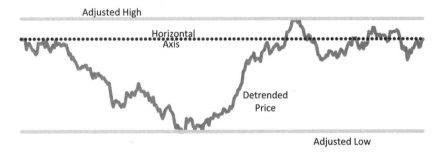

Figure 11.2
Flattened Trading Range

range will stay the same but now equals the ordinary high-minus-low range for the adjusted series. See Figure 11.2.

In the case of Brownian motion, the adjusted series is known as a Brownian bridge. "Brownian" refers to a continuous-time random walk with no discrete jumps. The "bridge" refers to it being tied down at both ends rather than one. For a t-distribution, there's no formal name, partly because continuous time muddies the very notion of a t-distribution; we need to shift to Brownian motion with occasional discrete jumps.

The mean range of a Brownian bridge works out to twice the mean absolute change, or $\sqrt{\pi/2} \cong 1.25$ times the cumulative volatility. The standard relative error of an average of T i.i.d. samples works out to

$$SRE(Brownian\ Bridge\ Range) \cong \frac{0.217}{\sqrt{T}},$$ (11.1)

which is less than a third of the SRE for an ordinary T-period standard deviation estimator. To put it another way, the width of the current day's trading channel can, in principle, estimate volatility better than ten days of closing prices, even when the regime stays the same.

Practical Approximations

A range measure filters a larger data set for the difference between two extremes. For more precision we can incorporate finer data directly into an ordinary variance calculation. For any Brownian displacement Δx, if we measure the displacements over n subintervals and add their squares, this estimates variance n times as precisely as $(\Delta x)^2$ does. By subdividing the subdivisions, we can in principle measure current volatility to arbitrary precision in infinitesimal time.

In practice, precision at short time scales is limited. Brownian approximations break down. Bid-ask spreads distort our measures. We lack sufficiently fine-grained data or run out of storage capacity for it.

Adjusted trading range offers a good proxy. On intervals of a day or longer it typically dwarfs big-ask spreads. The human eye (more precisely, the brain using visual data as input) can quickly identify the main patterns and exceptions.

When we don't have enough information to calculate the adjusted trading range directly, we can estimate it using logarithmic high/low/open/close (HLOC) data. A first approximation is

$$adjRange \cong high - low - \frac{1}{2} \cdot |close - open|,$$ (11.2)

which is the standard range less half the absolute return. The Appendix explains the intuition and makes some refinements to improve the projections of volatility.

To illustrate the application, let's return to the SPX example from the previous chapter, using HLOC data from Yahoo Finance. Highs and lows

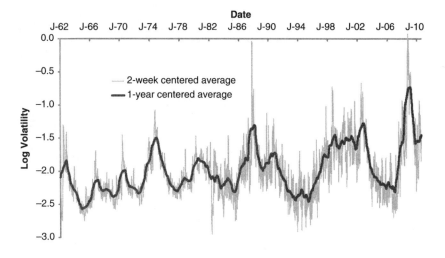

Figure 11.3
Rolling Range-Based SPX Volatility

are available from 1962 onward; opens were recorded until recently as the previous day's close. Figure 11.3 depicts the (log) volatility calculated from two-week and one-year averages of range-based measures. Both averages are centered as best possible. In practice we wouldn't obtain the full year of data until six months after the date we're pinning it to.

If risks were stable, the one-year average line should look relatively flat, typically within 10% (0.1 log unit) of its mean. Instead it swings by more than a factor of 6 (1.8 log units). Eighteen months in 2007 and 2008 sufficed to traverse most of that range. Yet volatility can be range-bound for years at a time or shift in a relatively smooth trend. There are also fluctuations of a few months' duration that are too big to dismiss as random noise and too irregular to treat as a fixed cycle.

Volatility does seem to revert to mean over a five-year horizon. However, it is not clear the mean is stable. Indeed, the chart suggests a rising long-term trend, although our vision may be distorted by the crisis near the end and the limited liquidity near the beginning.

At the very least, the chart challenges the presumption that advanced technology, lower transaction costs, and better educated traders must inexorably grind volatility down. While those developments do bring prices closer to consensus, they also make it easier to trade on fine differences in

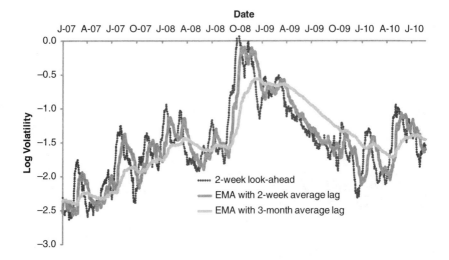

Figure 11.4
Range-Based Predictors of SPX Volatility

opinion and small nuggets of information. A sophisticated market need not be a calm one.

Indeed, judging from Figure 11.3 alone, it seems hard to predict anything about volatility other than its relative continuity and eventual pullback from extremes. Hence, most of what we call volatility forecasting is simply trying to track it closely and project a short-term continuation or reversion. That's more the rule than the exception in finance.

Two range-based estimators are charted in Figure 11.4 for 2007 through 2010, along with the average range-based volatility looking two weeks ahead. An EMA with an average lag of two weeks significantly outperforms an EMA with an average lag of three months. In September 2008 it is an excellent barometer of crisis, as it indicates volatility has doubled. In 2009 it is an excellent barometer of tensions easing. Dynamic mixtures can provide similar early warnings with fewer fluctuations during calm.

Why Is Volatility Volatile?

Financial econometricians have for a generation recognized that the volatility is volatile. Engle (1982) developed tractable models under the name Autoregressive Conditional Heteroskedasticity, or ARCH. Bollerslev (1986) introduced a Generalized ARCH or GARCH model, which has spun out numerous variations.

The basic idea of GARCH is to treat the variance σ^2 of a random walk as following a random walk itself. To keep σ^2 from wandering off to infinity or down below zero, GARCH models its drift as mean-reverting and its volatility as a power function of σ. A basic specification in continuous time is

$$d\sigma^2 = a(1 - b\sigma^2)dt + c\sigma^m dz, \qquad (11.3)$$

where a, b, c, and m are positive constants and dz represents standardized Brownian motion with zero drift and unit rate of variance. Relationships like these are known as GARCH processes.

In most GARCH processes $m = 1$, although Heston (1993) developed a popular option pricing model in which $m = \frac{1}{2}$. For $m = 1$, equation (11.3) matches equation (8.1), with σ^2 replacing the default risk θ. It follows that σ^2 will have a long-term equilibrium gamma distribution.

This suggests modeling tail risks with a normal-gamma distribution. However, that's not nearly as tractable as the t-distribution, which implicitly assumes the inverse variances are gamma distributed. Moreover, the differences are mild, as the logarithm of a gamma-distributed variable is approximately normally distributed, and the logarithm of the inverse variable will have the same distribution with the signs reversed. In either case, financial market tail risks will decay log-linearly or slower.

Empirically, GARCH models work like mixtures of EMAs. However, unlike the dynamic mixtures I recommend, most researchers look for a single best fit for the period as a whole. Indeed, many researchers speak of GARCH processes as if they are stable drivers of volatility and not just convenient estimators. This is misleading in theory and dangerous in practice.

To start with the practical danger, let's return to the historical chart of range-based SPX volatility and cover up the last two years. Suppose we estimate fixed GARCH parameters for the previous 46 years. No matter how sophisticated the model we choose, the best fit will almost surely breed false confidence in avoiding the volatility experienced in fall 2008. While dynamic estimators may be no less myopic, at least they will adjust quickly to new evidence. Also, we can inject more caution by keeping tabs on past episodes of false confidence.

On the theory side, GARCH is less a causal explanation than a descriptor looking for a cause. If the price-to-dividend ratio stays constant or changes only gradually, one might attribute GARCH behavior in prices to an underlying GARCH process in dividends. However, this just shifts the puzzle somewhere else. Why should dividend noise behave like GARCH?

In fact GARCH behavior demonstrates the power of beliefs. Recall our discussion in Chapter 7 of beliefs about default risk. They are inherently unpredictable, because the change in the mth cumulant κ_m of beliefs depends on the next higher-order cumulant κ_{m+1}. For beliefs about log dividends, the analogous result is even more striking:

$$\text{volatility}(\kappa_m) = \frac{|\kappa_{m+1}|}{\text{volatility } (dividends)}. \tag{11.4}$$

Not surprisingly, the mth cumulant of prices turns out to move with the mth cumulant of beliefs about dividends. It follows that the variance of market prices will be volatile except in the rare case when beliefs are completely unskewed.

To confirm that completely unskewed beliefs are rare, note that skewness will be volatile except when kurtosis is zero, and more generally that κ_m cannot stay zero unless κ_{m+1} stays zero. The only way volatility can stay nonvolatile is for beliefs about drift to stay perfectly Gaussian. In practice that's impossible.

In short, we don't need to assert the volatility of price volatility. Learning under uncertainty implies it. However, the controlling parameters will hardly ever be constant. Neither can we completely predict their evolution.

Rational Exuberance

It's not just the volatility of volatility that reflects rational learning. The average level of volatility does too. This merits more discussion, as much of behavioral finance clings to the notion that markets are excessively volatile.

The notion dates to Shiller (1981), who compared the volatility of SPX with the volatility of dividends accruing to SPX. With a constant price-to-dividend ratio, the volatility of log prices should match the volatility of log dividends. With a price-to-dividend ratio that discounts temporary shocks, the volatility of log prices should be less than the volatility of log dividends. Shiller found that, on the contrary, market prices were much more volatile than dividends.

This finding sparked enormous debate. Orthodox finance inclined to minimize the importance of the aberration. Behavioral finance took it as proof of gross investor irrationality. Shiller (2006) characterizes the problem as "irrational exuberance." That is, emotion causes investors to exaggerate the importance of minor news. Taleb (2004) attributes the exaggeration to investors being "fooled by randomness."

Each of us needs only review his own life to realize that emotion or foolishness often prevails. However, experience also confirms the adage about fools getting parted from money. From an evolutionary perspective, it is hard to understand why a rational minority does not come to dominate the market.

In fact, as Kurz (1994a, 1994b, 1996) first showed, rational learning is bound to induce excess volatility. If a dividend is better than expected, it may be a sign we weren't expecting enough. Perhaps the firm's growth prospects are improving. Perhaps some bad luck before caused us to understate growth prospects. Rationally updating our beliefs using Bayes' Rule, we'll expect slightly more growth going forward than we would if the dividend were poor. With higher growth, we're willing to pay a higher price-to-dividend ratio.

The next dividend may be unexpectedly poor. We then lower our expectations and the price-to-dividend ratio we will offer. If we imagine news about dividends arriving continuously, its noisiness will constantly jiggle the price-to-dividend ratio.

Hence, market price volatility will sum two components. The first is the volatility of dividends. The second is the volatility of the price-to-dividend ratio caused by learning. Shiller's analysis ignored the second component.

How much extra volatility will learning induce? That depends on what we believe and how intensely we believe it. From equation (11.4), the volatility of the mean belief depends on the variance of beliefs. The less certain we are about growth, or the more we disagree with each other, the more the consensus will shift with new evidence.

The price impact, in turn, depends on how long we expect the new growth trend to last. If growth is expected to revert to mean within a month, even huge disagreements will have miniscule impact. If growth trends are expected to persist for decades, the volatility when we're highly uncertain will dwarf the news itself. The observed patterns of excess volatility are broadly consistent with economic cycles lasting a few years.

In hindsight, this can look quite irrational. We'll see a few long trends and a lot of confused wandering around them. The same news will evoke vastly different responses, depending on the context. Yet high volatility isn't necessarily unhealthy. It just means that the market feels perplexed about the future and is eagerly sifting new evidence for insight.

Risk-Adjusted Investment

Enlightenment is the flip side of disillusionment. So if the difficulty of predicting market volatility discourages, look at the bright side. Let it encourage more attention to tracking current volatility and to adjusting investment appropriately.

For independent investments, the best single adjustment applies the fraction Kelly criterion mentioned in the previous chapter. It says to bet in proportion to expected net-of-funding return μ divided by variance σ^2, or equivalently to the Sharpe ratio $S \equiv \frac{\mu}{\sigma}$ divided by the volatility. For example, if volatility doubles, investors should look to trim their investment unless μ quadruples or S doubles.

Of course, the practical application hinges on keeping transaction costs under control. One simple approach sets a wide target range stretching across the ideal holding. It rebalances only when the actual holding falls outside the target range, and trades only enough to bring the holding back to the edge of the range. More sophisticated variants set inner and outer target ranges with fractional trading in between. We also need to bear in mind the tax impact of frequent adjustments.

Nevertheless, the swings in market volatility are so extreme that it seems cruel not to alert retail investors to them. Financial investors rightly encourage retail investors to focus on the long run and to diversify their holdings. Mutual funds and unit trusts arose to supply this exposure. In recent years, exchange-traded funds and some EU-regulated funds have delivered more exotic risk-reward exposures. Intermediaries need to take the next step and offer more clearly risk-adjusted exposures.

It is easy to convert any liquid stock index into a volatility-adjusted index. Just construct a predictor of next-day volatility using information at hand, adjust the what-if holding of the index to aim for unit volatility, record the result, and repeat. Initially the predictor might not be very good, as we've seen with VaR. But we can make it better by folding range measures, implied volatilities, and information from other assets into dynamic mixtures. Given enough practice and publicity, some investment advisors may take enough comfort to use volatility-adjusted indices as benchmarks for their own performance.

That's where the fun begins. The network externalities that favor a few leading currencies or credit ratings will also encourage markets to focus on a few volatility-adjusted benchmarks. Given enough appeal, brokers will offer financial derivatives mimicking their performance. That will reduce transaction costs and broaden their appeal.

This is bound to make markets function better. For starters, I see evidence that volatility smoothing improves Sharpe ratios long-term. To confirm this requires analysis of dozens of major equity indices around the world, along with adjustments for funding costs, dividends, and taxes. To avoid short-circuiting the deeper treatment this deserves, let me just offer this as a conjecture.

If testing confirms the conjecture, it represents a major market anomaly. While in principle everyone could take advantage of the anomaly, large-scale attempts to do so might wipe it out. Moreover, having retail investors trim equity holdings when volatility surges and expand when volatility recedes could aggravate market fluctuations. There's no way these innovations can yield all gain and no pain.

Still, even if long-term equilibrium leaves average Sharpe ratios unchanged, the world as a whole stands to benefit. Many hedge funds serving the ultra-rich already manage their volatility closely. Assisting retail investors in doing so would help level the playing field. By tempering sharp drawdown in crisis, volatility smoothing would also help enlist broader participation in financial markets at less personal risk.

For those who fear that market fluctuations get worse, please bear in mind that—

- The key to trimming market swings lies in dampening the credit cycle, not in slowing investor response.
- If our savings and regulatory institutions can't let social imagination play, let's redesign them with sturdier buffers.
- Early warning of market uncertainty may help policymakers avert market panic.

～

"You're right, Prometheus. Trading range indicates volatility much better than the net return does. With finer precision, no one can doubt that volatility is volatile. It shows the crucial importance of tracking changes short-term."

"There is some longer-term mean reversion as well," said Prometheus. "I'm glad Osband used your equation to explain the combination. Too many theorists simply invoke GARCH as a deus ex machina."

"Speaking of gods, that excess volatility reminds me of the climb up Mt. Olympus," said Pandora. "Men didn't know the way. They searched and got lost. Zeus had plenty of time to gather lightning bolts and strike them down."

"What does that have to do with excess volatility?"

"The best path always looks straighter in hindsight. Looking back, analysts see things that past markets could not."

"They'll know more if they study the path itself. Chartists have done that for generations. Economists should pay more attention. Perhaps they are irrationally under-exuberant."

"Perhaps they are," said Pandora. "However, I don't blame them for having their guard up. Chartists speak a lot of gobbledygook, while traders exaggerate their prowess. It's going to take a lot of work to mend the divide."

"That's not the only divide. Orthodox theorists versus behaviorists. Keynesians versus monetarists. Fans of quantification versus skeptics. Regulators versus deregulators. Twentieth-century frictions still rule."

"Let's not understate the progress. Finance theory embeds risk at its core. It didn't always. Mean-variance analysis of portfolios dates to the 1950s. Analytic formulas for derivative prices date to the 1970s."

"Finance theory still tends to assume the risks are generally known. They aren't. They can't be. Even the beliefs can't be completely known. Your equation proves it."

"Yes, financial risk and uncertainty are twins. Finance theory needs to embed both at its core, along with the learning that describes their interaction."

12

Conclusions

Pygmalion held such high standards for women that none could meet them. Driven crazy with loneliness, he sculpted what he thought was an ideal woman of ivory. He clothed it, wedded it, and took it to bed. Aphrodite, taking pity on him, substituted a real woman for the sculpture and blinded him to her imperfections.

Unfortunately, Pygmalion's blessing made him insufferable. Bragging of his intolerance for flaw, he encouraged wave after wave of idolatry. People clung to their narrow images of perfection and begged the gods to make them real. They forgot that reality transcends imagination.

For those of us in finance, it is high time to remember.

As we return to work or studies, as we review our investments or speak out as citizens, I hope we find both new respect and new skepticism for financial markets. Winston Churchill once described democracy as the worst form of government except for everything else. We can say the same about financial markets as predictors of future returns. They disgrace with error, and dazzle with error correction.

Fair value can never be more than what we're learning it to be. Learning adds risk. Moreover, we can never completely get a handle on learning risk; it's too complex and unpredictable. The best we can do is track its evolution, project it forward with broad confidence intervals, and correct the mistakes we see.

When it comes to specific conclusions, each of us is entitled to draw her own. Here are mine. Mostly they recapitulate comments made earlier.

Risk-astrophe

Financial catastrophe in 2008 blindsided the world. It destroyed trillions of dollars of nominal wealth in a few months. It shattered confidence. It shuttered production.

It wasn't supposed to happen. Yes, the theoretical possibility was recognized. Any system founded on beliefs risks their rejection. Markets can have bubbles. Bubbles will pop. But there weren't supposed to be so many bubbles, much less so many popping at once. What happened to our risk controls?

The answer is that they did control risk, only not in the way we wanted. They redirected risk toward safe sectors, only to make them unsafe from the concentration. They kept small risks under control, only to induce even riskier leverage. They deterred uncoordinated blowups, only to make a coordinated blowup more devastating.

But the answer still begs why. Did we measure risk wrong? Did we measure the wrong risks? Did we use the measures wrongly? Did we wrongly expect too much from risk measures?

Yes. Yes. Yes. Yes.

We stumbled because we forgot an eternal trade-off. People can seize opportunity only by taking on uncertain risk. Metaphorically I ascribe this to an ancient bargain between Zeus and Pandora. Having emerged from the box of treasure and woe, risk can never be compartmentalized again. Mankind can aspire to mastery of the universe but never achieve it. To err big is human.

Finance continually pushes us to the edge of this bargain. Its willingness to price uncertain risks and trade them encourages innovation. But that doesn't mean asset markets know the true risks. Market-clearing prices are just consensus beliefs, weighted by the money attached to convictions. Truth enters only in dribs and drabs, via observations that give noisy evidence on the current path and foggy glimpses into the future.

Consequently, whether we focus on objective risks or beliefs, we will never completely tame financial markets. They are bound to evolve in surprising ways and make us scramble to control them. If we try to regulate them tightly, the way some think is right, we will quench the fires of discovery and innovation that make our world so special.

Risk-pertise

One thing the financial world sorely needs is more risk-analysis expertise. Current standards are grossly lopsided. Most risk managers have detailed knowledge of individual trade exposures, largely redundant with that of the traders they're checking on. However, when it comes to aggregating those exposures into portfolio risks as whole, they often know barely more than outside regulators.

In my experience, less than a quarter of risk managers understand the precision of the estimators they use, much less the trade-offs between estimators. Most measure their reports by the number of pages they contain, not the insights they provide. Spurious information obscures the connection between portfolio tail risks and common risk drivers.

The further one gets away from trading, the worse it gets. Consider the Madoff scandal, the biggest private-sector Ponzi scheme of all time. Nearly as disgusting as the fraud itself was the lapsed oversight of regulators and feeder funds. Already by 2000, Madoff's performance record was, from a statistical perspective, too smooth to be true. Yet when investigator Harry Markopolos reported this to the SEC along with other circumstantial evidence, he met with incomprehension (Markopolos 2010).

This is pathetic. Centuries ago, before people understood the germ theory of disease, barbers doubled as surgeons because they knew how to use knives. How much longer will people oblivious to statistics be allowed to judge reasonable financial doubt?

Risk managers and regulators who've worked their way up without deep risk-pertise are unlikely to think they need it now. Let us focus instead on training future cohorts. At least three professional associations already sponsor certification programs for financial risk analysts. These kinds of programs need to be expanded and deepened.

Personally I'd like to see a three-year program, with each year offering Master's-level training in a different field: economic history, statistics, and finance. Toss in some cross-disciplinary seminars, case studies, and internships on trading floors. Perhaps China or India, with fewer vested interests in the status quo, will seize the opportunity to lead in training.

Having skilled cohorts at hand won't force risk takers to take heed. Finance should learn from Ulysses. When he wanted to hear the Sirens lure him to ruin, he had his crew tie him to the mast, stopper their ears with wax, and row past regardless of his orders. Since few higher-ups will voluntarily abridge their powers the way Ulysses did, and since the potential social damage from mishandling risk is so high, let's try to embed more responsibility into the decision-making process.

That's a tall order. No regulations can measure up. Indeed, they might divert more effort to checking boxes than to thinking outside them.

However, let's consider the starting point. We can't legally run a trucking company without hiring licensed drivers, providing them with safety equipment, and ensuring our trucks don't spill toxic waste on the roads. We can legally run a huge investment firm trafficking in tens of billions of dollars in potentially toxic derivatives without being required to hire any licensed risk professionals, defer to expert judgment, or avoid behavior we know is unsound.

On balance I think the problems are best addressed through extending the "actuary approach" long used in the insurance industry. Like doctors and lawyers, actuaries have to pass rigorous exams administered by a professional board. They also pledge a fiduciary responsibility to the public.

Needs for actuary approval discourage misrepresentation of risks or intentional underfunding of reserves. Actuaries carry enough prestige and professional backing that employers are wary of twisting their arms. However, actuaries do work for their companies and have incentives to take thoughtful risks.

This is not a call to manage the rest of finance like insurance. Market risk is wilder and woollier than ordinary life-and-casualty risk; it needs room to roam. I am simply recommending that we raise qualification standards, hold risk managers accountable for substance as well as form, and provide external backing.

Perpetual Debt Deferral

The biggest single systemic risk in finance is domestic sovereign default. It strikes not only at sovereign debt holders but also at confidence in the rules of the economic game. However, paying off debt is burdensome. As an alternative, suppose a sovereign resolves to service all principal and interest by issuing new debt. No lender gets defaulted on; no generation ever feels the burden of repayment. It's like issuing a perpetually deferred perpetuity.

Perpetual deferral is a game of musical chairs in which most of the chairs and players are concealed from view. By allocating a bit more GDP toward repaying debt or growing a bit faster, perhaps the sovereign will start supplying chairs faster than new players arrive. Until then, the knowledge that some players bring their own chairs and don't need to sit in them right away gives us confidence in finding a seat.

Most developed countries are currently playing the biggest perpetual deferral game of all time. Judging from history, they will most likely fail. Previous debt spirals have nearly always culminated in default.

The United Kingdom and the United States were the most prominent exceptions to this rule. They undertook huge debts in wartime and worked them down relative to GDP in peace, with the support of prospering citizenry grateful for victory. The context today is very different. The debts pay for leisure and health care, the structural balance between net benefit takers and net taxpayers is worsening, and every generation insists that it not be a net payer.

Yet they don't have to fail. World productivity is growing at record rates. Debt stocks can expand in proportion without raising the percentage burden on GDP. The expansion amounts to a kind of seigniorage that governments can tap. More importantly, by raising retirement ages and private copayments for health care, it is relatively easy to get public finances back on track.

Hopeful uncertainty helps explain developed governments' ability to raise enormous sums at low rates, even as fiscal imbalances worsen. Other factors enter, too: the Chinese government's willingness to lend, fear about the business climate for private investment, and search for safe havens from debt blowups elsewhere. Still, uncertainty lies at the core.

The implication for good policy is clear. Don't take this benevolent uncertainty for granted. It can turn quickly, as it has for the PIIGS. Perhaps it should. When I said it was relatively easy to get public finances back on track, I meant relative to the effort needed to fight a war or holocaust. When it comes to gathering motivation it's extraordinarily difficult. The greatest single demotivator is the ease of rolling over debt.

More transparent accounting of the costs and risks can help. Stop exempting public agencies from private sector standards for estimating the NPV of future obligations. To put teeth in this, let's make accomplices liable for knowingly abetting concealment. For example, some investment banks have reaped billions of dollars from helping governments and public agencies cook their books. This ought to be a crime.

Bank Regulation

A lot of bank regulation pretends that a steady stream of future revenues can substitute in crisis for cash on hand. Hundreds of years of banking experience tell us otherwise. Yes, developments in financial markets make more assets more liquid most of the time. But they can't prevent emergencies where cash is king. Banks that can't tide themselves through emergencies aren't worth banking on.

Ensuring the smooth functioning of the payments system should be a top priority. To that end, let's reduce duration mismatch. Make banks that depend heavily on demand deposits shorten their lending profile. To secure extra buffers they'll have to offer new savings products or seek longer-term capital.

Few banks want to do that. They profit from offering liquidity on the back of illiquidity. Many economists applaud. They feel that borrowing short to lend long encourages productive investment. Conventional wisdom accepts high duration mismatch and just seeks to make lending safer.

I demur. Given the importance of stable liquidity, we should be wary of pumping it up on false pretenses. Besides, the world isn't short of aggregate saving, except where tax and benefit policies discourage it.

What the world is short of, and will always be short of, is lending under both high risk and high uncertainty. That's where banks can help. In the course of handling payments, they learn about real businesses and their customers. They learn about real homeowners and their jobs. The more idiosyncratic the risk and the harder it is for third parties to neatly categorize, the more banks ought to excel relative to alternatives.

Hence we should welcome banks making lots of relatively risky loans, provided the risks aren't too common and the spreads cover costs. Securitization should enhance this comparative advantage, by allowing banks to resell the most standardized exposures of their lending books. Better-matched duration will reduce vulnerability to panic. Add another layer of protection by tightening leverage caps.

Regrettably, the global banking reforms summarized in Basel I and Basel II moved in the opposite direction. They excused nearly any duration mismatch or leverage, provided it was "safe." The safest categories, in Basel's view, were developed country debt and home mortgages. Not surprisingly, that's where the investable money went.

It made people feel richer, as low bond rates buoyed equities and low mortgage rates buoyed housing. The flip side was less investment in manufacturing and private-sector services, even as foreign imports soared. It exacerbated the hollowing out of productive capacity in the developed countries, a trend Landes (1999) had decried even before.

The worst part was aggravation of the credit cycle. Trillions of dollars funneled toward the same low-risk loans initially vindicated their safety. As valuations soared, loans came to be backed more by prospects for favorable rollover and further appreciation than by real earning power. Basel helped a mountain of debt disguise itself as a mountain of real wealth.

Credit Rating

The main problem with credit ratings is how we use them. We need to stop idolizing assurances of safety. Even experts can't know. They are extrapolating from too little data into environments than can easily change. The estimates don't deserve the reserves-not-needed pass that current regulations give them.

That doesn't mean we should cripple rating agencies. Credit rating is a valuable service. It summarizes information relevant to servicing and makes it easier to compare credits. Sharing information economizes on investigation and helps build a consensus.

I don't even mind that regulators delegate some of their powers to rating agencies. On balance, that breeds more competence and less corruption than an in-house monopoly. While it tempts credit rating agencies to shade their ratings, concern about reputation usually provides a reasonable offset.

Clearly that offset failed in the last bubble. Rating agencies deserved to be shamed. Their defective modeling of portfolio risk contributed heavily to insecuritization.

Still, I blame banking regulations at least as much for providing such skewed incentives. The leverage gradient for credit ratings is way too steep. The extra uncertainty at high credit grades calls for extra buffers. My ballpark estimate is that gradients should be no more than half as steep as they are now.

To make rankings more useful, credit rating agencies should be obliged to indicate their uncertainty. Mathematically this corresponds to reporting the variance of default risk estimators as well as the means. As rating agencies and users are accustomed to non-numeric credit grades, the most palatable way to inform of uncertainty would be to report a credit grade range.

Rating agencies already hint of uncertainty through credit watches, warnings, and outlooks. Issuing upper and lower credit grades would make this routine. It would encourage timelier adjustments and discourage outcry, since no single grade would look quite so bold.

Upper and lower credit grades will be particularly useful for rating issuers with implicit guarantees. The PIIGS in Europe, overstretched U.S. states and municipalities, and the Fannie/Freddie mortgage giants are unlikely to service their debts on their own. No higher authority explicitly guarantees their debts. However, they can surely tap external assistance, and possibly enough assistance to avoid default. High and low credit grades should therefore reflect the default risks with and without assistance.

Ratings of credit portfolios need a more fundamental makeover. The dominant methodologies are wrong. They ignore common drivers—e.g., a credit bubble's impact on mortgages.

With common drivers, defaults tend to cluster. This makes portfolio tail risks decay much slower than for the standard binomial and normal benchmarks: indeed, more log-linearly than log-quadratically. A mixed gamma-Poisson distribution, also known as negative binomial, provides a much better benchmark.

Value at Risk

Value at Risk is the most beautiful name ever invented for a bad financial concept. It suggests certainty where there is none. It portrays a floor on crisis exposure as a ceiling. It pretends to a precision and robustness it doesn't have.

The rational essence of VaR is a percentile calculation: a threshold loss expected to be exceeded some fraction of the time. Reserve concerns favor setting the fraction at 0.1% or lower, so as not to threaten a crisis every year. Direct estimation tends to be so unreliable that the fraction is usually set at 5%. However, a 5-percentile is significantly less precise than an ordinary standard deviation, without providing any more insight into tail risk.

An even worse problem is the typical one-to-two-year sampling horizon for VaR. That's far too long to provide useful warning of market storms. Forecasters of market risk need to learn from the experience of weather forecasters. Medium-term projections don't work; too many things can go awry. Focus instead on up-to-date tracking, short-term projection, and error correction.

Granted, short-term forecasts can be myopic. Financial risk analysts need to stay aware of economic history, sovereign debt pressures, and other macro factors. It's analogous to a weather forecaster staying aware of seasonal changes and climate.

The trouble with standard VaR is that it tells us neither weather nor climate but some jumble in between. Standard VaR reports are like weather reports updating us on the twelfth worst weather experienced over the past year. They won't help us plan our day. They won't help us plan for disaster.

Decades ago, regulators banned advertisement of cigarette filters as protection against tobacco carcinogens. Let them now ban the advertisement of VaR as protection against financial carcinogens. Let's advertise, instead, our evolving uncertainty and forecasters' best efforts to understand it.

We can improve dramatically on VaR by tracking slanted trading ranges or "price channels." Good traders have done this for generations. With modern technology it's easy to evaluate a host of different methods, mix them dynamically for better tracking, and make this information widely available. Simple calculations with trading range data put VaR to shame.

Publishing volatility-adjusted indices would be a practical way to alert investors to market risk. Over time, these could become investible instruments themselves. Such instruments could help level the playing field for smaller investors.

21st Century Finance

In the late nineteenth century, Rayleigh's Law in physics predicted that looking into a hot black box should blind the viewer with X-rays. When this didn't happen, no one complained that radiation was foolish. Physicists humbly recognized that if practice consistently defies existing theory, existing theory must be wrong.

Eventually someone came along who thought outside the box about the box. He found a single way to explain the evidence: nature must restrict energy discharge to discrete pulses. Max Planck's discovery marked the birth of quantum theory.

Fast-forward a hundred years. Finance researchers have discovered numerous puzzles where practice defies existing theory. However, finance theory has not reinvented itself the way physics did. Instead it has split into rival camps. In a sense, orthodox finance studies optimal "economically rational" rules of conduct while behavioral finance studies the violations. Synthesis is reduced to estimating the empirical mixture.

I believe that uncertainty and learning can account for most apparent violations of economic rationality. Pandora's Equation, which shows that each update of a cumulant of beliefs depends on the cumulant one order higher, provides a key to understanding. Demonstration of its full power falls outside the scope of this book. However, we did see how easy it is to—

- Account for excess volatility, using the updating equation for mean beliefs.
- Account for GARCH-type behavior, using the updating equation for the variance of beliefs.
- Account for the high volume and frequency of trading, using the turbulence of cumulant updating.
- Account for the appeal of charting, again using the turbulence of cumulant updating.

Pandora's Equation can help resolve even more puzzles when coupled with two more findings. One is Martin's (2010) demonstration that higher cumulants of beliefs are crucial to the determination of discount rates. The other, developed in Chapter 8 using an Ising-type model, is that a miniscule deference to others can congeal a robust consensus on risk.

These findings are interconnected. If all beliefs were Gaussian normal, the paradoxes wouldn't exist. If cumulant updating were self-contained, we couldn't explain why markets are so turbulent. If we never deferred to consensus, we couldn't build viable financial markets to tide us through the turbulence.

Uncertainty and learning point to a finance theory worthy of the twenty-first century. Such a theory can in turn offer new insights on learning. We have seen that markets can function like composite brains and that their turbulence is more rational than it appears. We have seen hints that brains themselves can function like markets. Someday, finance theory will help guide the construction of learning machines beyond current imagination.

This may seem far-fetched. Remember, though, that quantum theory in its early stages gave few hints of the treasures in store. Embracing Pandora's risk opens a gateway to better understanding and practical mastery.

~

"He finished the book," said Pandora. "What do you think?"

"It was better than I expected. Maybe we taught him something after all. I still think he didn't write enough about your equation," said Prometheus.

"Some will say he wrote too much. At least he motivated it. It's more important to ask the right questions than to answer the wrong ones."

"He doesn't always. No man does."

"It's a start. I'm more worried about who will read it, and whether they take it to heart and head. We've got to get finance theory out of its rut."

"It's easy. Theorists just need to emphasize the contradiction between the aim of finance and the arrow of time. Finance wants to discount future returns. Time forces reliance on past and present returns. Beliefs mark a synthesis. Your equation describes the inherently unstable dynamics."

"That's a great explanation," said Pandora, "if you're a Hegelian Marxist. There aren't many of them in finance."

"They like equations. He should have focused on your equation. I think it would have better conveyed the key theme of the book, in one simple line."

"Of that we can't be certain."

APPENDIX

Chapter 1: Introduction

As the Introduction is largely self-explanatory, I will take the opportunity to assemble some useful information on probability. It will come in handy later. Let me draw particular attention to cumulant generating functions, which will reappear frequently in our analysis.

I will also introduce some notational conventions that reduce clutter. For readers feeling rusty, let me start with a simple refresher.. For m a positive integer, the factorial $m!$ refers to $m \cdot (m-1) \cdot \cdots \cdot 2 \cdot 1$, and $0! \equiv 1$, where $'\equiv'$ means "is defined as". Exponentiation $\exp(x) \equiv e^x$ refers to the sum $\sum_{k=0}^{\infty} \frac{x^k}{k!} \equiv 1 + x + \frac{1}{2} x^2 + \cdots$. The natural logarithm $\log(x)$ transforms e^x back to x. The symbols $<<$ and $>>$ mean, respectively, "much less than" and "much greater than".

Probability Distributions

Informally, probability measures relative frequency. Formally, probability is a measure on subsets of a set Ω of events. It ranges from 0 for an empty set to 1 for the full set. Given a bunch of nonoverlapping subsets, the probability that one event in their midst occurs equals the sum of probabilities on each subset.

When outcomes can be ordered by value, the cumulative probability $F(x)$ refers to the probability of the set $\{y \leq x\}$. If the set is discrete, $F(x)$ just sums the probabilities $f(y)$ for every distinct member. If the set is a continuum, $F(x)$ can be interpreted as the integral of a probability density $f(y)$. We can also mix the two, using the Lebesgue-Stieltjes notation $dF(x)$ to denote either the discrete jump at $F(x)$ or the differential $f(x)dx$.

Expectations

The expectation of a random variable $g(x)$ refers to its probability-weighted average $\int_\Omega g(x)dF(x)$. We sum $g(x)f(x)$ where f is discrete and integrate $g(x)f(x)$ where f is continuous. For simplicity I will borrow standard physics terminology to write the expectation as $\langle g(x) \rangle_f$ and usually drop the subscript as understood.

Cumulative probability can be viewed as $F(x) \equiv \langle I(y \leq x) \rangle_f$, for I an indicator variable that equals 1 if true and 0 if false. The q-percentile denotes the y for which $F(y) = \frac{q}{100}$, also written as $y = F^{-1}(q\%)$. Value at Risk (VaR) is often interpreted as the 5-percentile.

The most common expectation is the mean $\langle x \rangle$. The expected squared deviation from the mean $\langle (x - \langle x \rangle)^2 \rangle = \langle x^2 \rangle - \langle x \rangle^2$ is known as the variance var(x). The standard deviation is the square root of the variance.

Converting x to $\dfrac{x - \langle x \rangle}{\sqrt{\mathrm{var}(x)}}$ measures an outcome in standard deviation units. This is known as standardization. Standardized random variables have zero mean and unit variance.

Higher Moments and Cumulants

The expectation $\langle x^m \rangle$ is known as the mth moment. The moment-generating function $\langle \exp(bx) \rangle$ summarizes the moments neatly, since its mth derivative at $b = 0$ is just $\langle x^m \rangle$. Not all moments need exist, and occasionally two different probability distributions can match in all moments. For these reasons, theorists generally prefer to work with the characteristic function $\langle \exp(ibx) \rangle$, where $i \equiv \sqrt{-1}$. See Feller (1971: chaps. 7 and 15) for examples.

Often it is easier to work with the natural logarithm $\kappa(b) \equiv \log\langle\exp(bx)\rangle \equiv \sum_{m=0}^{\infty} \frac{\kappa_m b^m}{m!}$, known as the cumulant generating function (CGF). Again, it is preferable technically to work with the complex counterpart $\log\langle\exp(ibx)\rangle$.

The various κ_m are known as cumulants. The first four cumulants are, respectively, the mean, the variance, $\langle(x-\kappa_1)^3\rangle$, and $\langle(x-\kappa_1)^4\rangle - 3\kappa_2^2$. For a standardized random variable, κ_3 is known as the skewness and κ_4 as the kurtosis. The higher the order of the cumulant or moment, the more information it adds about the extremes of the distribution.

CGFs are always convex—i.e., they lie on or above any tangents. Sometimes they are so convex they turn infinite at finite b. The more convex a CGF is, the more the associated distribution is influenced by the "tail risks" at its extremes.

Gaussian Distribution

Only one probability distribution has a finite number of nonzero cumulants (Marcinkiewicz 1938). It is the Gaussian or normal distribution, with CGF $K(b) = \kappa_1 b + \frac{1}{2}\kappa_2 b^2$. The corresponding density $f(x) = (2\pi\kappa_2)^{-\frac{1}{2}}\exp\left(-\frac{(x-\kappa_1)^2}{2\kappa_2}\right)$ is bell-shaped. While unbounded in range, it fades rapidly beyond $\kappa_1 \pm 3\sqrt{\kappa_2}$.

The special case of zero mean and unit variance is known as the standard normal distribution. It is charted in Figure A.1. As a symmetric distribution, all its odd moments are zero. For even m the moments are $(m-1)\cdot(m-3)\cdots 3\cdot 1$.

Table A.1 gives the odds of losing more than s standard deviations, which I will abbreviate as an "s-tail." In practice, when a 5-tail or higher is reported, most likely the underlying distribution is not Gaussian or its standard deviation is understated.

Most distributions have fatter s-tails than normal. The main exceptions are strictly bounded. Distributions with all positive cumulants will have especially fat upper tails: their risk divided by the corresponding Gaussian tail risk will rise without bound as s grows.

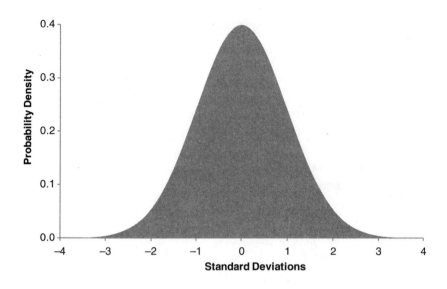

Figure A.1
Standard Normal Distribution

Table A.1
Gaussian Loss Risks

s	Odds of s-tail
2	1 to 44
3	1 to 740
4	1 to 32 thousand
5	1 to 3.5 million
6	1 to 1 billion
7	1 to 780 billion

Multivariate Probability

Sometimes the probability is a function of several variables. The most notable joint statistic is the covariance $\text{cov}(x,y) \equiv \langle xy \rangle - \langle x \rangle \langle y \rangle$, the mean product less the product of the means. Equivalent expressions include $\langle (x - \langle x \rangle)(y - \langle y \rangle) \rangle$, the expected product of deviations from the mean. The correlation $\text{corr}(x,y) \equiv \dfrac{\text{cov}(x,y)}{\sqrt{\text{var}(x)\,\text{var}(y)}}$ refers to the covariance after standardization.

Tail risks for portfolio returns depend not only on higher individual cumulants but also on higher cross-cumulants. Direct estimation of the latter is typically intractable (Osband 2002: chap. 7). This has a huge bearing on portfolio risk assessment, as we shall see in Chapter 9.

The only multivariate distribution with a finite number of non-zero cumulants has CGF $K(B) = M'B + \frac{1}{2}B'\Sigma B$, where M is a k-vector mean, Σ is a k-by-k matrix of covariances, and B is a k-vector argument. It is known as multivariate Gaussian. Its density is

$$f(X) = (2\pi)^{-k/2}|\Sigma|^{-1/2}\exp\!\left(-\tfrac{1}{2}(X - M)'\Sigma^{-1}(X - M)\right),$$ where X is a k-vector

of observations and $|\Sigma|$ is the determinant of Σ.

Conditional Probability and Independence

Conditional probability $f(A|B)$ measures the probability of a set of outcomes A given that another set of outcomes B has occurred. It is defined as $\dfrac{f(A \cap B)}{f(B)}$, the probability that both A and B occur divided by the probability that B occurs. In effect, it chops probability down to the set B and rescales it to sum to one.

Sometimes the conditioning has no influence: $f(A|B) = f(A)$ for all the sets we're examining. This is known as independence. Independence makes probability tractable, by allowing us to filter out a lot of information as irrelevant. Independent variables with identical distributions are known as i.i.d.

The most important independence in finance is independence over time. A classic random walk describes a series of backward and forward steps, each one independent of each other. Brownian motion describes the limit when steps are frequent and tiny with variance per unit time held constant. Generalized Brownian motions, in which the mean and variance might change over time, are known as diffusions.

Cumulant Laws

Independence is most easily analyzed using cumulants. The CGF for a sum of independent variables is readily shown to equal the sum of the individual CGFs. It is also readily shown that $\kappa_1(ax + d) = a\kappa_1(x) + d$ for any two scalars a and d, while $\kappa_m(ax + d) = a^m\kappa_m(x)$ for any integer $m > 1$. For a standardized sum of i.i.d. variables with mean μ and variance σ^2,

$$\kappa_m\left(\frac{\displaystyle\sum_{i=1}^{n} x_i - n\mu}{\sigma\sqrt{n}}\right) = n^{1-m/2}\kappa_m\left(\frac{x - \mu}{\sigma}\right)$$

(A1.1)

$$= \begin{cases} 0 & \text{for } m = 1, \\ 1 & \text{for } m = 2, \\ n^{1-m/2}\sigma^{-m}\kappa_m(x) & \text{for } m \geq 3 \end{cases}$$

For $m > 2$, $n^{1-m/2}$ vanishes as n gets large. Hence K(b) approaches $\frac{1}{2}b^2$, which corresponds to the standardized Gaussian density. This is the heart of the Central Limit Theorem.

The Central Limit Theorem implies that a Brownian displacement Δx over time Δt has a Gaussian density with mean $\kappa_1\Delta t$ and variance $\kappa_2\Delta t$. In the Brownian context, κ_1 is known as the drift and $\sqrt{\kappa_2}$ as the volatility. Usually drift and volatility are reported on an annualized basis.

The Central Limit Theorem also implies an asymptotically normal distribution for the average estimation error from i.i.d. estimates. The mean deviation will be zero for an unbiased estimator. The variance of the estimator will shrink inversely to the number of samples.

The Central Limit Theorem is the most useful single tool in financial risk analysis. It is also the most misused. Logarithmic changes in price are often presumed sufficiently i.i.d. to approximate as Gaussian. The resulting probability density for price, known as lognormal, usually fits the central region of the distribution reasonably well. However, Central Limit approximations weaken considerably in the tails.

Uncertainty

In practice, nothing is completely independent. At most we have conditional independence, which presumes some features stay constant. Weighing which conditions to ignore or take into account is a great challenge.

In most natural science, the subject matter is relatively uniform or can be made relatively uniform though controlled experiments. Testing often involves billions of effectively independent observations. The Central Limit Theorem applied to estimation squeezes our uncertainty toward the limits imposed by quantum mechanics.

Finance works with much fewer relevant observations and with much more interdependence. Uncertainty becomes as vital to our modeling as risk. Indeed, they are closely intertwined. Most of what we call market risk is just other people's uncertainty.

Bayes' Rule

We associate objective risk with a notional probability measure, even after conceding the values might be unstable and hard to identify. We can do the same for subjective uncertainty. Given a feasible set of mutually exclusive hypotheses $\{\theta_i\}$, we can describe relative convictions by nonnegative probabilities $p(\theta_i)$ summing to one. When new information x arrives, the "prior" beliefs can be updated to "posterior" beliefs through repeated application of conditional probability:

$$p(\theta \mid x) = \frac{f(\theta \cap x)}{f(x)} = \frac{f(x \mid \theta)p(\theta)}{\sum_i f(\theta_i \cap x)} = \frac{f(x \mid \theta)p(\theta)}{\sum_i f(x \mid \theta_i)p(\theta_i)}. \qquad (A1.2)$$

This is Bayes' Rule. Since the denominator is needed only to make the probabilities sum to one, Bayes' Rule is usually expressed more simply as $p(\theta \mid x) \propto f(x \mid \theta)p(\theta)$. In words, the posterior is directly proportional to the prior times the probability the evidence would occur if the prior were true.

Bayesian updating can be messy in practice. To appreciate this, note that each moment of p gets updated using a different formula:

$$\left\langle\theta^m\middle|x\right\rangle = \frac{\sum_i \theta_i^m f(x\,|\,\theta_i)p(\theta_i)}{\sum_i f(x\,|\,\theta_i)p(\theta_i)} = \frac{\left\langle\theta^m f(x\,|\,\theta)\right\rangle}{\left\langle f(x\,|\,\theta_i)\right\rangle}. \qquad (A1.3)$$

If f is polynomial in θ, each moment's update will depend on higher moments, making for a potentially endless chain. However, (A1.3) implies a one-line updating of the moment-generating function

$$\left\langle e^{bx}\middle|x\right\rangle = \frac{\left\langle e^{bx} f(x|\theta)\right\rangle}{\left\langle f(x|\theta)\right\rangle}, \qquad (A1.4)$$

which for some combinations of f and p is tractable. These combinations are known as conjugate pairs. See Bernardo and Smith (2000) for fuller discussion.

Uncertainty over Hidden Measures

Just as probability theorists are loath to identify objective risk with noisy relative frequencies, they are loath to identify subjective uncertainty with noisy market prices. To ground subjective probability better, imagine that various objective probability measures $\{F_\theta\}$ might apply, each indexed by a different θ. Another probability measure G determines θ.

In other words, θ is a conditioning variable for the larger space, while F_θ indicates the conditional probabilities. However, if θ cannot be observed, it must be inferred from the observations x. These inferences mold beliefs.

For more sophistication, randomness can evolve over time as a "stochastic process." For example, the drift and volatility of a Brownian motion might change. Our information θ evolves alongside as a "filtration." Liptser and Shirayev (1977) provided a masterly treatment. For a more accessible introduction, see Brzeźniak and Zastawniak (1999).

Equilibrium Disorder

Modeling uncertainty as filtration subsumes the Bayesian approach within an objective framework. However, it does not expunge the core indeterminacy that vexes analysts of uncertainty. How do we know the umbrella distribution G?

There is no perfect answer. Usually G is chosen for tractability. Classical probability theory implicitly presumes a degenerate G, with all weight on one particular value of θ.

An alternative approach identifies G with a kind of equilibrium disorder. The equilibrium tends to be the maximum disorder or "entropy" consistent with some environmental constraints. Boltzmann (1886) pioneered the probabilistic interpretation of entropy. Shannon (1948) extended entropy to cover information processing more generally.

Entropy comes in several varieties, reflecting a mixture of calculation difficulties and conceptual nuance. Cover and Thomas (1991) elaborate in their textbook on information theory. Nevertheless, the various entropies share a common aim in searching for order within disorder. This book will search for similar kinds of order within financial disorder.

Rational Beliefs

Because learning is error prone, subjective uncertainty won't track objective risk perfectly. Both the tracking and the deviations can affect market prices. To emphasize this, Kurz (1974) subdivides uncertainty into two types. "Exogenous" uncertainty transmits objective risk. "Endogenous" uncertainty transmits forecasting errors and reactions to others' errors. Kurz (1994a, 1994b, 1996) widens rational expectations to encompass beliefs that are rational given the observed evidence. He traces most of the noisiness of market pricing to the endogenous uncertainty of rational beliefs.

> In a rational beliefs equilibrium the beliefs of agent are, in general, wrong in the sense that they are different from the true probability of the equilibrium process. These beliefs are, however, rational. Consequently, in a rational beliefs equilibrium agents make forecasting mistakes and these play a crucial role in the analysis. (Kurz 1997)

David (1997) and Veronesi (1999, 2000) derive similar results, drawing on the regime-switching models of Liptser and Shirayev (1977) and Hamilton (1989).

Chapter 2: The Ultimate Confidence Game

Fiat Money

Economists have long debated whether pure fiat money, devoid of intrinsic value, is viable. A consensus is developing that it is not. Goldberg (2005) has debunked some colorful stories of primitive societies relying on stones and seashells. As for government IOUs, their legal tender guarantees usefulness in paying taxes and in settling other debts.

Cochrane (2005) likens fiat money to equities, with government fiscal surpluses playing the role of corporate profits. I find that way too optimistic, as there's no legal claim, enforcement is a nightmare, and many governments don't run surpluses. Shubik (1999) emphasizes the distinction between money and a credit contract. Governments implicitly agree, for they treat the seigniorage from money issuance as profit. However, many governments are sufficiently well off or concerned about their reputation to provide de facto backing.

Another strand in the literature emphasizes money's use as a store of value. Samuelson (1958) presents a basic model of fiat money appreciating in a rational bubble. Wallace (1980) provides a more sophisticated treatment.

I emphasize the evolutionary dynamics. A commodity gains favor as a means of exchange, capitalizes on its own liquidity, and substitutes proxies with successively less intrinsic value. Fiat money is the limiting case. While the limit is not zero, it's a lot less than what the fiat money sells for.

Perpetual Options

Options grant the holder a right to buy or sell. Perpetual options never expire. The lack of expiry simplifies the mathematical treatment. It collapses the partial differential heat equation characteristic of options theory to an ordinary second-order differential equation. The solution, first worked out by McKean (1965), specifies an optimal threshold: hold the option on one side of the threshold and exercise it on the other. Wilmott (2006: chaps. 9 and 10) provides a lucid treatment of perpetual options and stopping rules.

However, standard models aren't very satisfying for analyzing the perpetual put embedded in money. Cash tends to be so inferior that we sell it immediately. That's largely because standard options theory assumes friction-free markets. Why pay extra for liquidity when everything is liquid?

To compensate, we can assume a "convenience yield" for money. That tends to yield a knife-edge result. Once the convenience yield is high enough not to sell money right away, we're tempted to hold money forever. Moreover, the very assumption of a convenience yield tends to obscure the convenience we're trying to analyze.

Guo and Zhang (2004) offer a more sophisticated model of a perpetual American put, where risks change randomly over time. Here I will stick with two simpler models, which convey the intuition fairly well even though each is incomplete. One model focuses on the search for bargains, the other on consumption smoothing.

Search for Bargains

If exchange were restricted to barter, each of us would have to find someone who offers what we want and wants what we offer. Exchange via money makes shopping a lot easier. Each good or service we encounter offers for our money some marginal satisfaction x, which we can view as a sample from the distribution F of all such x. Suppose that we examine n commodities in sequence, with each examination costing δ in deferred pleasure. Suppose that at any point we can stop shopping, buy anything we have investigated, and consume it. What is our optimal strategy?

On average, the best commodity of n will represent the top $\dfrac{100}{n+1}$ -percentile of F. Hence the nth investigation stands to move an extra $\dfrac{100}{n} - \dfrac{100}{n+1} \cong \dfrac{100}{n^2}$ percent into the upper tail. When the expected gain falls below δ, stop shopping and pick the best bargain.

The gain, as Wolpert (2009) shows, tends to be directly proportional to σn^{α}, where σ is the standard deviation of F and α is a positive constant or near-constant. It follows that the expected holding time for money will be proportional to $\sigma^{1/\alpha}$.

The fatter-tailed the distribution, the lower α will be and the longer the likely search. For a uniform distribution, $\alpha = 2$. For a Gaussian distribution, $\alpha = 1 + \frac{1}{2}\ln \ln n$. For an exponential distribution, $\alpha = 1$. For a Pareto distribution proportional to $x^{-\beta}$ with $\beta > 1$, $\alpha = 1 - \dfrac{1}{\beta}$.

In any case the option value of money grows with σ. This helps explain precautionary demand. Anticipation of increased volatility helps explain speculative demand.

Note too that money has a countercyclical attraction. Not only is it more useful when markets are turbulent, but also the turbulence prompts commodity sellers to pay a premium for it. This provides insurance to risk-averse consumers and makes money a welcome asset at less than the risk-free rate.

Opportunity Costs

Economics studies trade-offs between choices. Opportunity costs measure those trade-offs. If you could be earning 2% after-tax on a term savings account, then holding cash to term has an opportunity cost of at least 2%. Optimization matches marginal costs to marginal benefits.

In a world without risk or uncertainty, choosers generally behave as if they maximize an increasing concave utility function U subject to budget constraints. Increasing means that more makes them happier. Concave means that they would rather mix two baskets than oscillate between one and the other. When consumption has a scalar measure c, the relevant conditions can be summarized as $\dfrac{dU}{dc} \equiv U'(c) > 0$ and $\dfrac{d^2U}{dc^2} \equiv U''(c) \leq 0$.

U is not defined uniquely, as adding any scalar or multiplying by any positive scalar leaves decision making unchanged. Mathematically that tells us to focus on $U''\!/_U$, and its multivariate analogues. The simplest case is $U(c) \equiv c$, which lets us proxy utility by net monetary gains.

The Cost of Waiting

The single most important opportunity cost in finance is the cost of waiting. Economists typically divide these waiting costs into two parts: a deferral element that depends only on time and a satiation effect that depends only on variations in consumption. If our inherent preferences don't change over time, this yields a structure $U \equiv \sum_{t=0}^{\infty} \beta^t u(c_t)$ for some discount factor β. Empirical estimation suggests an annual β of around 0.98, so that waiting costs about 2% per year.

Often it is more convenient to focus on the logarithmic impatience $\delta \equiv -\log(\beta)$ and rewrite utility as $U \equiv \sum_{t=0}^{\infty} e^{-\delta t} u(c_t)$. This generalizes naturally to the continuous-time variant $U \equiv \int_{t=0}^{\infty} e^{-\delta t} u(c_t) dt$, where c_t is reinterpreted as a rate of consumption.

Elasticity of Intertemporal Substitution

The elasticity of intertemporal substitution (EIS) measures the percentage shift in the savings-to-consumption ratio per percentage point change in the effective interest rate. With time-separable utility, the EIS can be shown to equal the inverse elasticity $\dfrac{d \log c}{d \log u'(c)} = \dfrac{u'(c)}{c u''(c)}$ of the marginal utility of consumption. Empirical estimates of the EIS range from under 0.2 in Barsky et al. (1997) to 2 in Gruber (2006). Engelhardt and Kumar (2009) claim 90% confidence that EIS lies between 0.5 and 1.

Expected Utility

Since we never know for certain what the future will bring, we need to replace the various $u(c_t)$ with expectations. The simplest method substitutes expected consumption $\langle c_t \rangle$ for each c_t, but this makes no allowance for risk aversion. The next simplest method substitutes expected utility $\langle u(c_t) \rangle$ for each unknown $u(c_t)$.

Expected utility allows us to define a certainty equivalent $m_t \equiv u^{-1}(\langle u(c_t) \rangle)$, which indicates what a risky return is worth in terms of sure things. The more concave u is, as measured by u''/u', the greater the gap between expected return and certainty equivalent. This gap is known as the risk premium.

A time-separable $\langle u(c_t) \rangle$ is a special case of a more general expected utility theory. People who don't abide by general expected theory aren't fully economically rational, since they will knowingly take sucker bets bound to cost them money (Green 1987). Unfortunately for theory, and possibly for humanity as well, people do violate these axioms. How regularly and deeply are matters of great interest and debate.

Relative Risk Aversion

For ease of calculation, finance theory commonly assumes that tolerance for risk scales proportionately with wealth. That is, $\dfrac{d \log u'(c)}{d \log c} = -\gamma$ for some nonnegative scalar γ known as the relative risk aversion (RRA) coefficient. This implies a power utility specification

$$u(c) \equiv \begin{cases} \dfrac{c^{1-\gamma} - 1}{1-\gamma} & \text{for } \gamma \geq 0,\ \gamma \neq 1, \\ \ln(c) & \text{for } \gamma = 1. \end{cases} \qquad \text{(A2.1)}$$

also known as constant relative risk aversion (CRRA) utility.

With CRRA utility, $u'(c) = c^{-\gamma}$. For a modest fractional change η in consumption, $u(c + \eta c) - u(c) \cong \eta c u'(c) + \frac{1}{2}\eta^2 c^2 u''(c) = (1 - \frac{1}{2}\gamma\eta)\eta c u'(c)$. If η is a small wobble with mean zero and standard deviation σ, the certainty equivalent is $-\frac{1}{2}\gamma\sigma^2 c$.

When large consumption shares are at risk, the RRA has a huge impact on behavior. A value less than 1 is considered small. It implies that no risk is too big to warrant taking, if the upside is big enough. A value greater than 10 is considered high. It rules out taking even a 5% risk of losing 30% of wealth, regardless of the potential upside.

My sense of market behavior is that—

- Given 95% chance of overwhelming gains, most investors are willing to wager more than 75% of wealth but not everything.
- Given even odds of doubling their wealth, most investors are willing to lose a quarter to half of their wealth if they fail (See Figure A.2).

Both of these suggest an RRA on the order of 1 to 3. This is broadly consistent with the empirical findings of Friend and Blume (1975), Constantinides (1990), and many others.

With time-separable utility, the RRA is the inverse of the EIS. I interpret the bulk of empirical evidence as falling roughly in that range, and hence will use time-separable CRRA for benchmark estimates. However, this has some troubling implications, as the notes to the next chapter will show.

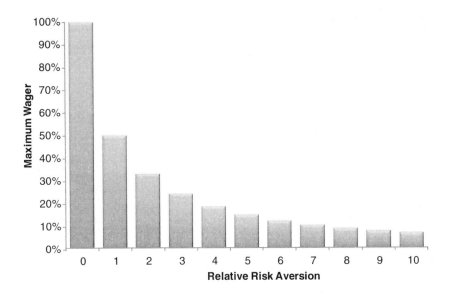

Figure A.2
Value of 50% Chance to Double Wealth

Consumption Smoothing

Risk aversion encourages people to smooth their consumption. But since reality rarely matches plans, ex post consumption may wobble even when ex ante consumption does not. Money can help moderate that.

With ample money paying zero interest and no uncertainty, a consumer with the preferences described above should equate $u'(c_t)$ to $e^{-\delta}u'(c_{t+1})$ for all t, implying that CRRA consumption optimally declines at logarithmic rate δ/γ. Imagine that consumption without money equals $1 + \eta$ today and $e^{-\delta/\gamma} - \eta$ the next period. Applying a second-order Taylor expansion, the absolute difference in expected utility works out to

$$\left| (1 - \tfrac{1}{2}\gamma\eta)\eta + e^{-\delta}(1 - \tfrac{1}{2}\gamma(-\eta)e^{\delta/\gamma})(-\eta)(e^{-\delta/\gamma})^{-\gamma} \right|$$
$$\cong \left| \eta - \tfrac{1}{2}\gamma\eta^2 - \eta - \tfrac{1}{2}\gamma\eta^2 e^{\delta/\gamma} \right| \tag{A2.2}$$
$$= \tfrac{1}{2}(1 + e^{\delta/\gamma})\gamma\eta^2 \cong \gamma\eta \cdot \eta u'(1).$$

Hence money yields approximately the same gain as if the cash set aside earned interest at rate $\gamma\eta$. If γ is moderate and η is even a few percent, this will substantially exceed typical interest rates. It provides a powerful incentive to hold emergency reserves of cash or low-interest demand deposits.

Reality Check

The previous calculation cheats, by ignoring the risk that the extra liquidity isn't needed. Weighing against that is the risk that the extra liquidity isn't needed. Suppose, for example, that an immortal consumer can consume the optimal stream $1, e^{-\delta/\gamma}, e^{-2\delta/\gamma}, \ldots$ Unwisely, she saves η too much initially and realizes it just after. Her optimal response is to spread the extra out over subsequent periods, again declining at logarithmic rate δ/γ. This boosts consumption from the second period on by a fraction $\eta\left(e^{\delta/\gamma} - 1\right) \cong \eta\delta/\gamma$. The net change in expected utility works out to approximately

$$\left(1 - \tfrac{1}{2}\gamma(-\eta)\right)(-\eta) + \left(1 - \frac{\eta\delta}{2\gamma}\right)\eta\left(e^{\delta/\gamma} - 1\right)\sum_{n=1}^{\infty} e^{-n\delta}\left(e^{-n\delta/\gamma}\right)^{1-\gamma}$$

$$= -(1 + \tfrac{1}{2}\gamma\eta)\eta + \left(1 - \frac{\eta\delta}{2\gamma}\right)\eta = -\tfrac{1}{2}\left(\delta/\gamma + \gamma\right)\eta \cdot \eta u'(1). \tag{A2.3}$$

Hence, the loss from needless saving will absorb just over half of the gain from prescient saving. Nearly half of the gain remains. Thus, even relatively modest noise can justify a transaction demand for liquidity.

Liquidity is even more important to buffer large losses or to capitalize on others' misfortune. The more polite terms are "precautionary demand" and "speculative demand." In these cases the second-order Taylor approximation for utility tends to fail. The notes to the next chapter will tackle higher-order expansions.

Infinite Geometric Series

The second line of (A2.3) required the simplification of an infinite geometric series. The basic formula is

$$\sum_{t=0}^{\infty} z^t = \frac{1}{1-z} \quad \text{for } |z| < 1, \tag{A2.4}$$

which can be verified by multiplying both sides by $1 - z$. A simpler proof notes that $Z \equiv \sum_{t=0}^{\infty} z^t = 1 + zZ$ and then solves for Z. The continuous-time variant is even neater:

$$\int_0^{\infty} e^{-yt} dt = \frac{1}{\lambda}. \tag{A2.5}$$

Alternatively we can write $Y \equiv \int_0^{\infty} e^{-yt} dt \cong 1 \cdot dt + (1 - y\,dt)Y$, which in the limit requires $1 - yY$ to vanish.

Currency Inertia

Suppose two currencies are available, with base holding costs of δ_1 and δ_2 per time period, where each cost reflects consumer impatience plus inflation or depreciation. Mahserg's Law favors whichever currency has the lower δ_i. However, some sellers may not accept both currencies. Let us assume a probability p_i each period of finding a desired good from sellers accepting currency i.

The expected cost C_i of using currency i is δ_i with probability p_i and $\delta_i + C_i$ with probability $1 - p_i$. Solving $C_i = \delta_i + (1 - p_i)C_i$ yields $C_i = \frac{\delta_i}{p_i}$. Hence we must have

$$\frac{\delta_2}{\delta_1} < \frac{p_2}{p_1} \tag{A2.6}$$

to justify a switch to currency 2. If currency 1 is currently universally accepted, the percentage savings in holding cost must exceed $1 - p_2$ to justify a switch.

Now let us allow for currency conversion at transaction cost c. As long as $c < \frac{\delta_i}{p_i}$, it is worth making the conversion instead of waiting. We then have $C_i = \delta_i + (1 - p_i)c$, which requires

$$\frac{\delta_2}{\delta_1} < 1 + \frac{p_2 - p_1}{\delta_1} c < \frac{p_2}{p_1} \tag{A2.7}$$

to justify using currency 2. Thus a low conversion cost can actually increase currency inertia.

Foreign Exchange (FX) Reserves

Most of the data on FX reserves comes from the International Monetary Fund (IMF 2010). However, some governments don't report their FX reserves to the IMF or started reporting only recently. I assembled series on China's and Taiwan's FX reserves from Web reports on holdings of China's and Taiwan's central banks. To backfill gaps in the IMF table, I interpolated from scattered reports.

Figure 2.1 in Chapter 2 leaves out FX reserves held by major Middle Eastern and African oil producers. These are reportedly approaching $1 trillion, with nearly half held by the Saudi Arabian Monetary Authority (CIA 2010). However, estimates for earlier in the decade are hard to come by and inconsistent. The CIA's estimates for Saudi reserves increased tenfold in a year because of reclassification.

Chapter 3: Great Expectations

Asset Valuation

It is said that a bird in hand is worth two in the bush. Asset valuation extends such comparisons to value any risky or uncertain future payment stream in terms of cash at hand. The adjustment applied to each conditional expectation is known as its discount factor. The sum of discounted values is known as the net present value, or NPV.

Discounting is to finance theory what thinking is to philosophy. Everybody does it, but even the experts aren't sure how to do it right. Moreover, practice refutes many otherwise appealing notions. For controversies over discounting, two excellent references are Cochrane (2004) and Mehra (2008).

Simple Discounting

The simplest discounting model assumes a constant rate of interest r. In effect, that says something worth 1 today is worth $1 + r$ next period and $(1 + r)^T$ T periods from now. Inverting that, a dollar paid T periods from now is worth $(1 + r)^{-T}$ dollars today. Multiply each payment by the appropriate discount factor and sum to calculate the NPV.

Applying (A2.4), an asset paying 1 each period has an NPV of $\frac{1}{r}$. If payments grow at rate g after the first period, the NPV works out to $\frac{1}{r-g}$. This implies a dividend at rate $r-g$ and a capital gain at rate g, which sum to the benchmark interest rate r.

Logarithmic Versus Percentage Change

Logarithms can be tidier to work with percentages. If we define $\tilde{r} \equiv \log(1+r)$ as the logarithmic interest rate, we can rewrite the T-period discount factor as $e^{-\tilde{r}T}$ and evaluate the NPV of a continuous dividend stream as $\int_0^\infty e^{-\tilde{r}t} \langle c(t) \rangle \, dt$. For a logarithmic growth rate $\tilde{g} \equiv \log(1+g)$, the dividend-to-NPV ratio will be $\left(\int_0^\infty e^{-\tilde{r}t} e^{\tilde{g}t} \, dt \right)^{-1} = \tilde{r} - \tilde{g}$.

Given a logarithmic change $\tilde{x}$, the corresponding percentage change can be calculated as $x = \exp(\tilde{x}) - 1$. Second-order Taylor approximations $\tilde{x} \cong x - \frac{1}{2}x^2$ and $x \cong \tilde{x} + \frac{1}{2}\tilde{x}^2$ are excellent for growth rates of less than 10%.

Consumption-Based Pricing

The main challenge for analysis of discount factors is to relate their levels to market equilibrium. Consumption-based pricing models focus on equilibrating consumption and savings. Given time-separable utility, $\left\langle \beta(1+r_{t+1}) \dfrac{u'(c_{t+1})}{u'(c_t)} \right\rangle$ must equal 1 for all t. Assuming CRRA utility, this simplifies to $\left\langle \beta(1+r_{t+1})(1+g_{t+1})^{-\gamma} \right\rangle = 1$ where g_{t+1} denotes the percentage growth of consumption. We can rewrite this in logarithms as

$$\log\langle \exp(\tilde{r}_{t+1} - \delta - \gamma\tilde{g}_{t+1}) \rangle = 0. \tag{A3.1}$$

Consumption-Based Pricing with Near-Normal Risks

By near-normal risk I mean that a second-order Taylor approximation can capture it. In that case

$$\log\langle \exp(z)\rangle \cong \log\langle 1 + z + \tfrac{1}{2}z^2\rangle$$
$$\cong \langle z\rangle + \tfrac{1}{2}\langle z^2\rangle - \tfrac{1}{2}\langle z\rangle^2 = \langle z\rangle + \tfrac{1}{2}\operatorname{var}(z). \qquad \text{(A3.2)}$$

This holds with equality for lognormal distributions. Applying the name "near-normal" to equation (A3.1) and rearranging terms,

$$\log(1 + \langle r\rangle) \cong \langle \tilde{r}\rangle + \tfrac{1}{2}\operatorname{var}(\tilde{r})$$
$$\cong \delta + \gamma\langle \tilde{g}\rangle - \tfrac{1}{2}\gamma^2 \operatorname{var}(\tilde{g}) + \gamma \operatorname{cov}(\tilde{g}, \tilde{r}). \qquad \text{(A3.3)}$$

Of the four terms on the right-hand side, the first three define the risk-free rate r_f:

$$\tilde{r}_f \cong \delta + \gamma\langle \tilde{g}\rangle - \tfrac{1}{2}\gamma^2 \operatorname{var}(\tilde{g}). \qquad \text{(A3.4)}$$

If equity growth r_{eq} matches consumption growth, their covariance is just their variance, implying

$$\log\left(1 + \langle r_{eq}\rangle\right) - \tilde{r}_f \cong \gamma \operatorname{var}(\tilde{g}). \qquad \text{(A3.5)}$$

This difference is known as the equity risk premium. It denotes the extra return investors demand to take on aggregate economic risk.

Rate Puzzles

Let's plug in some numbers. Consumption growth tends to wobble at most a few percent per year, suggesting a variance of 2% squared or less. With $\delta = 1\%$, $\gamma = 2.5$, $\langle \tilde{g}\rangle = 1.5\%$, and $\operatorname{var}(\tilde{g}) = 0.0004$, the real risk-free rate will be 4.74%, while the risk premium will be 0.1%.

This is weird. The risk-free rate is humongous, while the risk premium is miniscule. To restore any semblance to reality, we need to shift about three percentage points from the risk-free rate to the risk premium.

As Mehra and Prescott (1985) emphasize, no small tweak comes close to achieving this. If (A3.5) is correct, the RRA is most likely 20 or higher. That seems preposterous. Suppose we can draw a card from an ordinary deck, with one joker thrown in to make 53. We win infinite riches unless we draw the joker. Are we willing to pay 20% of wealth for the chance? Not at an RRA of 20; we would find it too risky. See Figure A.3.

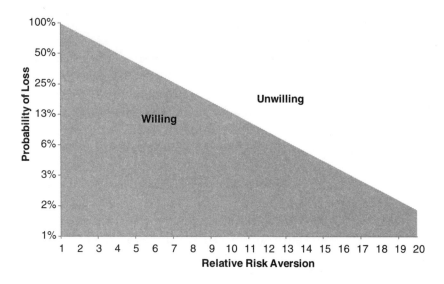

Figure A.3
Willingness to Risk 20% Loss for Infinite Reward

The risk-free rate $\tilde{r}_f$ can be even harder to fit, as Weil (1989) notes:

- Boosting the RRA from moderate levels makes it even harder to explain the risk-free rate, unless $\gamma > \dfrac{\langle \tilde{g} \rangle}{\mathrm{var}(\tilde{g})}$. The threshold is almost surely in the double digits.
- A high RRA makes the risk-free rate hypersensitive to expected growth. A 0.2-percentage-point increase in $\langle \tilde{g} \rangle$ is hard to separate from measurement error, Yet it hikes $\tilde{r}_f$ by over four percentage points when the RRA exceeds 20.
- An RRA of 1 or less is out of line with survey data and makes a high-risk premium even harder to explain.

Habit

One response is to drop time-separable utility. Greenig (1986) retains the form $U = \sum_{t=0}^{\infty} \beta^t u_t$ but reinterprets each u_t to depend on past consumption as well as present. This distinguishes the EIS from the inverse RRA, making a low risk-free rate easier to model.

Constantinides (1990) replaces absolute consumption in $u(c)$ with consumption relative to past habit. Abel (1990) reinterprets habit as a social norm: envy or "keeping up with the Joneses." Campbell and Cochrane (1999) tweak Abel's specification to better fit the empirical data and draw out a rich set of implications.

Social experience, reinforced by the psychological research summarized in Gilbert (2006), suggests that people do indeed measure satisfaction at least partly in relative rather than absolute terms. Fuhrer (2000), among others, finds strong evidence of macroeconomic impact.

Note that habit creates a negative externality. If Jones consumes more today, he will be harder to please tomorrow, and Smith—who wants to keep up with Jones—will be harder to please as well. Society might benefit from compressing income differentials and discouraging conspicuous consumption, even if growth drops. Indeed, it might be useful occasionally to destroy wealth in order to enhance satisfaction in the subsequent recovery.

Recursive Utility

Another explanation defines utility recursively. Drawing on earlier work by Kreps and Porteus (1978), Weil (1989) and Epstein and Zin (1989, 1991) specify utility U_t as an "aggregator" of immediate consumption c_t and the certainty equivalent of next-period utility U_{t+1}. They assume a power function for certainty equivalence and constant elasticity of substitution for the aggregator, yielding the compound form

$$U_t = \left(c_t^{1-\alpha} + \beta \langle U_{t+1}^{1-\gamma} \rangle^{(1-\alpha)/(1-\gamma)} \right)^{1/(1-\alpha)}, \tag{A3.6}$$

where γ denotes the RRA and α denotes the inverse EIS. When $\alpha = \gamma$, this reduces to standard CRRA. A high α implies a low risk-free rate regardless of γ.

Recursive utility has a peculiar side effect, first noted by Kreps and Porteus (1978). It imparts utility to the timing of information, outside its direct impact on consumption. Censors might add value by filtering and redirecting information.

Recursive utility is also hard to calculate. Closed-form expressions are rarely available. However, Duffie and Epstein (1992) provide formulas for updating recursive utility in continuous time, which might provide tractable approximations.

Half-Answers

As we have just seen, either habit or recursive utility can explain a low risk-free rate and low sensitivity to growth, at the cost of more complex modeling. A third explanation, offered by Bansal and Coleman (1996), emphasizes the relative liquidity of risk-free assets. The convenience yield offered in emergencies cuts the return required in ordinary times.

None of these explanations account for a high risk premium. Using second-order approximations, they still yield an equation like (A3.5), which implies an absurdly high RRA. At best they provide half-answers.

Tail Risks

The risk premium puzzle is best addressed squarely. While small wobbles in consumption don't rattle moderately risk-averse investors, big losses do. So let's model sensitivity to risks in the tails of the distribution.

Not any tail risk will do. Small independent losses can coincide by chance. In the limit, i.i.d. risk generates a normal bell curve, unbounded yet defined by mean and variance alone. The tail risks I am referring to stand out from the bell curve. Typically a common driving factor—a war, natural disaster, or market crash—overrides the independence that prevailed before. Osband (2002) calls this "iceberg risk" and modifies the classic Markowitz (1952) model of portfolio optimization to incorporate it.

To illustrate the impact, let us assume consumption has mean zero and standard deviation of 5% a year. With an RRA of 3, a second-order approximation suggests a certainty equivalent loss of only 0.4%. However, if the standard deviation arises from a 0.34% chance of an 85% fall, the actual certainty equivalent loss could be as high as 6.5%. Rational investors might shift their portfolios a lot to avoid that.

Rietz (1988) first linked the risk premium explicitly to a small risk of disasters. Barro (2006) revives and improves Rietz's argument. Using historical data to estimate model parameters, he attributes the gap between bond rates and the lower implied risk-free rate to default risks experienced in crisis. Gabaix (2010) extends the Rietz-Barro framework to incorporate a time-varying intensity of disasters. He uses this to explain the risk premium, the risk-free rate, and eight other puzzles of finance.

Cumulant Expressions

Martin (2010) notes that the certainty equivalent of CRRA utility is closely related to the CGF, which we can express as

$$\kappa(1-\gamma) \equiv \log\left\langle\exp\left((1-\gamma)\tilde{g}\right)\right\rangle. \tag{A3.7}$$

Instead of applying second-order approximations, Martin substitutes K directly into Lucas's (1978) equilibrium equations for asset prices. Given a dividend stream of c_t^λ for some constant power λ, and assuming risk is i.i.d., the price-to-dividend ratio p_λ simplifies to

$$p_\lambda = \sum_{t=1}^{\infty}\exp\left(-\left(\delta-\kappa(\lambda-\gamma)\right)t\right) = \frac{1}{\exp\left(\delta-\kappa(\lambda-\gamma)\right)-1}. \tag{A3.8}$$

The logarithmic dividend-to-price ratio $\log\left(1+\frac{1}{p_\lambda}\right)$ is even simpler at $\delta - K(\lambda-\gamma)$. For a risk-free bond, $\lambda=0$, so

$$\tilde{r}_f = \delta - K(-\gamma). \tag{A3.9}$$

For aggregate wealth paying consumption as its dividend, $\lambda=1$ and the consumption-to-wealth ratio works out to $\delta - K(1-\gamma)$. The logarithmic expected return on wealth adds an additional $K(1)$, implying a risk premium of

$$K(1) + K(-\gamma) - K(1-\gamma). \tag{A3.10}$$

A Taylor series expansion of K confirms that (A3.9) and (A3.10) match (A3.4) and (A3.5) to second order. However, the higher cumulants play a significant role, except for Gaussian distributions where they're all zero. Tail risks can easily explain the rate puzzles.

Martin performs a similar analysis for the recursive utility in (A3.6). The risk-free rate adds an additional term in $\dfrac{\gamma-\alpha}{1-\gamma}K(1-\gamma)$, which provides more modeling flexibility. The risk premium and its explanation remain exactly the same.

Instability

As Martin notes, marginal risks of severe losses can significantly change the risk premium in (A3.10). He finds that unsettling, and seeks to infer expectations from observed discount rates and consumption-to-wealth ratios.

In practice, expectations will adjust with the evidence of outliers. Every day of continued calm tends to trim the perceived risk of breakdown, usually by just a little. Observed breakdowns tend to raise the perceived odds of repeat, usually by a lot. These responses can be wholly rational. But they imply that both the risk premium and the risk-free rate will be volatile.

Martin's model is not set up to address this. When risk is i.i.d. as it assumes, uncertainty about the parameters eventually evaporates. The easiest way to modify this is to allow for Markov switching across a variety of risk regimes, or probability distributions for risk. Markov switching means that the probability of switching from one state to another doesn't depend on the states before.

Markov regime switching messes up the tidy expressions in (A3.8)–(A3.10). We need more tractable specifications of the CGF to solve for key rates. Simple disaster risk helps do that. Gabaix's modifications reintroduce complexity in a tractable way.

Veronesi (2004a) achieves tractability without jumps. He assumes dividends followed lognormal Brownian motion with changing drift. Solving the pricing equations, he managed to account for a host of market phenomena. But the solution has at least one disconcerting property. For time-separable CRRA utility with $\gamma > 1$, a jump to higher growth tends to induce a sell-off.

This property turns out to have little to do with either risk or uncertainty. From (A3.4), the discount rate with no risk equals $\delta + \gamma \tilde{g}$, implying a price-to-dividend ratio $\dfrac{1}{\delta + (\gamma - 1)\tilde{g}}$ that declines with g. Veronesi incorporates habit to make valuations vary with growth rather than against it.

A Rietz-Barro-Gabaix-type specification doesn't need that. Since disaster causes a discrete shock, all sufferers recognize it immediately and can't benefit from shifting out ex post. Indeed, with Gabaix's specification, faster recovery after the disaster draws investors back in. As a consequence, growth in their models tends to boost asset prices even with moderate risk aversion and time-separable utility.

Uncertain Synthesis

Small risks of big losses, coupled with evidence that markets in the second half of the twentieth century were unusually calm, whittles down the risk premium we need to explain (Veronesi 2004b). Cogley and Sargent (2008) demonstrate that a lingering fear of the Great Depression, which Bayesian updating gradually eased, could make investors appear much more risk averse than they were. The lower the risk aversion we need to posit, the less anomalous the evidence on EIS looks, and the less need we have for complex utility specifications trying to build in extra inertia.

We also know that empirical stock returns are at least ten times more volatile than aggregate consumption. If we treat stocks as an asset paying stock returns rather than consumption, it is fairly easy to explain the observed risk premium. Given a risk-free asset, an RRA of γ, and a risky lognormal stock portfolio offering a log risk premium μ for volatility σ, Osband (2002: chap. 20) shows that the optimal investment share ω^* in the risky asset is

$$\omega^* = \frac{\mu}{\gamma\sigma^2} \equiv \frac{S}{\gamma\sigma},$$ (A3.11)

where $S \equiv \mu/\sigma$ is known as the Sharpe ratio. If no risk-free asset is held in equilibrium, ω^* must equal 1, implying $S = \gamma\sigma$. With stock market volatility about 15% and an RRA of around 2, we would expect an equilibrium Sharpe ratio of about 0.3, which is close to what we observe (Cogley and Sargent 2008: table 6).

Indeed, if we take into account the tail risks of market returns, the observed Sharpe ratio seems too low. Perhaps investors realize that most of the tail risks cancel out longer-term. Perhaps they realize that equities are only a slice of the risk assets available.

In any case, market volatility clearly creates substantial risk for participants, so if we can explain it we can explain all or most of the risk premium. Indeed, market volatility is easy to explain in terms of learning, as Kurz and Beltratti (1996) and Weitzman (2007) emphasize.

Chapter 4: Sustainable Debt

The Cost of Servicing Perpetuities

Suppose a perpetuity worth B earns the risk-free rate r every period. By symmetry, it is as if the perpetuity earns r next period plus another perpetuity worth B. Hence $B = \dfrac{B+r}{1+r}$, which implies $B = 1$.

If a borrower repays a perpetuity next period with a combination of the original perpetuity, a deduction g from the interest rate normally due, and a fraction g of a new perpetuity, then absent default risk the value B shouldn't change. Figure A.4 presents a chart of various net interest paths for perpetuities.

Applying (A2.4) to a cash repayment that starts at $r - g$ and grows at rate g, the present value is readily calculated as

$$\sum_{t=1}^{\infty} \frac{(r - g)(1 + g)^{t-1}}{(1 + r)^t} = \frac{r - g}{1 + r} \cdot \frac{1}{1 - (1 + g)/(1 + r)} = 1. \quad (A4.1)$$

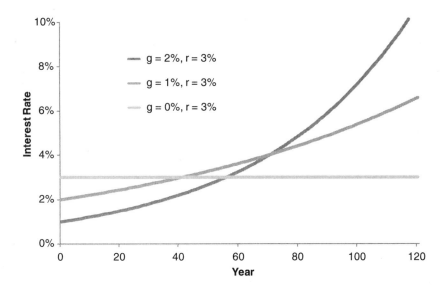

Figure A.4
Possible Interest Paths for Perpetuities

The continuous-time variant makes this clearer:

$$\int_0^\infty (\tilde{r} - \tilde{g}) e^{\tilde{g}t} e^{-\tilde{r}t} dt = \frac{\tilde{r} - \tilde{g}}{\tilde{r} - \tilde{g}} = 1. \tag{A4.2}$$

Hence, issuing perpetuities or letting the stock of perpetuities mount shouldn't change the debtor's burden in NPV terms. However, on closer inspection these equations apply only for $g < r$. At $g = r$ the net payment is zero every period, for an NPV of zero. At $g > r$ the net interest payment is negative, and increases so fast that that the NPV diverges to minus infinity.

Explaining Something for Nothing

By issuing perpetuities that are never repaid on aggregate out of the borrower's own funds, the borrower is transferring resources as permanently as taxes would. Yet the lenders will value the aggregate perpetuities and interest on perpetuities as 1 initially and compounding at rate r thereafter. How can we reconcile the something lenders think they are getting with the nothing or infinitely less than nothing that the borrower is paying?

The simples answer is that it can't be. With $g \geq r$, the present value of wealth is infinite. People should optimally consume more now, indeed infinitely more. Since supply is finite, r must rise above g to restrain demand, eliminating the sovereign's free lunch.

A second answer qualifies this no. While no bond is truly risk free, the sovereign may be able to approximate it in limited quantities. To reassure lenders, the sovereign occasionally winds large debts down well below servicing capacity. Bond seigniorage comes mostly from the low interest rates owed, although there may still be elements of a perpetually deferred perpetuity.

A third answer contends that the public sees through the sovereign's disguises and deducts the NPV of its tax burden from its wealth. Barro (1979) calls this the "Ricardian equivalence theorem on public debt." This is a bit of a misnomer, for while Ricardo (1820) advocated a full accounting for future tax burdens of debt, he believed that lenders to the sovereign underestimated the burdens. Empirical research, reviewed in Briotti (2005), tends to back Ricardo's observation, provided the debt burden is not too high.

A fourth answer contends that a perpetually deferred perpetuity, like the fiat money it embellishes, is a kind of "rational bubble." Tirole (1985)

confirms that theoretical models of economies with overlapping generations are prone to rational bubbles, and suggests they are widespread in
real economies. However, the inherent fragility of bubbles would again
argue for occasional wind-down of sovereign debt exposure.

Worthless Debt Bubbles

Equations (4.1)–(4.3) for worthless debt imply that $B' = cB = \theta B = \theta_0 B^{m+1}$,
where B denotes the bond stock, c denotes the instantaneous credit spread,
and θ denotes the instantaneous default rate. The initial conditions are
$\theta(0) = \theta_0$ and $B(0) = 1$. If we multiply through by $-B^{-m-1}$ and integrate, we
see that $B^{-m} = 1 - m\theta_0 t$. Rearrangement and substitution yield equations
(4.4) and (4.5), except for the survival probability F. By definition, F decays
at rate $\theta(t)$, so $F' = -\theta F$, which implies

$$(FB)' = F'B + FB' = -\theta FB + F\theta B = 0. \tag{A4.3}$$

Hence FB is constant, and from the initial conditions the constant must
be 1. Since B^{-m} can't be negative, default is certain by time $T \equiv \dfrac{1}{m\theta_0}$. The
expected time of default works out to a fraction $\dfrac{1}{m+1}$ shy of T:

$$\int_0^T t\theta F dt = \int_0^T t\theta_0 (1 - m\theta_0 t)^{-1+1/m} dt$$

$$= t(1 - m\theta_0 t)^{1/m} \Big|_0^T - \frac{mT}{m+1}(1 - m\theta_0 t)^{1+1/m} \Big|_0^T = \frac{mT}{m+1}. \tag{A4.4}$$

At that time the interest rate will be $(m+1)\theta_0$, and likely only a modest
multiple of the base rate. Hence the debt stock will likely still appear con-
trollable at default. However, the expected bond stock at default is infinite
because of the extraordinary surge close to T:

$$\int_0^T B\theta F dt = \int_0^T \frac{\theta_o}{1 - m\theta_0 t} dt = -\frac{1}{m} \ln(1 - m\theta_0 t) \Big|_0^T = \infty. \tag{A4.5}$$

Disturbing Features

Because default is certain by time T, any lender appears better off not lending at all. At least commit to withdraw by time $T - \varepsilon$ for some positive ε.

However, this isn't a sustainable equilibrium. By offering a tiny positive expected profit, the borrower tempts the lender into betting for an additional $\varepsilon/2$ time, and again for $\varepsilon/4$ time, and so on until default occurs.

The repetition recalls the St. Petersburg Paradox. A risk-neutral gambler is induced to take a potentially infinite series of double-your-wealth-or-lose-everything bets. All the bets are fair, yet the gambler is bound to lose everything.

Usually people try to explain away the paradox by noting that the gambler likely isn't risk neutral or that the casino has limited funds. The real nub of the issue is a mathematical curiosity. The probabilistic "certainty" of default veils an infinitesimal chance of an infinite payoff, which may or may not be something we should ignore. To confirm that is the core problem, note that the expected value is infinite for bets with 99.99% chance of success, yet with probability 1 the gambler will leave the casino empty-handed.

Our worthless-debt model adds two twists. First, the odds of loss rise over time and eventually approach one. Second, each bet is played sufficiently faster than the preceding that an infinite series can get completed in finite time. While the St. Petersburg Paradox implicitly includes the last constraint as well, the violations of physical law get brazen close to T.

Hence, the worthless-debt game can't truly generate something for nothing. Either the borrower gets stuck with a huge debt it can't refinance or the lenders earn much less than expected. Moreover, the very notion of a default term structure that both sides fully agree on is fanciful to an extreme.

Nevertheless, the model offers useful insights into the lure and limitations of rollover. On the one hand, it distinguishes between rollover risk and fundamental solvency risks the way traders do, when most models of rational expectations treat them as essentially the same. On the other hand, it demonstrates that debt can't be rolled over indefinitely without fundamental backing, even in an otherwise ideal setting.

Generalization

To confirm that the simplicity of the model isn't misleading, this section incorporates impatience, growth, salvage value, and fiscal tightening. Dropping the tilde (~) to avoid clutter, let r and g denote the logarithmic risk-free rate and growth rate, respectively. Let a fraction $1 - \ell$ of face value be paid out in salvage on defaulted bonds, so that ℓ denotes the fractional loss. Over a short interval dt, creditors expect to receive roughly

$\theta(1-\ell)dt + (1-\theta\ dt)\ (1+(r+c)dt)$, which they compare to the risk-free proceeds $1 + rdt$. The equilibrium condition (4.1) gives way to

$$c(t) = \ell\theta(t) \tag{A4.6}$$

Let the sovereign always pay off a fraction q of the bond stock by running a primary (noninterest) budget surplus. A negative q corresponds to a primary budget deficit. The logarithm of the nominal bond stock grows at rate $c(t) + r - q$. However, the nominal bond stock now matters less than its ratio to GDP. Redefining B as that ratio, we replace equation (4.2) with

$$B'(t) = (c(t) + r - g - q)\ B(t) \tag{A4.7}$$

Equation (4.3) describing the evolution of default rates becomes

$$\theta(t) = \theta_0 B_0^{-m} B^m(t), \tag{A4.8}$$

where B_0 denotes the initial ratio of bond stock to GDP. Combining (A4.6)–(A4.8),

$$B'(t) = \ell\theta_0 B_0^{-m} B^{m+1}(t) + (r - g - q)B(t). \tag{A4.9}$$

To solve this, define new variables $v \equiv r - g - q$ and $a(t) \equiv B(t)e^{-vt}$. After some manipulation we obtain $-a^{-m-1}a' = \ell\theta_0 B_0^{-m}e^{mvt}$. Integrating both sides with respect to t, we solve for $a(t)$ and multiply by e^{vt} to yield

$$B(t) = B_0\left(e^{-mvt} - \frac{\ell\theta_0(1 - e^{-mvt})}{v}\right)^{-1/m}. \tag{A4.10}$$

Sustainability turns out to depend completely on v. If it is negative—i.e., if the GDP growth rate plus the primary surplus rate exceed the risk-free rate—the relative bond burden vanishes and with it the credit spread. If v is positive, default is inevitable by time

$$T = \frac{1}{mv}\log\left(1 + \frac{v}{\ell\theta_0}\right). \tag{A4.11}$$

This approaches $\dfrac{1}{\ell m\theta_0}$ as v approaches zero. The basic model is the limiting case with $\ell = 1$.

Chapter 5: The Midas Touch

Mathematical Models of Economic Cycles

Sismondi (1819) pioneered the notion that capitalism inevitably plunges into crises of overproduction. Marx (1887) portrayed crises as bound to worsen over time and eventually catalyzing a socialist economic order. In contrast, neoclassical economics emphasized markets' capacity for self-correction.

Not until after World War I did economists manage to recast these debates into mathematical forms. Aftalion (1927) showed that the time needed for capital construction could general economic cycles. Frisch (1933) introduced the more modern notion of converging cycles renewed by random shocks. Frisch and Holme (1935) analyzed a Lotka-Volterra-type model and incorporated Aftalion-type lags. Shocks made the system jump from one adaptive path to another.

Nowadays economists try to incorporate more forward-looking expectations of lags and shocks. Still, the older models provide useful insights about adjustment when capacity is uncertain. An economy's aggregate debt-servicing capacity is particularly hard to gauge. The models below draw out some implications.

Lotka-Volterra Model

Lotka (1925) developed the first mathematical predator-prey model, extending his earlier work with self-catalyzing chemical reactions. Volterra (1926) independently developed the same equations in an analysis of fish catches in the Adriatic. In the basic model, prey reproduce proportionately to population size and die at the rate of predation. Predators reproduce proportionately to the rate of predation and die proportionally to population. The rate of predation is proportional to the product of the two population sizes.

No one believes Lotka-Volterra models perfectly describe the world. They leave out too many factors and are too vulnerable to random variations at extremes. Still, they are widely used in biology for the crisp insights they provide into ecosystem dynamics. The landmark treatment in May (1973) largely rests on Lotka-Volterra-type models.

The basic idea is that if predator growth is a decreasing function of prey density, while prey growth is an increasing function of predator density, the following properties will likely hold:

- Changes in predator behavior affect average prey density far more than they affect predator density.
- Changes in prey behavior affect average predator density far more than they affect prey density.
- Predator-prey combinations will likely oscillate around a static equilibrium and are not guaranteed to converge to it.
- The short-term population response to a shock may run counter to the long-term response.

Static Equilibria

Rewriting equations (5.1) and (5.2) as

$$B'/B = a - (b-1)r$$
$$r'/r = Bd - c \tag{A5.1}$$

allows us to easily identify two static equilibria. One is $B = r = 0$, where debtors can borrow at risk-free rates but choose not to. If borrowers always whittle down their debt stock outside of emergencies by setting $a \leq 0$, that's where they'll head. But that is less a predator-prey game than the best way to avoid one. We will focus here on the other static equilibrium, which presumes a, $b-1$, c, and d are positive:

$$(\bar{B}, \bar{r}) = \left(\frac{c}{d}, \frac{a}{b-1} \right). \tag{A5.2}$$

Note that the equilibrium credit spread depends only on debtor behavior, while the equilibrium debt stock depends only on lender behavior. For example, we might view southern Europe's accession to the euro zone as an innovation that reduces both lenders' fear d of default and borrowers' compunction b to tighten in response to rising credit spreads. This causes both $\bar{B}$ and $\bar{r}$ to rise in equilibrium. If the European Union hikes fiscal support to compensate, this lowers a, which reins in $\bar{r}$ but has no impact on $\bar{B}$. If creditors fret about European Union backing, c may decline; this will trim $\bar{B}$ without raising $\bar{r}$.

Orbits

Before we tackle dynamics, let us simplify notation. By changing the measurement units of debt, credit spreads, and time, we can set $\bar{B} = \bar{r} = 1$. If we then shift to logarithms, the interior equilibrium shifts to the origin and allocations can range over the whole space. Specifically, defining

$$\tau \equiv \frac{t}{a}, \; x(t) \equiv \log\left(\frac{d}{c} B(\tau)\right), \; y(t) \equiv \log\left(\frac{b-1}{a} r(\tau)\right), \; \text{and} \; \alpha \equiv \frac{c}{a}, \quad \text{(A5.1)}$$ meta-

morphoses into

$$x' = 1 - e^y,$$
$$y' = \alpha(e^x - 1). \quad\quad\quad\quad\quad\quad\quad\quad\quad \text{(A5.3)}$$

Cross-multiplying these two equalities shows that $\alpha(e^x x' - x') = y' - e^y y'$. Integrating both sides with respect to time,

$$\alpha(e^x - x) + e^y - y = k \quad\quad\quad\quad\quad\quad \text{(A5.4)}$$

for some constant k. Every feasible k defines a path that the (x, y) observations stay on forever. Note that $e^x - x$ is convex, with minimum value 1 at $x = 0$. It follows that—

- Every path is bounded, with minimal and maximal y at $x = 0$ and minimal and maximal x at $y = 0$.
- The minimum feasible k is $\alpha + 1$, which applies only at the origin.
- Every higher k defines a closed orbit that surrounds all paths with lower k.

From equation (A5.3), motion along any orbit is counterclockwise. This has interesting implications for debt dynamics. Suppose a debt market close to a static equilibrium is hit by an innovation in one or more of its parameters. Regardless of the innovation, the equilibrium move in credit spread will match the direction of the immediate change in debt, while the equilibrium move in debt will run counter to the immediate change in credit spread.

Orbit Shapes

Translating back into (B, r) space, the orbits must remain closed with $B = \bar{B}$ defining the extremes for r and $r = \bar{r}$ defining the extremes for B. The closer an orbit gets to the origin, the farther out it must eventually venture, with both r and B well above the static equilibrium. That explains the progressively more oblong shape of outer orbits. In the extreme phase, observers unaware of the broader regularity would likely conclude the markets were broken.

Orbits in (x, y) space look more regular. For x and y both close to the origin, equation (A5.4) can be approximated as

$$\alpha x^2 + y^2 \cong k + \alpha + 1, \tag{A5.5}$$

which defines an ellipse. Outer orbits get oblong too, but with a tilt toward negative directions rather than positive. To confirm, note that by (A5.4) the extreme values have to satisfy equations of the form $e^x - x = Z$. For high Z, one solution will be close to $-Z$ while the other will be close to $\log(Z) \ll Z$.

Figure A.5 charts an example with $\alpha = 1$. Changing α will vertically squash or dilate the orbits.

Financial Phases

In the southwest quadrant, spreads shrink while debt expands. I label it "Surge" to highlight the impact on confidence and growth. Eventually, spreads get so low as to encourage excess debt; creditors start to get anxious. I label the southeast quadrant "Overstretch." The northeast quadrant reflects a credit "Crunch"; creditors raise rates even as debt starts to recede. Eventually it leads to a "Recovery" phase with a lean debt stock and declining spreads.

From (A5.3), change is quickest when both e^x and e^y are high. Hence, the Crunch phase is the briefest. Conversely, the Surge lasts longest, as its changes will be capped by the zero-one bounds on the exponentials.

For orbits near the origin, something akin to Kepler's second law applies. That is, a line from the origin to the current position traces out roughly equal areas during equal times. Therefore, the quadrant area inside an inner orbit is a first approximation to the time spent in the phase.

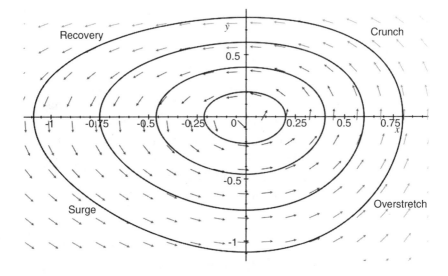

Figure A.5
Credit Orbits in (x,y) Space

However, outer orbits sweep areas far faster in Crunch than in Surge. Again, this reflects the exponential dependence in (A5.3). The practical implication is that a Crunch might spike so sharply that it seems more like an accidental breakdown than an integral financial phase. This seems consistent with the empirical evidence on booms, recessions, and crises.

Bolder Fiscal Response

The fiscal response per unit debt is modeled in (5.1) as $a - br$. To allow for incrementally bolder response as debts mount, let us modify this to $a - brB^\gamma$ for some positive γ. This changes the generic formulation (A5.3) to

$$x' = 1 - e^y \left(\frac{be^{\gamma x} - 1}{b - 1} \right),$$

$$y' = \alpha(e^x - 1). \tag{A5.6}$$

This change suffices to make the orbits spiral inward toward the equilibrium at the origin. Figure A.6 charts an orbit with $b = 1.5$, $\gamma = 0.1$, and $\alpha = 1$.

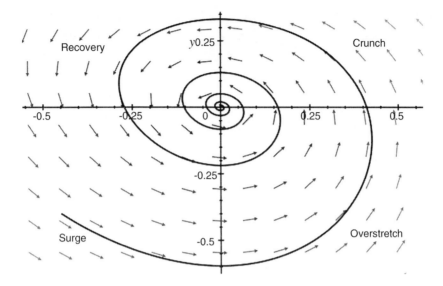

Figure A.6
A Self-Stabilizing Credit Spiral

To confirm local stability around the origin, let us apply the standard technique of checking that the eigenvalues of the associated Jacobian have negative real parts (Luenberger 1979: chap. 9). The Jacobian is the matrix J of partial derivatives evaluated at the equilibrium in question. Defining

$$\eta \equiv \frac{b\gamma}{b-1} > 0,$$

$$J = \begin{bmatrix} \dfrac{\partial x'}{\partial x} & \dfrac{\partial x'}{\partial y} \\ \dfrac{\partial y'}{\partial x} & \dfrac{\partial y'}{\partial y} \end{bmatrix}_{\substack{x=0 \\ y=0}} = \begin{bmatrix} -\eta & -1 \\ \alpha & 0 \end{bmatrix}. \qquad (A5.7)$$

The eigenvalues are the solutions to $|J - \lambda I| = 0$, for I the identity matrix, so

$$\lambda = \frac{-\eta \pm \sqrt{\eta^2 - 4\alpha}}{2}. \qquad (A5.8)$$

As these solutions will always have negative real parts, the equilibrium is indeed stable. For small γ, the square root will be imaginary, generating dampened oscillations like the one just depicted. If γ is large enough, the solutions will be real, so that paths converge to equilibrium without oscillation. Thus, a sufficiently bold fiscal response can indeed control the cycle.

Debt-Fueled Growth

As we have seen, debt can fuel growth by increasing liquidity or padding real wealth. Higher growth raises debt-servicing capacity and thereby soothes creditors. This makes y' a declining function of x', all else being equal. In that spirit let us modify (A5.3) to

$$
\begin{aligned}
x' &= 1 - e^y \\
y' &= \alpha(e^x - 1) - \delta x' = \alpha(e^x - 1) + \delta(e^y - 1)
\end{aligned}
\tag{A5.9}
$$

for some small positive constant δ. The Jacobian is $\begin{bmatrix} 0 & -1 \\ \alpha & \delta \end{bmatrix}$, so its eigenvalues

$$
\lambda = \frac{\delta \pm \sqrt{\delta^2 - 4\alpha}}{2}
\tag{A5.10}
$$

have positive real parts. All orbits spiral outward, so no equilibrium is stable.

Bolder Response and Debt-Fueled Growth

If we combine debt-fueled growth with bolder fiscal response, the Jacobian at the origin becomes $\begin{bmatrix} -\eta & -1 \\ \alpha + \eta\delta & \delta \end{bmatrix}$, with eigenvalues

$$
\lambda = \frac{\delta - \eta \pm \sqrt{(\delta - \eta)^2 - 4\alpha}}{2}.
\tag{A5.11}
$$

If $\eta > \delta$, the fiscal response will dominate everywhere and make any path converge toward the origin. A sufficiently high η or low α will rule out oscillation along the way.

If $\delta > \eta$, the origin will be locally unstable, so that inner orbits spiral out. However, the fiscal response will still dominate at very high debt levels, so that outer orbits spiral in. This generates a stable limit cycle in between. At least it does in simulations, and the model satisfies nearly all of the Kolmogorov (1936) stability criteria discussed in May (1973: chap. 4). Again, bear in mind that this limit cycle could be wide, and might appear divergent when both debt and credit spreads are running high.

Chapter 6: Safety in Numbers

Misplaced Complexity

Standard finance theory loves complexity. Here, for example, is a tidier version of Basel II's favored rule for estimating capital requirements K for sovereign, corporate, and banking exposures, given probability of default P, loss given default L, and maturity M, and where φ denotes the cumulative standard normal distribution:

$$\rho = 0.24 - 0.12\left(\frac{1 - e^{-50P}}{1 - e^{-50}}\right),$$
$$b = (0.11852 - 0.05478 \cdot \log(P))^2,$$
$$c = N\left(N^{-1}(P)\sqrt{\frac{1}{1-\rho}} + N^{-1}(0.999)\sqrt{\frac{\rho}{1-\rho}}\right), \qquad \text{(A6.1)}$$
$$K = L(c - P) \cdot \frac{1 + (M - 2.5)b}{1 - 1.5b}.$$

The original can be found in Basel Committee (2004), paragraph 272. In explaining its rationale, Basel Committee (2005) refers to Gordy (2003), Merton (1974), and Vasicek (2002). While these are sophisticated treatments, none of them tackle estimation error. In effect they average a subset of future shifts in risk while ignoring the fog that shrouds the future.

This chapter highlights the fog. Starting from the premise that all knowledge derives from observation, it treats risk estimation as a counting game. It allows two kinds of complexity only. First, it distinguishes a constant objective risk from subjective views on what that constant is. Second, it amends our counts to allow for tiny fractions. The next chapter will allow objective risk to change too.

Classic Estimation

In classic estimation, T independent observations are taken of a random variable x with true mean μ and variance σ^2. The sample mean $\bar{x} \equiv \dfrac{x_1 + \cdots + x_T}{T}$ will have mean μ and variance $\sigma^2 \big/ T$, and by the Central Limit Theorem will be approximately normally distributed for T large.

Moreover, $\bar{s}^2 \equiv \dfrac{(x_1 - \bar{x})^2 + \cdots + (x_T - \bar{x})^2}{T - 1}$ will be an unbiased estimator for σ^2.

Hence, a confidence interval stretching from $\bar{x} - m\bar{s}$ to $\bar{x} + m\bar{s}$ is often taken as a confidence interval for μ. It scales nearly inversely to the square root of T, so quadrupling the number of observations halves the confidence interval. Where the normal distribution applies, an m of 1, 2, 3, or 4 provides 68%, 95%, 99.7%, or 99.99% confidence, respectively.

In estimating default risk, x is generally taken to register 1 for default and 0 for payment. The mean μ will match the default risk. The variance will equal $\mu(1 - \mu)$, which will be close to μ when default is rare.

Bayesian Updating of Mean Beliefs

Bayesian analysis distinguishes between the true but unknown default risk Θ and the subjective convictions $p(\Theta)$. We will denote the mean belief by $E \equiv \langle \Theta \rangle$ and the variance of beliefs by $V \equiv \langle \Theta^2 \rangle - E^2$.

The text called the discrepancy between the observation and the mean belief the *news*. We will usually see it in ratio to its variance. With default risk, the ratio takes two values only:

$$\Delta J \equiv \frac{news}{\mathrm{var}(news)} = \frac{x - E}{E(1 - E)} = \begin{cases} +\dfrac{1}{E} & \text{if default,} \\ -\dfrac{1}{1 - E} & \text{if payment.} \end{cases} \tag{A6.2}$$

Applying (A1.3) with $f(1|\Theta) = \Theta = 1 - f(0|\Theta)$ and $m = 1$, the revised mean works out to $\dfrac{\langle \Theta \cdot \Theta \rangle}{\langle \Theta \rangle} = E + \dfrac{V}{E}$ after default and $\dfrac{\langle \Theta(1 - \Theta) \rangle}{\langle 1 - \Theta \rangle} = E \dfrac{V}{1 - E}$ after payment. A unified expression is

$$\Delta E = V \cdot \Delta J, \tag{A6.3}$$

which proves (6.2) and (6.3). The multiplier ΔJ explains why convictions shift more after default than servicing: default comes as more of a surprise.

Beta-Distributed Beliefs

If T observations witness D defaults, the revised mean works out to $\dfrac{\left\langle \Theta^{D+1}(1-\Theta)^{T-D} \right\rangle}{\left\langle \Theta^{D}(1-\Theta)^{T-D} \right\rangle}$. There is one kind of prior for which this is always easy to calculate. Called a beta distribution, it takes the form

$$p(\Theta | a,b) \propto \Theta^{\alpha-1}(1-\Theta)^{\beta-1} \tag{A6.4}$$

for some positive constants α and β. If we substitute D for α and $T-D$ for β, the mean and variance work out to $E = D\!\!\big/\!\!T$ and $V = \dfrac{E(1-E)}{T+1}$. Substitution into (A6.3) implies equation (6.1), where E after observation changes to either $\dfrac{D}{T+1}$ or $\dfrac{D+1}{T+1}$.

The beta distribution is the only distribution with this property. In general, no two distributions can always yield the same means after updating. If they do, their difference must have a zero mean under any beta distribution with integer parameters. Given any Θ between 0 and 1, we can concentrate the beta distribution's weight very close to it by choosing parameters $n\Theta$ and $n(1-\Theta)$ for n huge. Therefore the difference between the two distributions must effectively vanish in the neighborhood of Θ. Since this applies for every Θ, the two distributions must be substantively the same.

However, Bayesian updating does make other distributions more beta-like. For high D and $T-D$ this is intuitively clear, as the updating factors $\Theta^{D}(1-\Theta)^{T-D}$ dominate prior beliefs. More subtle arguments are needed for low D and T; we will reexamine this later.

Poisson Jumps

It is often convenient to model debt servicing as continuous, even if the payment required is zero, and to think of default as a rare event. D

becomes what is known as a Poisson process, which starts at zero and jumps by one with each default. I will modify this slightly to allow for a fractional starting point. Technically we should write $D(t)$ to denote its value at time t and write expressions like $D(t) = \lim_{\varepsilon > 0, \varepsilon \to 0} D(t - \varepsilon) + 1 \equiv D(t_-) + 1$ to denote a jump on default. However, the context will be so clear that I will continue to drop the time identifiers and describe D as jumping to $D + 1$.

Like in Chapter 4, θ will denote the instantaneous default rate. However, whereas Chapter 4 presumed the default rate was known even when it changed, Chapter 6 presumes it constant though unknown. It implies a default rate $1 - e^{-\theta}$ in one year, so to equate that to Θ we set $\theta = -\log(1 - \Theta)$. Whereas Θ can never exceed 1, θ can range from zero to infinity.

In continuous time I will reinterpret f, E, and V as $f(1|\theta) = 1 - f(0|\theta) \cong \theta dt$, $E \equiv \langle \theta \rangle$ and $V \equiv \langle \theta^2 \rangle - E^2$. The *news*–related variables I will redefine as

$$dJ = \frac{news \cdot dt}{\text{var}(news)} = \frac{dx - E dt}{E} = \begin{cases} -\dfrac{1}{E} & \text{if default,} \\ -dt & \text{if payment.} \end{cases} \tag{A6.5}$$

If default occurs in time dt, the revised mean is $\dfrac{\langle \theta dt \cdot \theta \rangle}{\langle \theta dt \rangle} = \dfrac{\langle \theta^2 \rangle}{\langle \theta \rangle}$, which jumps by $\dfrac{V}{E}$ like in the discrete case. If no default occurs, the revised mean is $\dfrac{\langle (1 - \theta dt)\theta \rangle}{\langle 1 - \theta dt \rangle} \cong \langle \theta \rangle + \langle \theta \rangle^2 dt - \langle \theta^2 \rangle dt$, so it shrinks by approximately Vdt. The unified expression is analogous to (A6.3):

$$dE = VdJ. \tag{A6.6}$$

Gamma-Distributed Beliefs

To tractably update beliefs about Poisson jumps, we need to modify the beta distribution. On the default side, θ replaces Θ. On the payment side, a nearly uninterrupted stream of servicing at rate $1 - \theta dt$ replaces $T - D$ discrete payments. In the limit, $f(\theta) \propto \theta^{D-1} (1 - \theta dt)^T \propto \theta^{D-1} e^{-\theta T}$. This is known as a gamma distribution with shape parameter D and inverse scale parameter T. It will recur so often in our analyses that I will write out its density in full:

$$f(\theta \mid D, T) = \frac{T^D}{\displaystyle\int_0^\infty y^{D-1} e^{-y} dy} \theta^{D-1} e^{-\theta T} \equiv \frac{T^D}{\Gamma(D)} \theta^{D-1} e^{-\theta T}. \qquad (A6.7)$$

The gamma function Γ always satisfies $\Gamma(D+1) = D\Gamma(D)$, except for $\Gamma(1) = 1$. When D is a positive integer, $\Gamma(D) = (D-1)!$.

The CGF $K(b)$ for a gamma distribution equals $-D \log\left(1 - \frac{b}{T}\right)$, which implies $\kappa_m = D(m-1)! T^{-m}$. In particular, $E = \frac{D}{T}$ while $V = \frac{D}{T^2}$. By (A6.6), a relevant default will boost E by $\frac{1}{T}$ in absolute terms and by $\frac{1}{D}$ in relative terms. Servicing will shrink E at rate $\frac{1}{T}$ in relative terms. We can use these relations both to calibrate the model and to test its internal consistency. If needed, a mixture of gamma distributions can provide additional degrees of freedom.

Gamma Shapes

On the range shown, the chart of beta distributions in the text describes gamma distributions as well. Figure A.7 presents another chart of gamma

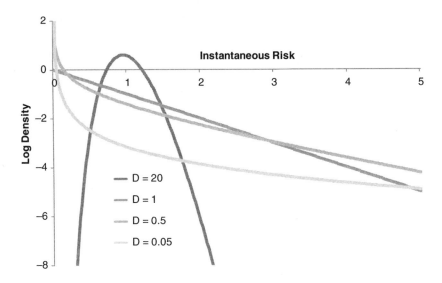

Figure A.7
Gamma Distribution Log-Densities with Unit Mean

densities, this one in logarithmic terms to highlight the tails. For simplicity, the mean is normalized to 1.

The curve for $D = 20$ looks quadratic with a mild positive skew; it approximates a normal density, which would be completely quadratic. $D = 1$ indicates exponential decay, where s-tail risk drops by 63% whenever s rises by 1. $D = 0.5$ gives the density of a Gaussian variable squared (chi-squared with one degree of freedom), implying that its 15-tail is fatter than a Gaussian 4-tail. The chart for $D = 0.05$ resembles, though does not equal, the distribution of a Gaussian variable to the fourth power.

Evidence for Low T and Fractional D

The better identified a risk is, the less a new observation should sway us. Gamma-distributed beliefs can accommodate that by setting T high. Standard finance theory implicitly assumes that whenever it treats a particular credit rating as correct. However, it generally ignores a corollary, namely that credit spreads based on high T shouldn't change much after default.

Practice clearly refutes high T for most sovereign and corporate debt. The text suggests a jump of at least 300 basis points (bps), implying a T of a few dozen years or less. For very short-term debt, a jump of 1,000 bps seems more likely, suggesting a T in single digits.

Since investment-grade credits are usually considered to have less than 1% default risk per year, their implied D must be much less than 1. Indeed, if this were not true, an outright default would not be the gross stain on investment-grade character that markets take it to be.

Another indication of fractional D is spread compression after default. For very short-term risks, spreads should be proportional to D/T before default and to $\dfrac{D+1}{T+\varepsilon}$ after. If we estimate the dispersion of relative spreads by the variance of their logarithms, the relative compression from default is approximately $\mathrm{var}(\log(D)) - \mathrm{var}(\log(D+1))$. That tends to be much higher for $D \ll 1$ than for $D \gg 1$.

For example, for a D that ranges from 4 to 40, the compression cannot exceed $\log\!\left(40/4\right) - \log\!\left(41/5\right) \cong 0.2$. In contrast, for a D that ranges from 0.04 to 0.4, the difference at extremes is $\log\!\left(0.4/0.04\right) - \log\!\left(1.4/1.04\right) \cong 2.0$. The high relative compression in spreads observed after default implies that the D is low.

Alternative Formulations

Viewing evidence of fractional default as fractional evidence of default makes it slightly easier to grasp. The next chapter will offer a more appealing interpretation in terms of mixtures of beliefs, where D is fixed and T varies. For a crude approximation, imagine that the market believes default risk is either $\dfrac{D+1}{T+1}$ or zero, with mean $D\!\!\!/_T$. The next observation will shift the consensus in the same way a beta distribution would. Granted, we'll be set up wrong for the next round, unless we posit regime switches that move the risk where we want it. But continual updating of beta distributions using equation (6.1) isn't viable either; otherwise D will ratchet up without bound.

In other words, to some extent the market acts as if it knows only two default risk classes. "Perfectly safe" is the base case and where everyone wants to be. But there's some decay to "high," with a value that changes gradually over time. Anyone identified as high risk through default immediately tries to shift back. Intermediate credit spreads basically reflect the difficulty of distinguishing "never will default" from "hasn't yet defaulted."

Portfolio Default Risks with Gamma Beliefs

If Poisson default risks at rate θ are watched for unit time, the number of defaults will follow what is known as a Poisson distribution, with a probability $\dfrac{\theta^k}{k!}e^{-\theta}$ of k defaults. If θ is sampled from a gamma distribution with parameters D and T, the number of defaults will follow a "gamma-Poisson" distribution. The CGF works out to $-D\log(1-(e^b-1)T^{-1})$, as the notes to Chapter 8 will confirm.

For comparison, a binomial distribution with D tries and probability $1\!\!\!/_T$ of default on each try would have a CGF of $D\log(1+(e^b-1)T^{-1})$. If T and D had negative signs this would match the CGF for the gamma-Poisson. For this reason the gamma-Poisson is also known as the negative binomial distribution and often is interpreted to describe as the number of successes until D failures occur. However, this makes no physical sense when D is not an integer, so such cases have garnered yet another name, a Pólya distribution.

Now imagine a portfolio of n i.i.d. credits, or more precisely n credits that we treat as such. The most efficient way to estimate their default risk is to pool the observations and use the joint D and T for each. That is, each credit is presumed to have the same Poisson default risk θ drawn from a gamma distribution with parameters D and T. The total number of defaults on all n credits will then be gamma-Poisson with parameters nD and T.

Underestimation of Tail Risks

Standard risk estimation for n i.i.d. credits assumes a binomial distribution with default probability E. The CGF is $n\log(1 + (e^b - 1)E)$. The CGF for the more appropriate gamma-Poisson distribution can be rewritten as $-nD\log(1 - (e^b - 1)D^{-1}E)$. This replicates a binomial when $D = -1$, although we have seen that a small positive D is more appropriate.

To see what difference this makes to tail risks, note that a binomial CGF is finite for all b, whereas the gamma-Poisson CGF gets unbounded as soon as b exceeds $\log(1 + DE^{-1})$. The smaller D is, provided it stays positive, the more convex the CGF gets and the more fat-tailed the distribution.

For a more algebraic demonstration, take a Taylor series expansion of the logarithm with $\beta \equiv (e^b - 1)E$ to see that

$$-nD\log\left(1 - \frac{\beta}{D}\right) = n\left(1 + \frac{\beta^2}{2D} + \frac{\beta^3}{3D^2} + \cdots\right). \tag{A6.8}$$

The coefficients of β are negative if and only if D is negative and its power is odd. Since all derivatives of β with respect to b are positive, switching the sign of a negative D must boost all the cumulants. Trimming a positive D will also boost the cumulants, since each coefficient divides by a positive power of D. The relative difference must rise with the order of the cumulant.

Hence, the appropriate portfolio distribution is much fatter-tailed than the standard binomial distribution. Granted, a higher n will make both distributions more normal. However, what most normalizes them is nD, and D will likely be much less than 1. For sufficiently high-grade portfolios, even $n = 1000$ might leave nD less than 1. In short, a gamma-Poisson distribution for an investment-grade portfolio will have unusually fat tails and grow normal abnormally slowly.

If D were fixed across assets, tail risks would basically depend on the distance in standard deviations from the mean, which in turn is roughly proportional to $\sqrt{nE}$. However, since D tends to be much tinier for high grades than low ones, the appropriate gradient is much flatter and potentially can flip for extreme risks.

Chapter 7: When God Changes Dice

Differential Terminology

The notes to the previous chapter muddied the distinction between discrete risk Θ and continuous-time risk θ by using f, E, and V to refer to either. The text muddies things more by using θ in either sense. For clarity the notes to this chapter will restore the Θ-versus-θ distinction and preserve the Δ-versus-d distinction. The Δ denotes change over discrete time, whereas d denotes a differential change or Poisson jump.

Bayesian Updating of Higher Moments

Any moment $\langle \Theta^m \rangle$ of default risk must by (A1.3) shift to $\dfrac{\langle \Theta^m \rangle}{\langle \Theta \rangle} = \dfrac{\langle \Theta^m \rangle}{E}$

after default and $\dfrac{\langle \Theta^m \rangle - \langle \Theta^{m+1} \rangle}{1 - E}$ after servicing. It follows that

$$\Delta \langle \Theta^m \rangle = \left(\langle \Theta^{m+1} \rangle - \langle \Theta^m \rangle E \right) \cdot \Delta J, \tag{A7.1}$$

where ΔJ is the *news*-to-variance ratio defined in (A6.2). The continuous time variant substitutes θ for Θ and dJ from equation (A6.5) for ΔJ.

Bayesian Updating of Variance

The definition $V = \langle \Theta^2 \rangle - E^2$ and equation (A7.1) imply that

$$\begin{aligned} \Delta V &= \Delta \langle \Theta^2 \rangle - 2E\Delta E - (\Delta E)^2 \\ &= \left(\langle \Theta^3 \rangle - E \langle \Theta^2 \rangle - 2EV \right) \cdot \Delta J - (\Delta E)^2 . \end{aligned} \tag{A7.2}$$

The multiplier on ΔJ works out to $\kappa_3 \equiv \langle(\Theta - E)^3\rangle$, which proves (7.1).

The expected change in the variance is $-\langle(\Delta E)^2\rangle = -\dfrac{V^2}{\text{var}(news)}$. The expected gain in precision (inverse variance) is $\Delta\langle\frac{1}{V}\rangle \cong -\dfrac{\langle\Delta V\rangle}{V^2} = \dfrac{1}{\text{var}(news)}$, which proves (7.2).

Bayesian Updating of Convictions

From (A1.2), a conviction p_i on regime i, with current risk Θ_i, must shift to

$p_i \dfrac{\Theta_i}{E}$ after default and $p_i \dfrac{1 - \Theta_i}{1 - E_i}$ after servicing. A unified expression is

$$\Delta p_i = p_i(\Theta - E) \cdot \Delta J. \qquad (A7.3)$$

This expresses the change in conviction as a product of three terms: the current level, a measure $\Theta_i - E$ of idiosyncrasy, and the surprise value of new evidence.

In fact, (A7.3) applies for any belief distribution; it implies the updating equation (A7.1) for all the moments of belief. I have ignored it until now because it's usually not tractable to calculate over a continuum. Only the beta distribution and its continuous-time gamma counterpart preserve their functional forms under Bayesian updating of default risk. In those cases, mean and variance updating (or their D and T rule equivalents) will suffice for identification. However, with a discrete number of regimes it can be easier to work with beliefs directly than with their moments or cumulants.

Modular Updating

The text emphasizes the convenience of breaking a complicated distribution of beliefs into modular parts. Let's see how this works. Suppose regime i with mean E_i places subjective probability $v_i(\Theta)$ on default risk Θ, while the aggregate estimator with mean E places subjective probability $w(i)$ on regime i. Let $p_i(\Theta) \equiv w(i)v_i(\Theta)$ denote the aggregate probability weight on

Θ stemming from regime i. "Modular updating" means that if we update v_i assuming it's the only regime, and update w assuming all the weight is concentrated at the means, the product gives the same result as updating p_i directly.

To verify this, let's treat the default and servicing cases separately. With default, $v_i + \Delta v_i = v_i^\Theta / E_i$ and $w + \Delta w = w^{Ei}/E$, so their product $wv_i^\Theta/E = p_i^\Theta/E$

gives the correct value for $p_i + \Delta p_i$. With servicing, $v_i + \Delta v_i = v_i \dfrac{1-\Theta}{1-E_i}$ and $w + \Delta w = w\dfrac{1-E_i}{1-E}$, so their product $p_i \dfrac{1-\Theta}{1-E}$ again gives the correct value

for $p_i + \Delta p_i$.

The total weight p on Θ can include contributions from many different regimes. There we aggregate through summation since

$$\Delta p = p(\Theta - E)\Delta J = \sum_i p_i(\Theta - E)\Delta J = \sum_i \Delta p_i .$$

Regime Switching

Imagine that a risk currently in regime i randomly switches to regime j at rate λ_{ij}. "Markov" switching means that the λ values are independent of any previous history. For simplicity let us also assume independence over time. Figure A.8 presents a simple flowchart for a two-regime case. I have portrayed each regime as a cloud to emphasize that knowing a regime ($w = 1$) need not pinpoint the actual risk ($q = 1$). Indeed, different clouds might cover exactly the same feasible range, as different beta distributions do. With overlap, a risk can change regimes without changing its current value.

We can imagine switches occurring at the edge of every trading interval—say at the stroke of midnight if dt is approximated by a day. Given a conviction p_1 on regime 1 before switching, "outflow" depletes it by roughly $p_1\lambda_{12}dt$ while "inflow" swells it by roughly $p_2\lambda_{21}dt$. For multiple regimes, the flows imply

$$dp_i = \sum_{j \neq i} p_j \lambda_{ji} dt - p_i \sum_{j \neq i} \lambda_{ij} dt . \tag{A7.4}$$

Equation (A7.3) looks backward while (A7.4) looks forward These updates should be performed sequentially. However, in the continuous-time limit, we can join them side by side as

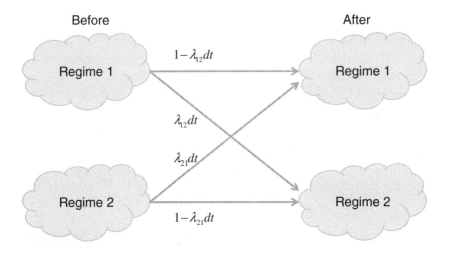

Figure A.8
Markov Switching with Two Regimes

$$dp_i = p_i(\theta_i - E)dJ + \sum_j p_j \lambda_{ji} dt, \qquad (A7.5)$$

where $\lambda_{ii} \equiv -\sum_{j \neq i} \lambda_{ij}$ denotes the total (negative) proportionate outflow rate.

More general forms allow for a continuum of states and for diffusions across them. Diffusions scale with the square root of time so they cannot be analyzed using (A7.5) alone. The notes to Chapter 8 will make additional adjustments.

Regime Switching Equilibria

For a risk that has just entered regime i, let us calculate its average sojourn time or "life" L_i before switching. With probability of roughly $|\lambda_{ii}| dt$ it will switch within the first instant dt, for expected life $\frac{1}{2}dt$. Otherwise, due to the Markov property it is as if the regime restarts at time dt, with an expected future life of L_i. Hence $L_i \cong |\lambda_{ii}| dt(\frac{1}{2}dt) + (1 - |\lambda_{ii}| dt)(L_i + dt)$, which in the limit implies $L_i = |\lambda_{ii}|^{-1}$.

The long-term equilibrium probability distribution over regimes must match aggregate outflows to aggregate inflows in (A7.4). This can be rewritten in matrix form as $(p_1 \cdots p_n) \begin{pmatrix} \lambda_{11} & \cdots & \lambda_{1n} \\ \vdots & \ddots & \vdots \\ \lambda_{n1} & \cdots & \lambda_{nn} \end{pmatrix} = 0$. For two regimes $p_1 \lambda_{12} = (1 - p_1)\lambda_{21}$, so $p_1 = \dfrac{\lambda_{21}}{\lambda_{12} + \lambda_{21}}$.

EMAs as Regime Switching Filters

Equation (A7.5) is strange in that it presumes knowledge of the various switching parameters λ while acknowledging ignorance of θ. To fix this, let's expand the notion of regimes. Let's define them not just over feasible default risks but also over the kinds of switching they entail. To make this tractable, the net flows should preserve the functional form of the beliefs. The simplest specification is a smoothly fading memory over a beta or gamma distribution, leading to the exponential moving average (EMA) updating rule (7.4).

In effect, this implies a beta or gamma distribution with fixed $T = \frac{1}{\lambda}$ and shifting D. Unfortunately I have not found a microlevel specification of regime switching that generates such a form. I can justify the reduced form only as an approximation.

Mixtures of EMA filters are even more useful approximations. Suppose we want to estimate risk as a weighted average "memory" of past observations. Since the past fades gradually in relevance, the most plausible weightings should decay smoothly over time. It turns out that all such weighting schemes can be expressed as mixtures of EMA filters.

By smooth decay, I mean that all derivatives decline toward zero with time elapsed. On reflection this amounts to making all odd-order derivatives negative and all even-order derivatives positive. Such functions are known as completely monotone. Bernstein (1928) and Steutel (1969) prove that any completely monotone density on the nonnegative real numbers can be expressed as a mixture of exponential densities. The EMA filter, as we have seen, is an exponential density over past information, so mixtures can capture any smoothly fading memory.

Since gamma distributions with $D < 1$ are completely monotone, they too can be expressed as mixtures of exponential densities with $D = 1$. Gleser

(1989) provides an explicit functional form, in which the means of the exponentials range from 0 to $\frac{1}{T}$ and higher means get higher weights. This is another way to make sense of fractional D, namely that exactly one default was recorded over a relevant time period of at least T and possibly much longer.

EMAs and Simple Moving Averages

The closest analogue to an EMA is a simple moving average (SMA) of the same duration. An SMA based on the last T observations has an average lag of $\frac{1}{2}(T+1)$, so we need to set $T = \frac{2}{\lambda} - 1$. The continuous-time analogue drops the -1.

For i.i.d. observations, the variance of the SMA estimator will be

$\sum_{t=1}^{T}\left(\frac{1}{T}\right)^2 = \frac{1}{T} = \frac{\lambda}{2-\lambda}$. This matches the variance $\sum_{t=1}^{\infty}\left(\lambda(1-\lambda)^{t-1}\right)^2$ for the

EMA. The variances for continuous time also match. Hence EMAs and SMAs of equal duration will be about equally noisy. The main differences in behavior come from the quicker short-term response of the EMA (about twice the immediate SMA response), which also implies noisier updating.

Most people find SMAs easier to understand than EMAs, and sometimes they are easier to work with analytically. Conceptually, however, they're schizoid. Each of them presumes that the regime changed the day before the window starts (otherwise, we should tap prior observations for higher precision) and definitely never changed again (otherwise the weights shouldn't be equal). Yet the next day we rewrite history and roll the one-and-only-one regime shift a day forward.

Effective Decay Rates

Comparison of equations (6.2) and (7.4) shows that the decay rate λ of an EMA equals $\frac{V}{E}$, the variance of beliefs divided by the variance of news. For a gamma distribution of beliefs, $T = \frac{E}{V}$. For a mixture of EMAs, we infer the effective λ and T from market responses.

The variance of a multiregime mixture equals the mean of the regimes' variances plus the variance of the regimes' means. Hence the effective decay rate seems higher and the effective observation time lower than the average for individual EMAs. Given $E = D/T$, a lower effective T in turn squeezes the effective D.

Bayesian Updating of Generating Functions

From equation (A7.1), every update of a moment of a distribution depends on the next-higher moment. A more compact description, along the lines of (A1.4), uses the moment-generating function to roll these separate updates together:

$$d\langle e^{b\theta} \rangle = (\langle \theta e^{b\theta} \rangle - \langle e^{b\theta} \rangle E)dJ. \tag{A7.6}$$

During any continuous stretch of servicing, $dJ = -dt$, which makes $d\langle e^{b\theta} \rangle$ infinitesimal as well. In that case the CGF will be updated as

$$d\kappa = \frac{d\langle e^{b\theta} \rangle}{\langle e^{b\theta} \rangle} = \left(\frac{\langle \theta e^{b\theta} \rangle}{\langle e^{b\theta} \rangle} - E \right)(-dt) = (E - \kappa')dt \cdot \tag{A7.7}$$

All the E in the last term does is constrain the intercept in the Taylor series expansion of K to zero. Hence we can rewrite the above more neatly as

$$d\kappa_m = -\kappa_{m+1}dt \tag{A7.8}$$

for any positive integer m. Provided debt is being serviced, each cumulant changes in direct proportion to the cumulant one order higher. The relations $dE = -Vdt$ and $dV = -\kappa_3 dt$ are just special cases.

On default, $\langle e^{b\theta} \rangle$ jumps to $\dfrac{\langle \theta e^{b\theta} \rangle}{E}$, so that the CGF gets updated as

$$dK = \log(K'/E). \tag{A7.9}$$

Again, E enters only to make the intercept κ_0 vanish. Otherwise $d\kappa_m$ will depend on all cumulants of order $m + 1$ and lower.

Limited Predictability

Recall that there is no maximum order to nonzero cumulants, unless beliefs are strictly normal. The restriction to nonnegative θ rules out normality. Hence the updating of cumulants is an endless ladder, with each higher order marking another rung.

The updating ladder becomes redundant if every cumulant is automatically the time derivative of the cumulant just below. For a gamma distribution with CGF $-D \log\left(1 - \frac{b}{T}\right)$, it is readily checked that $\kappa_{m+1} = Dm!\, T^{-m-1} = -\dfrac{\partial \kappa_m}{\partial T}$. At first glance, any CGF that depends on b and T only through the ratio $\frac{b}{T}$ should have this property. On closer examination, it's also crucial for cumulants to be linear in D, so that (A7.9) can treat default like the addition of an i.i.d. random variable. Moreover, no default risk can be negative. A gamma distribution appears to be the only distribution that fits these requirements.

For any other distribution, even the smallest discrepancy in a higher cumulant will percolate down to the mean via (A7.8), as long as debt is being serviced. From (A7.9), each default acts like a volcanic eruption that spews discrepancies to all higher-order cumulants. Toss in some random noise and it's a recipe for turbulence.

Turbulence doesn't prevent all predictability. Over short periods, markets should respond similarly to similar events. Over long periods, broader regularities should kick in, similar to the limit cycles observed in our models of aggregate debt and credit cycles. In simulations, beliefs show a strong tendency to revert to gamma distributions, with D and T that can shrink as well as grow. Chapter 8 will explore this further.

A Log-Odds Perspective

To see intuitively where the turbulence comes from, let us consider Bayesian updates on two possible risks Θ_1 and Θ_2, with probabilities p and $1 - p$ respectively. Applying (A1.2) to each probability and taking the logarithm of the ratio, we obtain

$$\Delta \ln\left(\frac{p}{1-p}\right) = \log\left(\frac{f(x \mid \Theta_1)}{f(x \mid \Theta_2)}\right). \tag{A7.10}$$

Good (1950, 1979) credited Turing with this formulation and termed the right-hand side the "weight of evidence." It is the logarithm of the so-called Bayes' factor. The left-hand side is known as the log odds ratio.

For default risk the weight of evidence takes two values: $\log\left(\frac{\Theta_1}{\Theta_2}\right)$ with default and $\log\left(\frac{1-\Theta_1}{1-\Theta_2}\right) \cong \Theta_2 - \Theta_1$ with servicing. Here their specific values aren't as important as their independence from p. It makes the log odds a random walk. The random walk will drift at constant expected rate toward whichever regime applies.

Denoting the log odds as q, we can rewrite the probability as $p = \frac{1}{1+e^{-q}}$. This is known as a logistic or sigmoid function and yields the S-curve shape in Figure A.9. Its slope as a function of p is $p(1-p)$, which is the driving factor in equation (7.3). The same evidence makes much more impact when observers are highly uncertain (p near ½) than when they are nearly certain (p near 0 or 1).

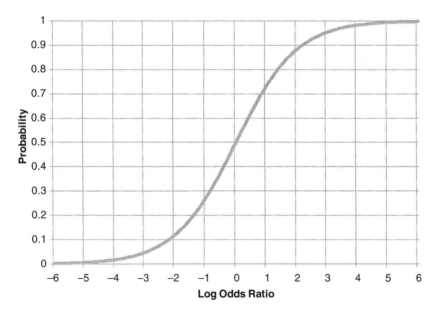

Figure A.9
Probability Versus the Log Odds Ratio

This transformation can make disagreements ebb and flow even when people track the same new information. Suppose, for example, that I am originally very pessimistic about state 1, which we agree is worth twice as much as state 2. I ascribe odds of 10,000 to one against its occurrence. You are even more pessimistic, ascribing odds of a million to one. That is a huge difference in log-odds. Nevertheless it will be hard to distinguish our views empirically. The fair values we assign will differ by less than 0.01%.

However, if the state is truly 1, our log odds will drift high enough to make our differences salient. Given a constant log odds gap of log(100) and sufficiently fine-grained evidence, there is bound to come a day when I am more than 99% convinced that state 1 applies while you are less than 1% convinced. There is a difference we can trade on! Moreover, while in this particular trade you will look the fool, I will someday look the fool if the state flips back.

In reality, neither you nor I will be exactly sure of the initial odds. Each of us will have a spectrum of beliefs. These spectra make for multiple tiny differences, so that our disagreements ebb and flow in varied ways.

Chapter 8: Credit-ability

Corporate Bond Default Rates

The chart in the text of U.S. corporate bond default rates is inspired by figure 1 in Giesecke et al. (2010). Since they do not list the default rates, I reconstructed data from several sources. For 1900–1943, tables A-2 and A-17 in Hickman (1953) summarize debt outstanding and new defaults by year. Table 21 in Atkinson (1967) extends the series through 1965. For 1966–1980, exhibit 26 in Emery et al. (2009) provides Moody's data. For 1981–2008, I averaged Moody's data with S&P data from table 6 in Vazza, Aurora, and Kraemer (2010). (Their correlation was 0.96). The estimate for 2009 comes from S&P alone.

For 1866–1899, I returned to Giesecke et al. Their tables 1 through 3 provide over 30 summary statistics for 1866–1899, including the first four moments, major quantiles, serial correlation, and means and maxima over shorter intervals. I used Excel Solver to find 34-point data sets with nearly identical statistics. While there is some wiggle room, all top candidates generate very similar charts.

The very high default rates in the late nineteenth-century United States reflect weak corporate governance. Corrupt managers routed bond proceeds to suppliers they controlled and let the mother company go bankrupt. Credit rating agencies arose in part to monitor this kind of fraud.

Factor Analysis of Default Risks

The simplest way to analyze default risks is to form an ordinary linear regression. The variable to be explained is the binary service-or-default observation. The explanatory variables are the various factors. The prediction becomes a point estimate for default risk.

This doesn't work very well. All the default risks have to lie between 0 and 1. The estimates don't and likely won't. Moreover, the highly nonnormal distribution of errors (our binary *news* variables) undermines standard confidence intervals.

The most favored alternative is logistic regression. It presumes that a linear combination of factors predicts the log odds $\log\left(\dfrac{\theta}{1-\theta}\right)$ rather than θ directly. Given the small risks we're dealing with, that's basically the same as $\log(\theta)$. This dovetails with the logarithmic scaling of credit ratings.

Whether formal or intuitive, logistic factor analysis makes credit ratings more reliable by boosting the effective number T of relevant independent observations. For household servicing of mortgages or credit cards absent economic crisis or natural disasters, the effective T and D seem high enough to justify standard Gaussian approximations. Corporate credit analysis requires more caution because of the smaller number of observations. Sovereign analysis is dicier still.

Unreliability at Extremes

In any statistical analysis, performance near the center of the distribution is easier to predict than performance of outliers. Errors in functional form or measurement mount when projected to extremes. Precision fades.

For a simple demonstration, suppose we're testing a single binary factor for influence on the log odds. Suppose we have D_0 defaults out of T_0 observations when the factor is inactive and D_1 defaults out of T_1 observations when the factor is active. Our point estimate of the difference in log odds turns out to have a variance of roughly $\dfrac{1}{D_1} + \dfrac{1}{T - D_1} + \dfrac{1}{D_0} + \dfrac{1}{T - D_0}$, which usually will be close to $\dfrac{1}{\min(D_0, D_1)}$. After discounting observations that aren't relevant, the minimum can morph into our familiar fractional D. Even at $\min(D_0, D_1) = 2$ a high confidence interval can span several alphanumeric notches.

Impact on Lending

While regulators generally discount credit ratings for uncertainty, they do not adjust nearly enough for differential uncertainty. This accentuates the problems noted in Chapter 6. It steers banks away from their natural comparative advantage in lending to households, small businesses, and other risky but high-margin activities.

When banks do engage in such lending, ratings arbitrage discourages from keeping the riskier tranches. They off-load them to the secondary market and worry less about monitoring performance. This tempts borrowers to deceive about their means and tempts lenders to bet wholly on appreciation of market collateral. These factors were huge contributors to the mortgage debacle.

Financial regulators are now risking an even worse debacle. The ratings game encourages banks to focus on the residual A-rated credits. These credits are disproportionately sovereigns with very high debts that are not yet in crisis. When crisis erupts and the sovereigns are downgraded, assets get marked down and capital requirements soar. The PIIGS downgrades would have immediately precipitated a banking crisis in Europe had not regulators bent the rules.

In defense of leniency, higher authorities have repeatedly shown their willingness to bail out subordinate authorities in return for greater centralization. However, these bailouts are highly uncertain. In fact, budgetary or constitutional constraints often forbid the higher authorities from promising bailouts. The uncertainty range proposed earlier for credit grades would help ratings agencies acknowledge this.

Pricing Longer-Dated Credit Risk

Suppose lenders have to discount a risky debt payment at future time t. To keep this simple, let us suppose that default risk is constant over time and independent of aggregate wealth. If the true default risk is known, the probability of payment is $(1-\Theta)^t$ in discrete time and $e^{-\theta t}$ in continuous time. If payment after default is zero and the risk-free rate is r, the present value for the continuous case will be $\langle e^{-rt}\, e^{-\theta t}\rangle$.

To convert that into standard investment terms, let us define a fair (logarithmic) credit spread $c(t)$ by whatever equates $e^{-(r+c)t}$ to $\langle e^{-rt}\, e^{-\theta t}\rangle$. The solution is

$$c(t)=-\frac{\log\langle e^{-\theta t}\rangle}{t}=-\frac{\kappa(-t)}{t}=E\cdot\frac{\log(1+t/T)}{t/T}. \qquad (A8.1)$$

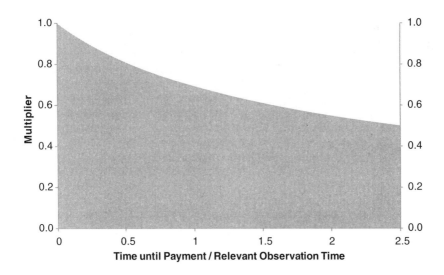

Figure A.10
Multiplier on Mean Default Risk

If there were no uncertainty, or equivalently if T were infinite, c would equal E, as it does for $t = 0$. Otherwise the credit spread must shrink for longer duration. The effect can be substantial, as Figure A.10 indicates. At $t = T$, the spread will be nearly a third less than at $t = 0$. That is the equivalent of half a credit grade on the Moody's scale.

Why does the multiplier drop below one? Mathematically, it stems from the convexity of $e^{-\theta t}$ in θ, which makes the mean discount factor exceed the discount factor of the mean. Raising t increases the convexity and thereby enhances the effect. It is analogous to the impact of higher interest rate volatility, which raises the expected price of a bond all else being equal.

For a more intuitive explanation, bear in mind that risk is presumed stable even though we don't know what is. If default is likely in the last year, it is likely in every prior year, trimming the opportunity cost of default in the last year. Conversely, if default is unlikely in one year, it is unlikely all the way through, making the credit more likely to pass through unscathed.

Caveats on Ratings Migrations

Ratings migration statistics are fuzzy around the edges. Companies pay for credit ratings and can ask that they be withdrawn. Presumably they are more likely to do so if they don't like their rating or fear a downgrade. Roughly 5% of investment-grade ratings and 10% of subinvestment-grade ratings are withdrawn each year. In a thoughtful review, Moody's analysts Hamilton and Cantor (2006) conclude that the overall bias from withdrawals is modest. However, they could not easily address the possibility that withdrawals anticipate the ratings agencies' first warnings of problems.

Another possibility is that credit downgrades shortly before default make the forecast record look better than it should. Since default is infrequent, even a few rush downgrades can significantly burnish the track record. Bear in mind, however, that the historical data reported in the main text associate default with the rating at the start of the year. That should mitigate problems.

Equilibria of Diffusions

Regimes shifts across discrete states are too coarse to describe diffusions. Diffusions are characterized by their instantaneous drift κ_1 and volatility

$\sqrt{\kappa_2}$, which may vary with position θ and time t. Here we will consider only cases where κ_1 and κ_2 depend on θ alone. We can write that as $d\theta = \kappa_1(\theta)dt + \sqrt{\kappa_2(\theta)}dz$, where dz denotes standard Brownian motion.

Often we're less interested in the motion of a single θ than the changes in the probability density $f(\theta, t)$. The Fokker-Planck equation describes the evolution:

$$\frac{\partial f}{\partial t} = -\frac{\partial(\kappa_1 f)}{\partial \theta} + \frac{1}{2}\frac{\partial^2(\kappa_2 f)}{\partial \theta^2}. \tag{A8.2}$$

We can derive this by equating $f(\theta, t)$ to the total migration to θ from the density at time $t - dt$, taking the limits and simplifying. Although straightforward, it is too messy to pursue here. See Risken (1996: chaps. 2 and 3) for detailed discussion.

Usually we can find a distribution g that satisfies (A8.2) without changing over time. It is called the stationary distribution. It tends to accord with the long-term average or asymptotic limit.

Setting the right-hand side of (A8.2) to zero for $f = g$, we can integrate it with respect to θ to see that $\dfrac{d(\kappa_2 g)}{d\theta} = 2\kappa_1 g +$ constant. Usually the extremes of the feasible range are quiet enough that the constant vanishes.

Rearranging terms, $\dfrac{d(\kappa_2 g)}{(\kappa_2 g)d\theta} = \dfrac{2\kappa_1}{\kappa_2}$. A second integration yields $\log(\kappa_2 g)$ on the left-hand side, with solution

$$g(\theta) = \frac{C}{\kappa_2(\theta)}\exp\left(\int_0^\theta \frac{2\kappa_1(\tau)}{\kappa_2(\tau)}d\tau\right). \tag{A8.3}$$

The constant C makes the density integrate to one.

Gamma Distributions as Long-Term Equilibria

For the model equation (A8.1), $\kappa_1(\theta) = a\theta^{2m-1}(1 - b\theta)$ and $\kappa_2(\theta) = c^2\theta^{2m}$. Substituting into (A8.3) and carrying out the integration

$$g(\theta) = \frac{C}{c^2}\theta^{\alpha - 2m}e^{-\alpha b\theta}, \quad \text{where } \alpha \equiv \frac{2a}{c^2}. \tag{A8.4}$$

Comparing with (A6.7), this is a gamma distribution with shape parameter $\alpha - 2m + 1$ and inverse scale parameter αb. More precisely, it is a gamma distribution provided α exceeds $2m - 1$. Otherwise all risk vanishes in the long run.

Parameter Fitting

To fit parameters using credit ratings, let us first transform equation (8.1) into a diffusion in logarithmic risk. Taking a second-order Taylor's approximation and simplifying, or just applying Itō's rule ,

$$d\log(\theta) = a\theta^{2m-2}\left(1 - \frac{1}{\alpha} - b\theta\right)dt + c\theta^{m-1}dz. \qquad (A8.5)$$

Most short-term changes in risk should come from the noisy dz term, which has intensity $\sigma\theta^{m-1}$. If $m = \frac{1}{2}$, as the popular Cox-Ingersoll-Ross (1985) model suggests, migration should be over four times more frequent among single/double/triple-A grades than among the corresponding single/double/triple-B grades. Instead, migration is marginally faster in lower grades.

The best fit for volatility requires $m > 1$. At first glance, it shouldn't be much greater than 1. However, since estimation error adds the most noise in the highest credit ratings, m needs an extra boost to compensate. In that case, lower credit ratings should on average improve (i.e., high θ drift down) significantly faster than high credits deteriorate. That doesn't seem to be the case. High credit ratings seem too sticky to reconcile (A8.5) with estimation error.

On balance, the least implausible model sets $m = 1$. To generate 25% annual migration across alphanumeric grades roughly 0.5 log units apart, c needs to be on the order of 0.5. Other back-of-the-envelope calculations suggest a on the order of 0.15 and b on the order of 0.02.

EMAs with Drift

We can easily incorporate long-term reversion into our dynamic EMA models. Here's a specification inspired by the previous discussion:

$$dE = \lambda(dx - Edt) + aE(1 - bE)dt. \qquad (A8.6)$$

To remind, dx equals 0 with servicing and 1 with default. If $a = 0$, this collapses to equation (7.4).

For $a > \lambda$, the E in (A8.6) will be bounded strictly away from zero. Nevertheless, the dynamic mixture can squeeze the aggregate E much lower by shifting its weight to higher-λ EMAs. This illustrates an important point. Making individual filters more stable and focused on the long term needn't make the aggregate estimate more stable. If the long-term estimates are sufficiently out of sync with short-term realities, a rational observer may rely even more on short-term forecasts than she would otherwise.

It is doubtful we need to consider many (a,b) pairs, since drift has a small influence relative to the volatility implicit in λ. The approximation $a = 0$ is likely adequate for most circumstances, taking us back to the simpler EMA filters of equation (7.4). Sometimes even a single gamma distribution of beliefs will do.

Ising-Type Models

Ising-type models explain phase transitions as cascades of local interactions among neighbors. The specific properties vary a lot with local geometry. For example, it's nearly impossible to induce a phase transition on a one-dimensional line, where each atom has only two neighbors. Calculations with more complex geometries can be fiendishly difficult. See Baxter (2007) for an overview of what master modelers have wrought.

The most tractable Ising-type model of phase transition imagines that each atom neighbors every other. First developed by Bragg and Williams (1934), it is known as the mean field model because the aggregate interactions with neighbors can be summarized as a single interaction with the mean. In material science it is hard to justify except as an extreme limit. In economics a mean field approach is more plausible, since we can imagine every belief interacting with every other belief via the market.

Our model treats an ordinal risk ranking between two issuers as a spin pointing up or down. In the standard Ising fashion, the product of spins records agreement or disagreement, and there's a small preference for agreement. The believer compares $\omega S + \dfrac{\varepsilon}{n} \sum_{j=1}^{n} S_j S$ for $S = \pm 1$ and reports whichever is bigger. In thermodynamics the choice would be probabilistic, though skewed toward the better values. Formulation (8.2) allows for human optimization, subject to processing constraints that limit reporting to ±1 instead of something more refined.

Distributions of Differences

How do we calculate the density of the difference $\omega = \theta_1 - \theta_2$ between two independent beliefs? The easiest way starts with the separate CGFs $K_1(b)$ and $K_2(b)$ for the two beliefs separately. (We're now back to viewing b as a variable rather than a parameter. I apologize for the potential confusion.). Since the CGF for $-\theta_2$ is $K_2(-b)$, the CGF for ω is the sum $K_1(b) + K_2(-b)$.

When the two sets of beliefs are identically gamma distributed with shape parameter D and inverse scale T, we calculate

$$K_\omega(b) = -D\log\left(1 - \frac{b}{T}\right) - D\log\left(1 + \frac{b}{T}\right) = -D\log\left(1 - \frac{b^2}{T^2}\right). \quad (A8.7)$$

The simplest case sets $D = 1$. Each belief has an exponential distribution, and their difference has a Laplace distribution. Figure A.11 charts the density.

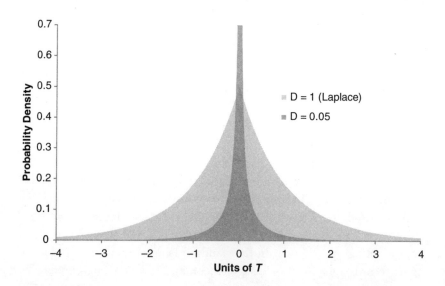

Figure A.11
Bessel Distributions for Differences of i.i.d. Gamma-Distributed Beliefs

A Laplace distribution is a double-sided exponential distribution. Compared to the Gaussian bell shape, it is much more concentrated at the center and has much fatter tails. As Broadbent and Kendall (1953) first noted (in a study of worm larvae!), it can be viewed as driftless Brownian motion stopped after an exponentially distributed time.

For general D, the CGF of (A8.7) corresponds to a Bessel distribution. Its density at x is proportional to $|x|^{D-\frac{1}{2}} K_{D-\frac{1}{2}}(T^{-1}|x|)$, where K denotes a modified Bessel function of the second kind (Kotz, Kozubowski, and Podgórski 2001). For $D \ll 1$ a Bessel distribution resembles a double-sided gamma distribution with shape parameter $2D$. Most of the probability mass will be concentrated near the origin, with unbounded density at the origin itself. However, it is extremely fat-tailed.

These properties are ideal for generating sticky rankings. Most believers will find both risks so tiny that they bend easily to the consensus. While those who disagree tend to disagree intensely, they are an isolated minority absent a default-triggered convulsion.

Chapter 9: Insecuritization

Exchangeable Default Risks

Let $P(n,k)$ denote the probability that exactly k out of n credit assets default. There are $\binom{n}{k} \equiv \dfrac{n!}{k!(n-k)!}$ distinct orderings that will generate this. If the assets are exchangeable, each of these orderings—say that the first k assets default, or the last k—will have the same probability $p(n,k)$, so

$$P(n,k) = \binom{n}{k} p(n,k).$$

There are two kinds of addition relations associated with these credits (or any exchangeable binary assets). The first involves the number of combination and adds down:

$$\binom{n}{k} + \binom{n}{k+1} = \frac{n!}{k!(n-k-1)!} \cdot \left(\frac{1}{n-k} + \frac{1}{k+1} \right)$$

$$= \frac{n!(n+1)}{k!(n-k-1)!(n-k)(k+1)} = \binom{n+1}{k+1}. \tag{A9.1}$$

This is the essence of Pascal's triangle.

The other addition relation involves the probabilities of particular orderings and adds up:

$$p(n, k) = p(n + 1, k) + p(n + 1, k + 1). \tag{A9.2}$$

This is the essence of an Osband (default risk) triangle. It simply says that if k out of k exchangeable assets default and another exchangeable asset is sampled, either k or $k + 1$ assets must default out of the $n + 1$ total. Each row is associated with an aggregate probability distribution, constructed by multiplying the entries on that row by the corresponding row of Pascal's triangle.

Binomial Triangles

If credits are independent with discrete default risk Θ, the probability $p(n,k)$ of k defaults followed by $n - k$ payments will be $\Theta^k(1 - \Theta)^{n-k}$. The adding-up condition (A9.2) is readily verified. Each row of the Osband triangle will scale geometrically at rate $\dfrac{\Theta}{1 - \Theta}$, so typically it will decline steeply. The aggregate probability distribution, known as binomial, will peak near $n\Theta$. The binomial looks like a discrete version of Gaussian except that it scrunches up near the edges. A better approximation for small risks is Poisson.

Variety of Osband Triangles

Write down any $n + 1$ nonnegative numbers. Build a pyramid up by addition and divide by the number at the top. To show that these candidate $p(n,k)$ values form a feasible Osband triangle, we simply need to verify that the corresponding $P(n,k)$ sum to 1 for every n.

Defining $\dbinom{n}{-1} \equiv \dbinom{n}{n+1} \equiv 0$, and applying (A9.1) and (A9.2),

$$\sum_{k=0}^{n} P(n,k) = \sum_{k=0}^{n} \binom{n}{k} [p(n+1,k) + p(n+1,k+1)]$$

$$= \sum_{k=0}^{n+1} \left[\binom{n}{k} + \binom{n}{k-1} \right] p(n+1,k) \tag{A9.3}$$

$$= \sum_{k=0}^{n+1} \binom{n+1}{k} p(n+1,k) = \sum_{k=0}^{n+1} P(n+1,k)$$

for every n. Since the first row sums to 1 by construction, all rows do.

We don't have to start at the bottom. We can start at either edge—the left edge of no default or the right edge of complete default—and extend down through subtraction. But then we have to check whether any $p(n,k)$ is negative. If so, we have to stop at the row above.

Portfolio Moments

For x_i the outcome for credit i, the mth moment $\left\langle \left(\sum_{i=0}^{n} x_i \right)^m \right\rangle$ of the portfolio is the expected sum of components that involve m or fewer different assets. All components can be calculated directly from the entries $p(1,1), \ldots, p(m,m)$ along the right edge. They require no information from rows further down.

Specifying the first m moments or their equivalents completely defines the risk pyramid down through the $m+1^{th}$ row. In particular, given mean $E \equiv p(1,1)$ and correlation ρ, the third row must set

$$p(2,0) = (1-E)(1-E+\rho E),$$
$$p(2,1) = (1-E)E(1-E), \tag{A9.4}$$
$$p(2,2) = E(E+\rho(1-E)).$$

Intuitively, it is as if default and payment are contagious. If the first credit defaults, a fraction ρ of previously safe credits shifts to risky. If the first credit pays, a fraction ρ of previously safe credits shift to safe. However, (A9.4) tells us nothing about the impact on probabilities if two or more credits default, apart from what's embedded in the adding-up condition. Osband (2002: chaps. 3 and 4) shows that a given mean and correlation can generate a wide range of tail risks.

Infinite Exchangeability

A subset of Osband triangles can be extended infinitely far. This corresponds to sampling from an infinite pool of exchangeable default risks. How can we confirm infinite exchangeability?

Clearly, binomial distributions are infinitely exchangeable. So are probabilistic mixtures (weighted averages) of binomial distributions. Denoting the mixing distribution by G, we can calculate

$$p(n,k) \equiv \left\langle \Theta^k (1 - \Theta)^{n-k} \right\rangle_G. \qquad (A9.5)$$

De Finetti's Theorem says that all infinitely exchangeable distributions for portfolios of binary assets must take this form.

Since $p(n,n) = \langle \Theta^n \rangle_G$, the right edge of the Osband triangle gives all the moments of G. We can use these to form the moment-generating function $\left\langle e^{b\Theta} \right\rangle_G = \sum_{m=0}^{\infty} \frac{p(m,m)}{m!} b^m$, which, given the restriction of Θ to the unit interval $[0, 1]$, uniquely defines G. In other words, we can read G from the right edge and use that to form a binomial mixture matching the target distribution. That is the intuition behind de Finetti's Theorem.

For a related question, suppose we are given the target moments and asked whether a probability distribution on the unit interval can generate them. According to the Hausdorff (1921) moment theorem, the answer is yes if and only if the moment sequence is "completely monotone." Complete monotonicity amounts to the nonnegativity of the various $p(n,k)$. Hence an Osband triangle embeds at least two important theorems about random variables.

Correlation as Ratio of Variances

The correlation ρ between two exchangeable default risks equals their covariance divided by their variance $E(1 - E)$. The covariance is the sum of two components. The first component is their mean conditional covariance, which is zero because the risks are conditionally independent. The second component is the covariance of their conditional means, which equals the variance since the two means match. Hence

$$\rho = \frac{\text{var}_G(\theta)}{\text{var}(x_i)} = \frac{p(2,2) - E^2}{E - E^2}, \tag{A9.6}$$

which confirms equation (9.1).

The mean and correlation tell us the first two moments of the mixing distribution and nothing more. That leaves a lot of room for tail risks in large portfolios to vary, though less than with strictly finite exchangeability. See Osband (2002: chaps 5 and 6) for more discussion.

Binomial Expansion Technique (BET)

The preceding result says to model a positive correlation with a nontrivial mixture of binomials. BET tries to circumvent this by regrouping the n correlated assets into M independent assets with the same default risk E. For every dollar bet on the correlated assets, $L = n/M$ times as much money must be bet on the independent assets to keep the portfolio means the same. To match the portfolio variance, $L^2 M$ must equal $n + n(n-1)\rho$. Hence $M = \dfrac{n}{1 - \rho + n\rho}$, which approaches $1/\rho$ as n gets large. This is the diversity score.

While misleading about the tails, diversity scores provide a handy way to think about the central impact of correlation. The calculations are readily extended to cover diverse asset sizes, default risks, and correlations that vary across asset classes. See Yoshizawa (2003) or Kiff (2005) for elaboration.

The biggest problem in implementing BET is that the step size for defaults is $1/M$, which always exceeds ρ. This forces ad hoc judgments on how best to interpolate safety thresholds. The simplest interpolation spreads the probability mass uniformly over the interval L and allows huge jumps across intervals. For more refinement, I interpolated a continuous piecewise linear density with nodes at the midpoint of jumps, and then rounded back to whole numbers of defaults.

Gaussian Approximation

Gaussian approximations sever most connections with binary risk to focus on means and variances. By the Central Limit Theorem, large portfolios of independent assets approach Gaussian in the center, and the fit gradually extends out to the tails. From (A1.1), the mth cumulant decays with $n^{1-m/2}$, so convergence is quickest with symmetric distributions and narrow tails. The risk distributions we deal with tend to be the opposite.

To avoid slurring good work by others, let me emphasize that my critique does not apply to mixed Gaussian distributions. Mixed Gaussian extends mixed binomial to model a continuum of outcomes. It is inherently flexible enough to approximate nearly any distribution. It also provides a tractable way to analyze complex regime switches (Osband 2002).

Correlated Binomial (CorBin)

CorBin assumes that the conditional correlation given an unbroken string of defaults is always ρ. To formulate this neatly, let $s_n \equiv \dfrac{p(n+1, n+1)}{p(n,n)}$ denote the conditional probability that the $n+1^{th}$ asset defaults given that n out of n other assets default. From (A9.4), $s_1 = E$ while $s_2 = s_1 + \rho(1 - s_1)$; indeed, we could define ρ as the value that makes the second equation hold. The distinctive CorBin assumption amounts to saying that $s_{n+1} = s_n + \rho(1 - s_n)$ for all positive integers n.

Hence every s_n and $p(n,n)$ element after the first can be calculated from the elements before. Since $1 - s_{n+1} = (1 - \rho)(1 - s_n) = (1 - \rho)^n(1 - s_1)$, we can also obtain a direct expansion:

$$p(n,n) = \prod_{j=1}^{n-1} s_j = \prod_{j=1}^{n-1} \left(1 - (1 - \rho)^{j-1}(1 - E)\right). \tag{A9.7}$$

This specifies the whole right edge $\{p(n,n)\}$ of an Osband triangle. All other entries are determined from these by successive subtraction. However, rounding errors tend to overwhelm standard spreadsheets after a few dozen rows. I used a program developed by Witt (2004) to handle the high-precision calculations needed.

Nonconvergence to Zero

I once wrongly presumed (Osband 2009, appendix) that (A9.7) must converge to zero as n approaches infinity. In fact, it never does, unless E or ρ

is zero. Let $p_{all} \equiv \lim_{m \to \infty} p(n,n)$ denote the probability that every credit defaults. Applying the Taylor series expansion $\log(1-z) = -\sum_{k=1}^{\infty} k^{-1} z^k$ and the geometric series summation (A2.4),

$$
\begin{aligned}
\log(p_{all}) &= -\sum_{j=0}^{\infty}\sum_{k=1}^{\infty} k^{-1}(1-E)^k (1-\rho)^{jk} \\
&= -\sum_{k=1}^{\infty} \frac{(1-E)^k}{k\left(1-(1-\rho)^k\right)} \\
&= -\frac{1-E}{\rho} \cdot \sum_{k=1}^{\infty} \frac{(1-E)^{k-1}}{k\left(1+(1-\rho)+\cdots+(1-\rho)^{k-1}\right)}.
\end{aligned}
\tag{A9.8}
$$

This clearly converges to a finite number since the last series sum is much less than $1/E$. For small E and ρ the series sum will be close to

$$
\sum_{j=1}^{\infty} \frac{1}{j^2} = \frac{\pi^2}{6} \cong 1.645.
$$

Are CorBin Random Variables Infinitely Exchangeable?

I have never found Witt's program to generate a negative value in an Osband triangle, except where data storage limitations rounds a miniscule entry above it to zero. Witt (2010a) provides plausible arguments for suspecting that there aren't any. However, they fall short of proof, as he acknowledges.

If CorBin represents a valid distribution for any number of variables, by de Finetti's Theorem it can be expressed as a binomial mixture, with (A9.7) specifying the moments of the mixing distribution. As the moment-generating function does not appear to have a simple reduced form, I have tried to identify the mixing distribution directly.

The atom at $\theta = 1$ provides one positively-weighted support for the mixing distribution. Since $p(n+1,n) = (1-s_n)p(n,n) \to (1-\rho)^{n-1}(1-E)p_{all}$, the next highest support point must be $1-\rho$, with weight $\dfrac{(1-E)p_{all}}{(1-\rho)\rho}$. These findings, coupled with direct inspection of (A9.7), suggest that the mixing distribution for CorBin is supported only at integer powers of $1-\rho$.

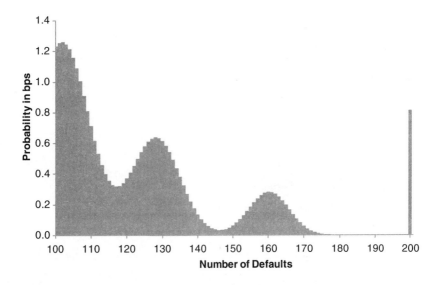

Figure A.12
CorBin Tail Risks with $n = 200$, $E = 2\%$, and $\rho = 20\%$

I have not managed to prove this conjecture. Nevertheless, the chart in Figure A.12 of extreme CorBin tail risks suggests it has merit. It assumes $n = 200$, $E = 2\%$, and $\rho = 20\%$. The undulation of a discretely separated binomial mixture is clearly evident. The local peaks come at 200, 160, 128, and 102, suggesting support at 1, 0.8, 0.8^2, and 0.8^3 (multiplied by 200 to generate the mode).

Beta-Binomial Distribution

Let us turn now to a mixing distribution that is far easier to work with and still very flexible. It is the beta distribution. We already encountered it as a natural way to model beliefs about default risk. It has two parameters, typically called α and β, though Chapter 6 associated them with D and $T - D$, for D the number of defaults and T the effective number of observations. For continuity I will maintain the terminology here, although the context and interpretation are different.

To remind, the beta distribution has mean $E = D/T$ and variance $\dfrac{E(1 - E)}{T + 1}$. If we use it as a mixing distribution for binomial distributions,

the induced correlation from (A9.6) will equal $\dfrac{1}{T+1}$. Hence the beta parameters can be estimated as $T = \frac{1}{\rho} - 1$ and $D = ET$.

The resulting mixture is called a beta-binomial distribution. It can be viewed as a sampling game with extra replacement. Imagine an urn with T balls, of which exactly D are red. For every ball picked from the urn, two balls of the same color are returned. If this is repeated n times, the beta-binomial distribution describes the probability of observing k red balls. The extra replacement represents a kind of contagion, in which both servicing and default tend to spread.

The beta-binomial probability of a given permutation has a daunting formula:

$$p(n,k) = \frac{\Gamma(D+k)\Gamma(T+n-D-k)\Gamma(T)}{\Gamma(T+n)\Gamma(D)\Gamma(T-D)}, \tag{A9.9}$$

where Γ is the factorial-related function we saw in (A6.7). Fortunately, most of this is a normalization factor independent of k. Starting from $p(n,0) = \dfrac{\Gamma(T+n-D)\Gamma(T)}{\Gamma(T+n)\Gamma(T-D)}$, the row can be filled in recursively as $p(n,k+1) = \dfrac{D+k}{T+n-D-k-1} \cdot p(n,k)$. Unlike a standard binomial, this will shrink at a decreasing rate and then start to rise, reflecting the dispersion of outcomes associated with variance/correlation/contagion.

Negative Binomial Distribution (NegBin)

The notes to Chapter 6 showed that when defaults are rare, discrete servicing can be approximated by a Poisson jump process. For a neat conversion, take the limit of the binomial CGF $n\log(1 + \Theta(e^b - 1))$ as Θ gets small to obtain the Poisson CGF $n\Theta(e^b - 1)$. Alternatively, approximate $(1 - \Theta)^{n-k}$ by $e^{-n\Theta}$ and $\dfrac{n!}{(n-k)!}$ by n^k. This converts the binomial probability $\binom{n}{k}\Theta^k(1 - \Theta)^{n-k}$ to the Poisson probability $\dfrac{(n\Theta)^k}{k!}e^{-n\Theta}$.

However, this isn't quite what we want. We need to convert the Θ defined on a unit interval to a $\theta \cong -\log(1 - \Theta)$ that can take any nonnegative value. Next we convert the beta distribution in D and $T - D$ to a gamma distribution in D and T, as explained in Chapter 6. The combination transforms the beta-binomial mixture into a gamma-Poisson mixture.

The moment-generating function for a mixture is the mixture of the conditional moment-generating functions: in this case, $\langle \exp(n\theta(e^b - 1)) \rangle_{gamma}$. The logarithm is just the standard gamma CGF with $n(e^b - 1)$ replacing b. We can write it as $-D\log\left(1 - \dfrac{e^b - 1}{T/n}\right)$. As noted earlier, that's just a binomial moment-generating function with the signs of D and T flipped, and hence is known as negative binomial or NegBin.

The probability of k defaults can be calculated directly through integration or inferred from the CGF. It is proportional to $\Gamma(D + k)\left(\dfrac{n}{n + T}\right)^k$. It can be interpreted as the probability of waiting $k + D$ periods for D failures, given odds of n to T on success.

Comparisons of Mixed Binomial Tail Risks

From the previous discussion, it should be clear that CorBin and NegBin have very different structures. There is no analogy in NegBin to the undulations in the tail and the strictly positive probability of universal default. However, with modest E and ρ and confidence thresholds of less than 99.99 percent, the estimated risk limits are close. CorBin tail risk decays slightly faster in the 99 to 99.99-percentile confidence range.

NegBin tends to exaggerate the likelihood of extreme outliers. The Poisson approximation it uses allows the same credit to default more than once in a given interval. When fit to the same mean and variance as NegBin, we would expect tail risks to decay slightly faster for beta-binomial than NegBin. Tests confirm that.

For completeness, Figure A.13 shows a full chart of log probability for NegBin, CorBin, and beta-binomial for the benchmark used in the text.

The CorBin risk tail generally falls between the beta-binomial and correlated NegBin tail. That's clearly the case in Figure A.13. If we raise the correlation to 20%, the undulation of the CorBin probability becomes so pronounced that it alternately breaks through one bound and the other.

Nevertheless, the correspondence is quite close in the ranges of most interest in finance. And where the curves diverge, the differences are usually so tiny in absolute terms that it's hard to tell which curve fits a given

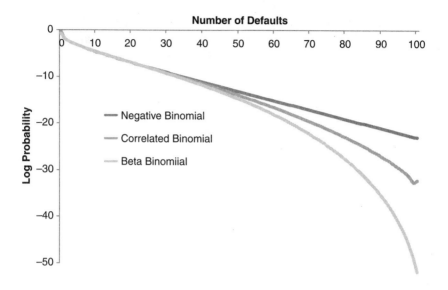

Figure A.13
Mixed Binomial Risks for $n = 100$, $E = 2\%$, and $\rho = 5\%$

data set best. As noted, a beta-binomial is more plausible than NegBin but less tractable. A correlated binomial is harder to work with than either but easier to summarize intuitively.

Any of these alternatives generate much fatter tails than Gaussian or BET. Tail risk for NegBin and its relatives is nearly log-linear where it matters. This is known as exponential decay. In contrast, Gaussian tail risk is log-quadratic, and BET tail risk is nearly so.

Copulas

Debt is never completely binary, as salvage after default varies. With multiple outcomes, no simple geometry can describe the potential intricacies of dependence. However, infinitely exchangeable random variables can always be characterized by mixing distributions over conditionally independent outcomes, as Hewitt and Savage (1955) have shown.

I like conditional independence because it is both intuitive and tractable. Many sophisticated portfolio risk analysts use copulas instead. In a sense, copulas sacrifice insight to improve fit. I explain briefly here.

Let H denote the cumulative probability distribution for a set of random variables $x_1, \ldots, x_n$ and let $F_i(x_i) \equiv H(\infty, \ldots, \infty, x_i, \infty, \ldots, \infty)$ denote the cumulative marginal probability distribution for each variable taken separately. According to a theorem proposed by Sklar (1959), there exists a multivariate function C such that

$$H(x_1, \ldots, x_n) = C(F_1(x_1), \ldots, F_n(x_n)). \qquad \text{(A9.10)}$$

This function is called a copula. It indicates the multivariate distribution when all variables are measured by percentile ranks.

When the defining functions are smooth enough, we can take multiple partial derivatives to establish that

$$h(x_1, \ldots, x_n) \equiv \frac{\partial^n H}{\partial x_1 \cdots \partial x_n} = \frac{\partial^n C}{\partial x_1 \cdots \partial x_n} \cdot \frac{dF_1}{dx_1} \cdot \ldots \cdot \frac{dF_n}{dx_n} \qquad \text{(A9.11)}$$
$$= c\big(F_1(x_1), \ldots, F_n(x_n)\big) \cdot f_1(x_1) \cdots f_n(x_n).$$

Hence the copula density is just the joint density divided by the density if the variables were independent. This is a neat way to divide dependence from the distribution of variables on their own. If we assume exchangeability, all the F_i or f_i will be identical and C or c will be invariant with respect to order. Hence, every symmetric copula must correspond to a mixing distribution over conditionally independent variables, even if we don't know which.

Copulas can be defined implicitly (as in the case of a normal distribution) or explicitly. Given the vast degrees of freedom and the infrequency of default, we never know which copula form is right. However, we may be able to exclude some forms as wrong or select from a constrained list. See Nelsen (2006) for an authoritative introduction.

The main shortcoming of copulas is that they obscure causality. For a simple example, consider two assets, each composed of a common market factor and an independent, asset-specific "idiosyncratic" factor. If the market calms down, the correlation will drop because the common factor becomes less volatile. If the market panics the correlation will surge. While we can measure the changes in correlation regardless, ignoring common factors makes it a lot harder to understand what's truly going on and can lead us to understate future risk.

Copulas measure all dependence, not just correlation. In particular they can identify extreme tail risk, which correlation cannot. However, like correlations, copulas aren't common drivers. They are simply measures of common drivers and their relation to other factors. To use copulas best, remember what not to use them for.

Chapter 10: Risks in Value-at-Risk

Tail Risks

Tail risks refer to the chances of outliers. To control for differences in scaling and baseline, outliers from different distributions are best compared in standardized terms. That is, for any outcome x (for simplicity I drop the prefix Δ), subtract the mean μ and divide by the standard deviation σ.

This chapter focuses on daily returns of major equity portfolio indices. Typically, μ will equal a presumed risk-free rate plus an unstable trend. Apart from high inflation or peak booms and busts, the daily μ will rarely exceed a few percent of the daily σ. As it doesn't affect any of the qualitative results in this chapter, I ignore it. Filtering out an unstable mean is in fact quite complex; I don't want the extra detail to cloud the intuition.

Mathematically, tail risks reflect the influence of higher standardized cumulants. Odd-numbered cumulants like skewness control the slant of risk, with negative values inflating loss tails at the expense of gain tails. In yet another simplification, this chapter assumes symmetric distributions, for which all odd-numbered cumulants are zero.

That makes tail risks a function of the even-numbered higher cumulants. Each higher order adds information about risk further out in the tails. However, each higher cumulant gets progressively more difficult to estimate reliably. That's because small percentage distortions get magnified when raised to higher powers.

Standard Relative Error

The bias of an estimator is the mean expected deviation from true value. The mean squared error (MSE) equals the variance of the estimator plus the bias squared. The root mean squared error $\sqrt{MSE}$ equals the standard deviation plus a nonlinear adjustment for bias. Because capital buffers typically set proportional to risk estimates adjusted for scale, I divide $\sqrt{MSE}$ by the estimator mean. That generates the root mean squared percentage error. The closest I have seen to an official name is "coefficient of variation for the root mean squared error." I rename it the standard relative error, or SRE for simplicity.

Kurtosis

For tail risks of a few standard deviations, most of the relevant information is embodied in the standardized κ_4, known as the kurtosis. Formally,

$$\text{kurtosis} \equiv \frac{\kappa_4}{\sigma^4} = \left\langle \left(\frac{x - \mu}{\sigma}\right)^4 \right\rangle - 3. \tag{A10.1}$$

For default risk with probability θ, the kurtosis is $\dfrac{1}{\theta(1 - \theta)} - 6$. Its minimum value is −2 at $\theta = \frac{1}{2}$, which is the least kurtosis possible for any distribution. For a Gaussian distribution it is zero, like every other higher cumulant. There is no maximum. Some continuous distributions with well-defined variance have infinite kurtosis.

From (A1.1), the kurtosis of a sum of independent variables shrinks linearly with the number of variables. Hence, if market returns were independent across time, kurtosis would shrink linearly with the holding period. While real market returns are not independent, they are sufficiently autonomous that kurtosis usually shrinks significantly with holding period.

Ordinary Standard Deviation Estimator

Suppose we're estimating the variance of financial returns as $V \equiv \dfrac{1}{T} \sum_{i=1}^{T} x_i^2$ and the mean is zero. The variance of V is $T^{-1}\langle(x^2 - \sigma^2)^2\rangle = T^{-1}(\langle x^4 \rangle - \sigma^4) = T^{-1}\sigma^4(2 + \text{kurtosis})$. Hence the percentage standard deviation of V is $\varepsilon \equiv \sqrt{\dfrac{2 + \text{kurtosis}}{T}}$. The percentage standard deviation of $\hat{\sigma} \equiv \sqrt{V}$ is approximately half of that, on the grounds that $\sqrt{\sigma^2(1 \pm \varepsilon)} \cong \sigma(1 \pm \frac{1}{2}\varepsilon)$. That explains equation (10.1).

However, $\hat{\sigma}$ is a biased estimator of σ, since a second-order Taylor series expansion shows that $\left\langle \sqrt{\sigma^2(1 \pm \varepsilon)} \right\rangle \cong \sigma(1 - \frac{1}{8}\varepsilon^2)$. The percentage bias is roughly $\dfrac{2 + \text{kurtosis}}{8T}$, so kurtosis needs to be less than half of T to keep this modest. In saying that 20 observations should generally be adequate for equation (10.1) to apply, I implicitly presume a kurtosis of less than 10.

Average Kurtosis

Does the kurtosis of daily portfolio returns really average less than 10? Not for a portfolio of illiquid credits sharing a common default risk. Many would argue that it's inappropriate for equity market portfolios as well.

Indeed, applying a standard kurtosis estimator to S&P 500 index (SPX) returns since 1950 yields a value of 29. The very data set I chose seems to refute me. However, I believe 29 grossly overstates the true kurtosis, for the following reasons:

- The standard kurtosis estimator—basically, (A10.1) adjusted for sampling error—assumes the volatility is constant. Clearly it isn't. If we apply the standard kurtosis estimator to a fixed window and roll the window forward every day, the average SPX kurtosis shrinks to 5.7 for a two-year window, 3.3 for a one-year window, and 2.0 for a six-month window. However, random Monte Carlo simulations suggest that this method can understate the true kurtosis by half on shorter samples of fat tails.
- Alternatively, we can start by standardizing each daily return using a rolling standard deviation. We then calculate kurtosis for the whole series. Using that approach, the kurtosis is 8.1 for a three-month standard deviation and 5.4 for a one-month standard deviation. Monte Carlo simulations suggest that these are likely overstated because of extra noise from standardization.
- The 20% loss on October 19, 1987 ("Black Monday") was over twice as big as any other. Perhaps we should exclude it as, so to speak, a one-time temporary invader from another financial planet. If so, the kurtosis for the whole series drops to

under 10 for the nominal returns and to under 5 for the standardized returns. However, high-kurtosis series are prone to jumps that seem out of character but in fact reveal key features.

Allowing for regime changes in means and variances generally trims the estimates of higher cumulants. So beware of kurtosis estimates based on constant variance. However, there is nothing sacrosanct about single-digit kurtosis. It's just an empirical observation on many large, liquid, equity-dominated portfolios.

Student's t-Distribution

If we draw T independent samples from a normal distribution, the sample mean $\bar{x}$ will be normally distributed with mean μ and variance σ^2/T. In other words, $z \equiv \dfrac{\bar{x} - \mu}{\sqrt{\sigma^2 / T}}$ will be a standardized normal variable. If we proxy an unknown σ^2 with the unbiased sample variance $\bar{V} \equiv \dfrac{1}{T-1} \sum_{i=1}^{T} (x_i - \bar{x})^2$, z ceases to be either normal or standardized. It has instead a distribution known as Student's t, named after the pseudonym used by Gosset (Student 1908) when he introduced it. (The brewery he worked for didn't want employees giving away trade secrets.).

The wobble in the denominator gives a t-distribution a larger standard deviation and fatter tails than a standard normal distribution. How much depends on $t \equiv T - 1$, known as the degrees of freedom. As t gets large, the t-distribution approaches standard normal; this follows from the convergence of $\bar{V}$ to σ^2. As t gets small, the tails get so fat that the cumulants are infinite for order t or higher. Where odd-numbered cumulants exist, symmetry sets them to zero.

A t-distribution can be viewed as a Gaussian mixture, where the means are identical but the variances differ. The inverses of the variances are gamma distributed with shape parameter $t/2$. In effect a t-distribution embeds fluctuations in volatility, and these make head and tails bulge relative to normal.

For $t > 2$, the variance is $\dfrac{t}{t-2}$. For $t > 4$, the kurtosis is $\dfrac{6}{t-4}$, in which case $t = 4 + \dfrac{6}{\text{kurtosis}}$. That is the transformation used in the text to express kurtosis *t*-distributions in terms of kurtosis. For example, a kurtosis of 0.5 to 12 confines the degrees of freedom to between 4.5 and 16.

Standardization of Student's t

The other transformation used was standardization. For example, the 5-percentile is 2.015 for a *t*-distribution with a kurtosis of 6 ($t = 5$). However, it represents only 1.561 standard deviations, which is less than the 1.645 for a normal distribution. In standard deviation terms, higher kurtosis elongates both the head and the tails at the expense of the shoulders in between. See Figure A.14.

In general, a *t*-distribution based on a standardized normal variable has variance $\dfrac{t}{t-2}$. We can scale a *t*-distribution to have mean μ and variance σ^2, in which case the density is

$$f(x) \equiv \frac{\Gamma(\frac{1}{2}t + \frac{1}{2})}{\sigma\sqrt{\pi(t-2)}\Gamma(\frac{1}{2}t)}\left(1 + \frac{(x-\mu)^2}{(t-2)\sigma^2}\right)^{-\frac{1}{2}(t+1)}. \qquad (A10.2)$$

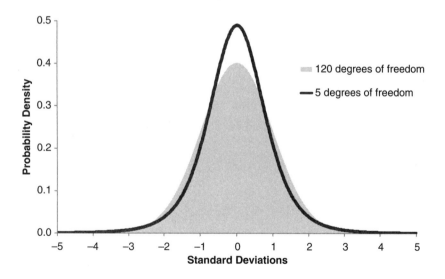

Figure A.14
Two Standardized *t*-Distributions

I will spare the reader the CGF, which is no simpler and depends on a modified Bessel function. Let me caution that (A10.2) is not the "non-central t-distribution" sometimes seen in the literature. Rather, it is the density we obtain when fitting a t-distribution to data of given mean and variance.

Kurtosis Estimation

If we know the mean and variance, the mean squared error of the best unbiased kurtosis estimator converges to $\dfrac{\langle z^8 \rangle - \langle z^4 \rangle^2}{T}$, for z standardized. For a t-distribution with less than eight degrees of freedom, that's not even finite. By using estimated means and variances, the standard kurtosis estimator keeps extremes in check. Still, its precision drops rapidly as kurtosis rises above 1 (t falls below 10). It also induces some biases that get more visible as kurtosis grows.

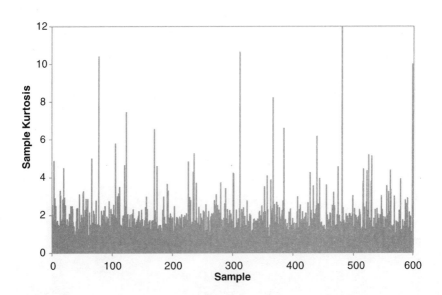

Figure A.15
Sample Kurtosis for $t=7$ with 600 Ten-Year Simulations

Imagine that we've successfully standardized index returns for 60 years and are sure that they're t-distributed with some fixed but unknown t. For a sample kurtosis of 2, our baseline estimate is $t = 7$. Still, we can't be 95% confident that $t = 6$ or $t = 8$ didn't generate it, corresponding to an actual kurtosis of 3 or 1.5. That is, a true kurtosis of 3[1.5] would with 5% probability generate a sample kurtosis as low[high] as 2 over 15,000 independent observations.

If we have only ten years of relevant data, we can't rule out $t = 5$ or $t = 9$ with 95% confidence. Figure A.15 depicts the sample kurtosis for 600 different simulations; the highest observation of 47 is clipped. In contrast, ten years of relevant data would shave the SRE for the ordinary standard deviation to around 2.5%.

If a t-distribution kurtosis is low we can identify it more easily. Suppose that with ten years of ideal data the sample kurtosis is 0.2, for a baseline estimate of $t = 34$. With 95% confidence we can rule out t below 16 or above 160, which narrows the range for true kurtosis to between 0.04 and 0.5.

Still, the estimator is much noisier than we would like. In practice, we're likely to infer a particular t-distribution proxy from observations on a broader asset class. Alternatively we can search for robust estimators that worry less about being right than about not being far wrong.

Robust Estimators

A Scottish Gentleman has been defined as someone who knows how to play bagpipes but doesn't. In similar spirit, statistical refinement sometimes amounts to knowing the best unbiased estimator and avoiding it. Robust estimators aim to provide respectable results even when the distributional form is misspecified and the data are dirty. Maronna, Martin, and Yohai (2006) provide a good overview.

The easiest case to analyze theoretically is the mean absolute deviation, which for daily portfolio returns is usually very close to the mean absolute value. This should scale linearly with σ, and for t-distributions the scaling factor is readily calculated through integration as

$$\alpha \equiv \frac{\pi^{1/2}(\tfrac{1}{2}t - \tfrac{1}{2})\Gamma(\tfrac{1}{2}t)}{(t-2)^{1/2}\Gamma(\tfrac{1}{2}t + \tfrac{1}{2})}. \tag{A10.3}$$

This grows from $\sqrt{\pi/2} \cong 1.25$ for a normal distribution to 1.29 for $t = 10$, 1.36 for $t = 5$, and 1.41 for $t = 4$. If we use 1.3 as a crude multiplier, the estimator has a lower SRE than the ordinary standard deviation for a kurtosis of 1 or higher ($t \leq 10$) and effective observation windows of two years or less.

We can make an absolute value estimator more robust and efficient in several ways. We can mix it with some of the ordinary standard deviation. We can posit different scaling factors, form a mixture, and dynamically adjust the relative weights using the updating equation (10.3).

Percentile Estimators

What is the probability density $g(x)$ that out of T i.i.d. observations, exactly $T - k$ observations exceed x and at least one observation equals x? The answer can be written as a product $f(x)T \cdot \binom{T-1}{k-1}(F(x))^{k-1}(1 - F(x))^{T-k}$, with the following interpretation:

- The density at the threshold is $f(x)$ and there are T candidates for the threshold, so the total density contribution is $f(x)T$. (Given continuous distributions the probability of two observations exactly at the threshold is an infinitesimal squared, so we needn't worry about overlap.)
- The probability that $k - 1$ observations don't exceed x and $T - k$ do is analogous to exchangeable default risk, with $F(x)$ as the risk per asset. The contribution is $(F(x))^{k-1}(1-F(x))^{T-k}$ for each of the $\binom{T-1}{k-1}$ distinct orderings.

Next let's grow T while keeping k close to $q\%$ of T. The density will cluster near its maximum at $y \equiv F^{-1}(q\%)$. In that neighborhood, $\dfrac{g}{Tf(y)}$ will be close to a binomial density with mean $q\%$ and variance $(T-1)q\%(1-q\%)$. Hence the q-percentile will have variance

$$\frac{(T-1)q\%(1-q\%)}{T^2(f(y))^2} \cong \frac{q\%(1-q\%)}{T(f(y))^2}, \tag{A10.4}$$

which confirms equation (10.2). Brown and Wolfe (1983) caution that this tends to understate the variance in small and medium-sized samples.

Relative SREs of Percentile Estimators

Given T, the SRE scales roughly with $\dfrac{\sqrt{q\%}}{f(y)y}$. For a normal distribution, the SRE peaks at the 5.8-percentile. The peak moves inward gradually as t-distribution tails get fatter, to 7.8% at $t = 10$ and 10.6% at $t = 4$.

The peak is more plateau than spike. Having the peak percentile widens the SRE on the order of a tenth. Hence, a 5-percentile comes close to maximizing precision among percentile measures, except where kurtosis is huge. However, each successive halving widens the SRE at an accelerating rate.

For a normal distribution, the SRE is 2.4 times as wide for a 0.1-percentile as for a 5-percentile. For fat t-distribution tails the decay is even greater. For $t \leq 5$ the SRE is over four times as wide for a 0.1-percentile as for a 5-percentile. As Dowd (2001) notes, even though fat tails make us more interested in measuring them, the worsening precision inclines us to extrapolate them from data closer in.

Holding q as well as T fixed, the SRE is inverse to the threshold times the density at the threshold. Both of these tend to rise as tails fatten. Comparing $t = 5$ with normal, SREs for the former are about one-third wider for a 5-percentile, two-thirds wider for a 1-percentile, and four-thirds wider for a 0.1-percentile.

EMAs of Standard Deviation

The text uses simple moving averages to make the results easier to understand. EMAs are logically more consistent, since they implicitly presume a constant daily probability of regime shift. They also are frugal with data storage, since we can update without needing to review earlier data. This makes them a favorite modeling tool in high-frequency finance (Dacorogna et al. 2001).

The classic EMA for variance calculates $\Delta V = \lambda(x^2 - V)$. The standard deviation can then be estimated as the square root:

$$\Delta \hat{\sigma} = \sqrt{V + \Delta V} - \sqrt{V} = \sqrt{\hat{\sigma}^2 + \lambda(x^2 - \hat{\sigma}^2)} - \hat{\sigma}. \qquad (A10.5)$$

For direct EMA updating of the standard deviation, again invoke the approximation $\sqrt{\sigma^2(1 \pm \varepsilon)} \cong \sigma(1 \pm \frac{1}{2}\varepsilon)$ to simplify the right-hand side. A bit of algebra shows that

$$\Delta\hat{\sigma} \cong \frac{1}{2}\lambda\left(\frac{x^2}{\hat{\sigma}} - \hat{\sigma}\right).$$ (A10.6)

Alternatively we can use the mean absolute value as a basis for estimation, leading to

$$\Delta\hat{\sigma} = \lambda(\alpha \mid x \mid - \hat{\sigma}),$$ (A10.7)

where α is given by (A10.3) after plugging in an estimate of kurtosis.

None of the above rules is optimal. Corrections for estimated means and other biases add additional terms. I am simply demonstrating the ease of applying basic EMAs to volatility estimations.

SAMURAI Updating

The SAMURAI approach mixes EMAs of varying duration and dynamically reweights them using a variant of equation (10.3). To express this more crisply, let $h(x)$ denote the latest outcome (which might be $x, x^2, \alpha|x|$ or something else) and E denote the aggregate forecast. The aggregate equals the mean $\langle E_i \rangle$ of individual model forecasts E_i, weighted by their probabilistic convictions $\{p_i\}$. The core updating rule is

$$\Delta p_i = \eta p_i(E_i - E)\frac{h(x) - E}{\text{var}(h(x))},$$ (A10.8)

for η on the order of 0.25 to 0.5. Surely η is positive and no more than 1.

The various Δp_i will sum to a multiple of $\sum_i p_i E_i - E\sum_i p_i = E - E = 0$

and hence keep the convictions summing to one. However, sufficiently large outliers in outcomes or beliefs might drive a weight below zero. The simplest patch switches any negative weight to a small positive one and then divides all the weights by their sum. Better patches trim extreme outcomes before computing their impact and replenish p_i close to zero.

Market Interpretation

For a market interpretation of (A10.8), imagine that each model is an independent gambler placing repeated small bets on a Brownian motion of unknown drift. Each bet pays out the distance y travelled and costs the consensus price E. Gambler i believes the drift is E_i, for a mean return of $E_i - E$. Of course, all these values change over time, as does the gambler's wealth p_i. How should the gambler bet?

There is a strong case for maximizing the expected logarithmic growth rate $\tilde{g}$ of wealth, since in the long run this will almost surely give the highest wealth. The insight dates back to Bernoulli (1738). Kelly (1956) rediscovered it independently in drawing out the implications of Shannon's (1948) theory of information, and provided a crisp application to binary bets. See Cover and Thomas (1991: chap. 15) for generalization. With a fraction ω of wealth bet on a small risky dx with drift μ and volatility σ,

$$\tilde{g} = \frac{\langle \log(1 + \omega dx) \rangle}{dt} \cong \omega \frac{\langle dx \rangle}{dt} - \tfrac{1}{2} \omega^2 \frac{\langle (dx)^2 \rangle}{dt} = \omega\mu - \tfrac{1}{2} \omega^2 \sigma^2. \quad \text{(A10.9)}$$

This is maximized when $\omega = \mu/\sigma^2$. That is the Kelly criterion for continuous time. Applying it to the case at hand generates (A10.8) with $\eta = 1$.

The Kelly criterion doesn't always seem effective. Even under ideal conditions, the probability of temporarily losing $100\ell\%$ of capital is $1 - \ell$. That's a larger risk of large drawdown than most gamblers can stomach.

To shave the risk, "fractional Kelly" takes a fraction $\eta < 1$ of the full Kelly bet. Thorp (2000), a mathematician who made a fortune applying fractional Kelly to casinos and stock markets, argues for η of about 0.5. Some gambling experts advise η as low as 0.25. Chin and Ingenoso (2007) show that under fractional Kelly, the chance of losing $100\ell\%$ of capital is $(1 - \ell)^{2/\eta - 1}$. For example, the 1-percentile loss is 99% under full Kelly, 78% under half Kelly, and 48% under quarter Kelly.

Expected utility maximization can justify fractional Kelly directly. Using the power utility specification (A2.1), the rate of expected utility increase works out to approximately $\omega\mu - \tfrac{1}{2}\gamma\omega^2\sigma^2$, where γ denotes the relative risk aversion (RRA). This is maximized for a fractional Kelly with $\eta = \gamma^{-1}$, confirming (A3.11). The recommended range for η corresponds to an RRA between 2 and 4, broadly consistent with other empirical evidence.

Computational Implications

Imagine a million forecasting models running in parallel, trying to predict the same thing. Some may be fully automated, some may depend wholly on human judgment, and some may mix the two. Even within a class they may differ enormously in the data they use and their methods of calculation. Or perhaps they differ only on fine points, like the choice of η above. How should we decide which forecasting model is best?

Absent more information, the best possible model is a dynamic mixture of all possible models. SAMURAI suggests a practical way to approximate that, without having to wire a trillion interconnections. Set up one additional computer as dealer. It keeps tabs on each model's credibility capital w, collects the various forecasts E_i, announces the credibility-weighted average E, lets each model decide how to bet (or assign bets to models that can't figure it out), and then divvies up the proceeds fairly.

Not once does the computer-dealer need to probe the innards of a model. It just needs to know the model's forecast and current credibility. The models don't need to communicate with anyone but the dealer. Never does the dealer reveal one model's forecast or credibility to another, except as folded into the aggregate.

This is very efficient and relatively private, unless the central computer gets hacked. But we can do better by starving the dealer of information about individual beliefs and credibility. This forces the dealer to act like an auctioneer. Suppose the dealer calls out a candidate price $\hat{E}$ and elicits candidate bets. The bets should sum to $\frac{\eta}{\sigma^2}\left(E - \hat{E}\right)$, making the forecast market net long if $\hat{E}$ is too low and net short if $\hat{E}$ is too high. Nudging the candidate price in response to net imbalance should converge to the right E.

In short, market-like mechanisms can improve our forecasts of market risk. Potentially they can achieve super-computer-type results at far less expense. By shifting weights when models break down, they also gain some of the flexibility and robustness typically associated with human brains.

From a computational perspective this is awesome. It also prompts an interesting conjecture about brains. How does evolution make them so good at what they do? Perhaps brains themselves are wired with market-like mechanisms.

Optimal Tracking of Brownian Motion

The SAMURAI approach is best justified as an emulation of Liptser and Shirayev's (1977) optimal filters for tracking Brownian motion. The closest analogue can be expressed as

$$dp_i = p_i(E_i - E)\frac{dx - E dt}{\sigma^2}, \qquad (A10.10)$$

where each E_i represents the mean drift for a particular regime. Ideally we should add terms $\sum_j p_j \lambda_{ji} dt$ as in (A7.5) to reflect expected switching across regimes. That's why I said that very small weights in (A10.8) should be replenished. But equations (A10.8) and (A10.10) do capture the most important terms.

The ratio $\dfrac{dx - E dt}{\sigma^2}$ is the unexpected component or *news* divided by the variance of *news*. This makes (A10.10) the Brownian analogue of the updating equation (A7.3) for default risk. The only difference is the nature of the news: continuous normal rather than discrete binary.

A rigorous derivation requires both measure theory and stochastic calculus. The following heuristic proof avoids both, but demands a willingness to treat any small Brownian dx as the sum of even tinier motions. While this doesn't alter any calculation of drift, it divides var $((dx)^2)$ by the number of moves being summed. This means $(dx)^2 \cong \sigma^2 dt$, with equality in the limit as variance vanishes.

One implication is that our uncertainty about true Brownian motion involves only the mean μ, as σ can be measured with certainty. Hence

$$f(dx \mid \mu = E_i) \propto \exp\left(-\frac{(dx - E_i dt)^2}{2\sigma^2 dt}\right)$$

$$\propto \exp\left(\frac{E_i}{\sigma^2} dx - \frac{E_i^2}{2\sigma^2} dt\right) \cong 1 + \frac{E_i}{\sigma^2} dx, \qquad (A10.11)$$

where the last step follows from a second-order Taylor series expansion. Bayesian updating using (A1.2) shows that $p_i + dp_i \cong Cp_i\left(1 + \frac{E_i}{\sigma^2} dx\right)$ for some factor C. Since the revised weights must sum to one, $C = \left(1 + \frac{E}{\sigma^2} dx\right)^{-1} \cong 1 - \frac{E}{\sigma^2} dx$. A bit more algebra establishes

$$dp_i \cong p_i \frac{E_i - E}{\sigma^2} dx \left(1 - \frac{E}{\sigma^2} dx\right)$$

$$\cong p_i \frac{E_i - E}{\sigma^2} (dx - Edt) \tag{A10.12}$$

with equality in the limit as required.

An extra multiplier η can be justified by treating the E_i as a shorthand for a more complex belief structure. For example, what looks like only two models might represent a beta distribution of beliefs stretching from E_1 to E_2. If regime switching preserves a fixed sum $\frac{1}{\eta} - 1$ of beta distribution parameters, optimal updating adds a multiplier η to (A10.10). A cruder variant posits that each model forms a weighted forecast of private belief E_i and consensus belief E, with weight η on the private belief.

Scoring Rules

Suppose we're using a summary statistic like mean or q-percentile to classify distributions. Knowing nothing about the underlying distribution f, we ask a better-informed agent to report the true value y^*. To encourage good reporting (which may include extra investigation as well as honesty), we score the agent $s(y, x)$ based on the actual report y and the outcome x, and try to design s so that $\langle s(y, x) \rangle_f$ is maximized at $y = y^*$ and no other. A "strictly proper" scoring rule s achieves this for every f. A statistic that allows such a rule is "elicitable."

Some statistics aren't elicitable. That includes the Conditional Value at Risk (CVaR), defined as the expected loss conditional on exceeding a specified percentile. Also known as the expected shortfall, it is more sensitive than VaR to extreme risks. But CVaR is even harder to estimate precisely than VaR when tails are fat. Add the difficulty of elicitation and CVaR doesn't seem too promising a reform path.

Osband (1985) discovered that all elicitable statistics have a common property. They must slice the space of feasible distributions into hyperplanes. Hyperplanes can be described by the directions they're orthogonal to. This amounts to finding a function $\phi(y, x)$ whose expectation is zero if and only if the distribution has statistic y. Given any such $\phi(y, x)$, multiplying by any nonzero function $\varphi(y)$ generates another.

Now suppose we can find a scoring rule that satisfies $\dfrac{\partial s(y, x)}{\partial y} = \varphi(y)\phi(y, x)$. The expected score has a single stationary point, since its derivative $\langle\varphi(y)\phi(y, x)\rangle_f$ vanishes if and only if $y = y^*$. As long as $\varphi(y)$ has the appropriate sign, y will generate a maximum. This gives a constructive procedure for generating a host of strictly proper scoring rules.

Every moment is elicitable, with $\phi(y, x) = x^m - y$. The full class of strictly proper scores can be written as

$$s(y, x) = \int^y v(z)dz + v(y)\,(x^m - y) + w(x), \qquad (A10.13)$$

where v is strictly increasing (its derivative corresponds to a positive φ) and w is arbitrary.

Every percentile is elicitable with $\phi(y, x) = q\% - I(x \le y)$, where I equals 1 when true and 0 when false. Using the same definitions of v and w, the full class of strictly proper scoring rules can be written as

$$s(y, x) = q\% \cdot v(y) - I\,(x \le y) \cdot (v(y) - v(x) + w(x). \qquad (A10.14)$$

The examples in the text set $v(y) \equiv y$ and $w \equiv 0$.

Prediction Markets as Scoring Rules

The previous argument also can provide insight into the form of (A10.8). Suppose we want to design credibility adjustments Δp_i to satisfy four conditions:

i) Each Δp_i depends only on p_i, E_i (which we will now assume is truthfully reported), the credibility-weighted average E, and the outcome $h(x)$.

ii) Each p_i takes sufficient account of the information at hand that Δp_i is not expected to change, provided E is the true mean.

iii) For any x and any combination of forecasts, the sum of credibilities stays constant.

iv) Adjustments should be independent of measurement scale.

Let X denote the vector of all possible outcomes. From (ii), $\Delta p_i(X)$ must be orthogonal to all distributions f that are orthogonal to $h(X) - E$. It follows that $\Delta p_i \equiv \xi(E_i, E, p)(h(x) - E)$ for some function ξ. A similar argument applied to (iii) shows that $\xi(E_i, E, p) \equiv v(E)p_i(E_i - E)$. From (iv), $v(E)$ must be inversely proportional to $\text{var}(h(x))$. The net result is (A10.8), albeit with no insight into η.

Chapter 11: Resizing Risk

Brownian Range

Given any random process x, the range R denotes the gap over a specified time interval t between the least upper bound and the greatest lower bound. In financial application, x typically refers to the logarithm of price, so the range equals the logarithm of the high/low ratio.

Given i.i.d. increments with zero drift, the range will be directly proportional to the cumulative volatility $\sigma\sqrt{t}$. Without loss of generality, we can set $t=1$. Feller (1951) first worked out its probability density under Brownian motion.

Parkinson (1980) observed that Brownian range generates far more precise estimators of variance than closes. He derived this from an explicit formula for the moments in terms of the gamma function Γ and the Riemann zeta function $\zeta(n) \equiv \sum_{k=1}^{\infty} n^{-k}$. For the moments we care most about it reduces to

$$
\begin{aligned}
\langle R \rangle &= \sigma\sqrt{8/\pi} \cong 1.596\sigma, \\
\langle R^2 \rangle &= \sigma^2 4\log(2) \cong 2.773\sigma^2, \\
\langle R^4 \rangle &= \sigma^4 9\zeta(3) \cong 10.819\sigma^4.
\end{aligned}
\tag{A11.1}
$$

It follows that a variance estimator

$$
V \cong 0.361 R^2
\tag{A11.2}
$$

has a variance of $0.41\sigma^2$, which is 4.9 times as precise as the standard estimator. By applying an updating rule along the lines of (A10.5) we can convert that into an EMA for volatility. Even better, although Parkinson did not mention it, volatility can be estimated directly as

$$
\hat{\sigma} \cong 0.627 R.
\tag{A11.3}
$$

This is 5.6 times as precise as the ordinary standard deviation estimator and 6.4 times as precise as an absolute return-based estimator.

Range Modified for Absolute Return

With nonnegative drift μ, the range will scale in the limit with the cumulative drift μt, making moments quick complex (Magdon-Ismail et al. 2002). Fortunately, we can finesse these issues by adjusting range for the observed absolute return. This improves precision even when the drift is zero.

Intuitively, if we have multiple unbiased estimators, an appropriately weighted average should typically have a lower variance than any single estimator. For Σ the covariance matrix of estimator, ω the vector of weights, and $\mathbf{1}$ a vector of ones, minimizing $\omega'\Sigma\omega$ subject to $\omega'\mathbf{1}=1$ requires $\omega = \dfrac{\Sigma^{-1}\mathbf{1}}{\sqrt{\mathbf{1}'\Sigma\mathbf{1}}}$. This is analogous to portfolio optimization. In a sense we're trying to maximize the Sharpe ratio of the estimator.

Applying this approach, Garman and Klass (1980) found such a high correlation between squared range and squared return $(\Delta x)^2$ that the optimal weight on the latter is negative. The following estimator is nearly optimal, and provides 7.4 times the precision of the returns squared:

$$V \cong 0.5\,R^2 - 0.386(\Delta x)^2. \tag{A11.4}$$

Like Parkinson, Garman and Klass did not consider the possibility that direct estimation of volatility might be better. In fact, the following direct estimator adds an extra 5% precision:

$$\sigma \cong 0.81R - 0.367|\Delta x|. \tag{A11.5}$$

While these computations can be numerically verified in Monte Carlo simulations, the formulas themselves give little clue for why they work. For a more intuitive appreciation we need to invoke the concept of a Brownian bridge.

Brownian Bridge

A Brownian bridge is a Brownian process that is tied down at both ends instead of just the beginning. Typically we view the motion as returning to the same point it started from. To convert an unrestricted Brownian motion to a Brownian bridge, just subtract the observed trend or "empirical drift" from the motion.

Since most of the observed trend is random, removing it makes Brownian bridges less noisy than the unrestricted motion they are based on. Brownian motions with very different end points get mapped to processes with the same zero end point, reducing the variation between them. While this trims the average range of a Brownian bridge, it trims the deviations from the average even more.

For a Brownian bridge spanning one unit of time, the following moments of the range R_{BB} can be calculated from formulas derived in Feller (1951), DasGupta and Lalley (2000), and Dudley (2002):

$$\langle R_{BB} \rangle = \frac{\sigma\sqrt{\pi}}{\sqrt{2}} \cong 1.253\,\sigma,$$

$$\langle R_{BB}^2 \rangle = \frac{\sigma^2 \pi^2}{6} \cong 1.645\,\sigma^2, \qquad \text{(A11.6)}$$

$$\langle R_{BB}^4 \rangle = \frac{\sigma^4 \pi^4}{30} \cong 3.247\,\sigma^4.$$

Using R_{BB}^2 to estimate the variance will have a precision exactly ten times that of the standard estimator. Since the estimator is independent of the squared return, we can combine them in the ratio ten to one to obtain 11 times the precision of the standard estimator:

$$V \cong 0.553 R_{BB}^2 + 0.091(\Delta x)^2. \qquad \text{(A11.7)}$$

Using the range to estimate volatility directly provides a bit more precision. Combining it with the absolute return achieves 11.4 times the precision of the standard estimator:

$$\hat{\sigma} \cong 0.744 R_{BB} + 0.085\,|\Delta x|. \qquad \text{(A11.8)}$$

We can add another few tenths of precision by tracking average log range and using it to estimate log volatility (just subtract 0.2). Then exponentiate and combine with ordinary estimators in ratio 10.8 to one. However, this method is extremely sensitive to "quiet" outliers; e.g., a market closure treated as an active trading day would generate a log range of $-\infty$.

For robustness and ease of calculation it's hard to beat (A11.8). The simpler variant $\hat{\sigma} \cong 0.798 R_{BB}$ still yields 10.6 times the precision of an ordinary standard deviation estimator. With even a modest likelihood of regime change, a month of one-day Brownian ranges provides better information on volatility than a year of daily closes.

Approximations to Brownian Bridge

Charting slanted trading range is a good away to estimate volatility. To the extent that prices follow Brownian motion, the vertical span of the channel matches the range of the corresponding Brownian bridge. By eyeballing that single measure, a trader can estimate volatility within a 22% standard deviation of the true value. This is an excellent first guess. Averaging over four nonoverlapping time periods can cut that in half. The eye also readily adjusts for obvious regime change and outliers.

When we have only occasional observations on a Brownian process, we can still try to approximate a Brownian bridge. Suppose, for example, we have at hand only logarithmic *high, low, open,* and *close.*

- When $\Delta x \equiv close - open$ is positive, the high likely occurs closer to the close than to the open; denote by $\frac{1}{2} + \tau$ its average time of occurrence. To convert the high to a Brownian bridge measure, we then subtract $(\frac{1}{2} + \tau)\Delta x$.
- By symmetry, the low will occur on average at time $1 - \tau$. To convert it to a Brownian bridge measure, we subtract $(\frac{1}{2} - \tau)\Delta x$.
- Hence, when Δx is positive, R_{BB} can be estimated as $R - 2\tau\Delta x$, for $R \equiv high - low$.
- When Δx is negative, we can by symmetry just run the day backward, for an R_{BB} estimate of $R + 2\tau\Delta x$. A unified expression good for any Δx is $R_{BB} \cong R - 2\tau|\Delta x|$.
- Monte Carlo simulations suggest $\tau = \frac{1}{4}$ when drift is zero, implying equation (11.2). However, this understates the Brownian bridge range, since the bridge high and low could not match nominal high and low. Moreover, correlation arguments suggest folding in some absolute return. That is why the coefficient ratio in (A11.5) is 0.45 rather than 0.5.

We can even approximate a Brownian bridge where data are missing. For example, one way to model the overnight change in price from close to open is to presume that market prices wander randomly overnight without being recorded. We can then infer an "overnight high" and "overnight low" as follows:

- Estimate the average absolute overnight change as a fraction of the daily absolute return. We can set this up as yet another EMA.
- Multiply that fraction by the latest estimated daily volatility to impute an overnight volatility.
- Estimate the overnight high (low) as 0.4 overnight volatility units above the maximum (below the minimum) of the close and open bounding the interval. This should on average simulate a trading range of 1.6 volatility units.

This interpolation of missing data can be further refined. While not perfect, it's better than leaving blanks. It is particularly useful for assets that trade infrequently or markets closed for long holidays.

Multiday Ranges

Price changes aren't really Brownian. At tick intervals they're not continuous. Even at daily intervals they're fat-tailed. If we construct a short-term bridge from cumulative fat-tailed risks, its range can be significantly more volatile than the range of a Brownian bridge.

The deterioration is at least comparable to that suffered by ordinary standard deviation estimators when kurtosis is high. It might be worse. It is hard to pin numbers without clearer specification of the cumulative process and the time interval. By the Central Limit Theorem, the impact of non-Gaussian deviations recedes as more independent shocks are folded together. The impact in simulations is quite noticeable.

In practice, I find that daily range-based measures rarely achieve half the precision of the Brownian ideal. Still, they significantly outperform standard estimators based on closing prices. They are particularly useful in constructing weekly estimators.

The easiest way to estimate weekly volatility is to multiply daily volatility by $\sqrt{5} \cong 2.24$. That's the single best starting point and often suffices. However, many assets are serially correlated. A one-day auto-correlation of ρ will boost weekly volatility by roughly 0.8ρ. If markets are very active and the correlations seem stable, that likely suffices. However, many analysts are sufficiently concerned about illiquidity or nonlinear effects that prefer, or are ordered to prefer, direct estimation of weekly or longer risks.

Multiday estimation is hard on precision. If we restrict ourselves to non-overlapping observations, the way classical time series analysis prefers, our weekly estimates utilize only a fifth as many samples as our daily estimates. While we may derive some benefits from dealing with thinner-tailed distributions, it is highly unlikely to outweigh the loss in sample size. If we extend the sample window to compensate, we run the risk of regime change making older data irrelevant.

The favored alternative is to introduce overlapping data. That allows nearly the same number of observations regardless of the holding period. However, overlapping observations are correlated, and correlation slashes the marginal benefits of extra samples.

Given i.i.d. Gaussian daily returns, Müller (1993) shows that doubling the number of observations through overlap increases estimator precision by at most one-third. The maximum precision gain is half, no matter how many overlapping intervals get stuffed in. In a sense, five overlapping weekly observations become the equivalent of an observation every 3.4 days.

Again, since kurtosis tends to shrink with holding period, the real trade-offs aren't that draconian. Nevertheless, range estimation offers a much better way to handle longer holding periods. A Brownian bridge estimated over a week should be much more precise than the average of five overlapping weekly squared returns. Overlapping Brownian bridges midweek offers a few more benefits. Bear in mind, too, that if we're inferring a Brownian bridge from partial data, a weekly chart will be five times as dense as a daily chart, so that errors recede in relative importance.

Adjusting the Multipliers

Between discrete jumps, serial correlation, volatility fluctuations, noisy measurement, and missing data, real-life conversion coefficients won't match the values in equations (A11.1) or (A11.6). The coefficients for mixed estimators like in equation (A11.8) won't be correct either. Furthermore, in practical application we won't know what's wrong or why.

Here is a vivid example from the SPX series. In an ideal driftless Brownian world, the mean absolute return should be exactly half the mean range. Figure A.16 charts the ratio over the last 46 years, with each mean

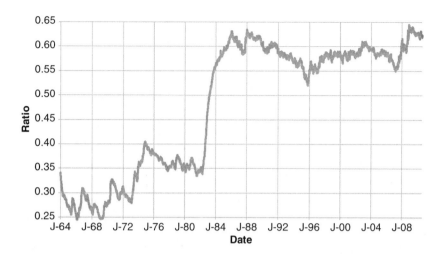

Figure A.16
Ratio of Mean SPX Absolute Return to Mean Range

calculated using an EMA with an average one-year lag. In Monte Carlo simulations, the ratio spends 99% of the time between 0.47 and 0.53. The SPX ratio behaves nearly the opposite. It is way too low until the early 1980s and too high after.

This is a sharp enough regime break that it temps to ditch the earlier data and refine the later estimates using futures prices. On reflection, I decided to stick with the original series, as it typifies the problems encountered in practice. I mitigated them by using EMAs with an average one-year lag to (i) adjust the multipliers on both range and absolute return relative to the ordinary standard deviation and (ii) update the covariance estimates used to calculate relative weights in the estimator.

This isn't the best method. It's not even the best method I can think of. I am simply noting it as one way to get things approximately right rather than precisely wrong.

Rational Updating of Brownian Beliefs

Let us shift from practical estimation back to theory. Given a countable set of Brownian motion regimes indexed by i, we can identify the subjective probability as p_i, the current drift as μ_i, and the instantaneous probability of switching to another regime j as λ_{ij}. For notational convenience let us also adopt the definition $\lambda_{ii} \equiv -\sum_{j \neq i} \lambda_{ij}$ used in (A7.5). All these can depend on time t, although the notation doesn't show that explicitly.

By combining the arguments used to justify (A10.10) and (A7.5), we can express the optimal updating rule as

$$dp_i = p_i \frac{\mu_i - E}{\sigma} dW + \langle \lambda_{\bullet i} \rangle dt, \qquad (A11.9)$$

where $E \equiv \langle \mu_i \rangle$ is the consensus mean, $dW \equiv \dfrac{dx - E\,dt}{\sigma}$ is standardized Brownian motion given beliefs, and $\langle \lambda_{\bullet i} \rangle \equiv \sum_j p_j \lambda_{ji}$ is the net inflow rate from regime switching. Note that dW equals the *news* measured in standard deviations. I will call it the *surprise*.

Equation (A11.9) basically applies even when the indices aren't countable. We just need p to represent a probability density and λ to represent a diffusion. See Liptser and Shirayev (1977) for a rigorous presentation. An informal description is

$$\Delta conviction = conviction \times idiosyncrasy \times surprise + \langle inflow \rangle, \quad (A11.10)$$

where *idiosyncrasy* refers to the deviation of belief from the consensus, as measured in standard deviations.

Because surprise gets weighted by a product of conviction and idiosyncrasy, it can get treated vastly differently at different times. An outside observer unfamiliar with the motivating beliefs could easily dismiss the updates as irrational. This equation turns out to account for most of the paradoxes in market behavior, although we will only scratch the surface here.

Cumulant Updating

Although (A11.9) looks neat, it requires a potentially infinite number of beliefs to be updated infinitely fast. It can't be calculated accurately except in special cases. To get more intuition for its properties, let's focus on the cumulants, starting with E. We can calculate dE by multiplying each dp_i term by μ_i and summing or integrating. This simplifies to

$$dE = \frac{\langle \mu^2 \rangle - E^2}{\sigma} dW + \left\langle \sum_i \lambda_{\bullet i} \mu_i \right\rangle dt$$
$$= \text{var}(\mu) \cdot \frac{news}{\text{var}(news)} + \langle RegimeShift \rangle. \tag{A11.11}$$

Again, this is completely analogous to earlier results in Chapters 6 and 7 for default risk. The only difference is the nature of the news. The more uncertain people are, or the more individually confident people disagree with each other, the more consensus will shift in response to news.

We can update all moments in this fashion, and summarize the results using a moment generating function:

$$d\langle e^{b\mu} \rangle = \left(\langle \mu e^{b\mu} \rangle - \langle e^{b\mu} \rangle E \right) \frac{dW}{\sigma} + \left\langle \sum_i \lambda_{\bullet i} e^{b\mu_i} \right\rangle dt. \tag{A11.12}$$

The update for the CGF $K(b) \equiv \ln\langle e^{b\mu} \rangle$ is a bit messier because of the second derivative's impact on drift. However, the volatility term is tidy. It is just the coefficient on dW above divided by $\langle e^{b\mu} \rangle$:

$$\text{volatility}(K) = \frac{\langle \mu e^{b\mu} \rangle - \langle e^{b\mu} \rangle E}{\sigma \langle e^{b\mu} \rangle} = \frac{K' - E}{\sigma}. \tag{A11.13}$$

This amounts to an infinite chain, where the volatility of each cumulant depends on the cumulant above. For any positive integer m,

$$\text{volatility}(\kappa_m) = \frac{|\kappa_{m+1}|}{\sigma}. \tag{A11.14}$$

For completeness, let me write down the full updating equation:

$$dK = \left[\frac{\left\langle \sum_i \lambda_{\bullet i} e^{b\mu_i} \right\rangle}{\langle e^{b\mu} \rangle} - \frac{(K' - E)^2}{2\sigma^2} \right] dt + \frac{K' - E}{\sigma} dW. \tag{A11.15}$$

The first term in the drift indicates the expected shift due to regime switching. I will call it K^{shift} for short. The other term follows from the second derivative impact embedded in Itō's rule. Equating higher-order terms of the corresponding Taylor expansions indicates that

$$d\kappa_m = \left(\kappa_m^{shift} - \frac{1}{2\sigma^2} \sum_{j=1}^{m-1} \binom{m}{j} \kappa_{j+1} \kappa_{m-j+1} \right) dt + \frac{\kappa_{m+1}}{\sigma} dW. \quad \text{(A11.16)}$$

For $m = 2$ this reduces to $d\,\text{var} = \left(\text{var}^{shift} - \frac{\text{var}^2}{\sigma^2} \right) dt + \frac{\text{skewness}}{\sigma} dW$, which accounts for the volatile autoregressive behavior known as GARCH.

Turbulence

Equation (A11.16) summarizes the notion that risk stays outside the box. I incline to call it Pandora's Equation, or at least one of its forms, alongside equations (A11.13)–(A11.15) and (A7.7)–(A7.9). Pandora's Equation deserves a book of its own, for it answers most of the puzzles of twentieth-century finance theory. Here I can provide only a few clues.

Mainstream finance seems not to recognize cumulant hierarchies, much less appreciate their importance. I have not found a single reference apart from my own articles. However, cumulant hierarchies are well known in statistical physics (Orszag 1970; Frisch 1996). They arise naturally in the course of analyzing the Fokker-Planck equation (A8.2) (Risken 1996) and other nonlinear interactions. They resemble the Bogoliubov hierarchy (Bogoliubov 1946), which analyzes an n-particle distribution in terms of an $n + 1$-particle distribution.

In fluid mechanics this is known as the moment closure problem (McComb 1990). The most striking physical manifestation is turbulence. Turbulence is less stable than either regular noise or deterministic chaos. Yet it does create temporary regularities.

Pandora's Equation indicates that markets are inherently turbulent. As discussed earlier, a probability distribution will always have an infinite number of nonzero cumulants unless it is perfectly Gaussian. Those nonzero cumulants will ricochet down the ladder via (A11.14). While the impact may dissipate as beliefs get more normal, anticipation of regime change tends to renew volatility.

Turbulence helps explain the popularity of charting methods. When even the most knowledgeable traders are unable to predict the market's full response to new information, everyone must work out approximations. Most of these will rest far more on short-term empirical regularities than on puzzled theory. Moreover, since these regularities are surely nonlinear, they call for humans' best nonlinear filters: their eyes.

Turbulence also invites a rethink of risk premia. The economic models described in Chapter 3 presume rational foresight of future risks. Our critique focused on the veil that obscures the future. Now we see that rational learning responses to that veil make market prices turbulent. Surely that adds to the premia.

Two-Regime Example

Even a small dose of uncertainty goes a long way in accounting for market behavior. The following model is adapted from David (1997). Let us posit two dividend regimes 1 and 2, with occasional shifts between them. In each regime, log dividends follow a random walk with volatility σ and drift μ_1 or μ_2. Let λ_{12} and λ_{21} denote the instantaneous switching rates. The discount rate is r.

Assuming no parameter changes over time, the fair (equilibrium) price-dividend ratios v_1 and v_1 will be constant. Given probability $p \equiv p_1$ of regime 1, $v(p) = v_2 + p(v_1 - v_2)$. The volatility of log($v$) equals $\dfrac{v_1 - v_2}{v(p)}$ times the volatility of p. Since p moves directly with dividends, the volatility of log price will be the sum of σ and price-dividend volatility, with no offset for partial or negative correlation.

Hence, correlated price-dividend volatility explains why fair prices are more volatile than dividends. Our next challenge is to explore the magnitude of the effects. Without loss of generality we can set $r = 0$, since all that matters are the excess drifts relative to the discount rate.

Suppose the regime starts out 1 with a dividend of 1. If the regime stays 1 over the next short interval dt, the dividend is expected to grow by $\mu_1 dt$ and asset value by $v_1 \mu_1 dt$. With probability $\lambda_{12} dt$ the regime shifts to 2, in which case the asset appreciates by $v_2 - v_1$. The dividend over the period is dt. (All these numbers are approximate; I've left out higher-order terms.). Fairness requires the expected return to equal zero in the limit, or $(\lambda_{12} - \mu_1)v_1 - \lambda_{12}v_2 = 1$. The parallel condition for regime 2 requires $-\lambda_{21}v_1 + (\lambda_{21} - \mu_2)v_2 = 1$. Solving this pair of equations,

$$v_1 = \frac{\lambda_{12} + \lambda_{21} - \mu_2}{\mu_1 \mu_2 - \lambda_{21} \mu_1 - \lambda_{12} \mu_2}$$

$$v_2 = \frac{\lambda_{12} + \lambda_{21} - \mu_1}{\mu_1 \mu_2 - \lambda_{21} \mu_1 - \lambda_{12} \mu_2}. \tag{A11.17}$$

In technical analysis, those values correspond to the edges of the price channel. The updating formula (A11.9) simplifies to

$$dp = (\lambda_{21} - (\lambda_{12} + \lambda_{21})p)dt + p(1-p)SdW, \tag{A11.18}$$

where $S \equiv \dfrac{\mu_1 - \mu_2}{\sigma}$ denotes the signal-to-noise ratio, which in turn is the difference of two Sharpe ratios. It follows that the ratio of "excess" learning-induced volatility to dividend volatility is

$$\frac{\sigma_{learning}}{\sigma} = \frac{p(1-p)S^2}{\lambda_{12} + \lambda_{21} - \mu_1 - \mu_2 + E}. \tag{A11.19}$$

For regimes that last longer than two years, the denominator will usually be less than 1. Hence, as long as S exceeds 1 and price isn't too close to the edge of its channel, price volatility will significantly exceed dividend volatility.

Equilibrium Uncertainty

Since beliefs are diffusing, they satisfy the Fokker-Planck equation. Applying (A8.3), the stationary distribution of beliefs turns out proportional to

$$p^{\xi_1 - \xi_2 - 2}(1-p)^{\xi_2 - \xi_1 - 2} \exp\left(-\frac{\xi_1}{p} - \frac{\xi_2}{1-p} \right), \tag{A11.20}$$

where $\xi_1 \equiv \dfrac{2\lambda_{21}}{S^2}$ and $\xi_2 \dfrac{2\lambda_{12}}{S^2}$. Although the expression is daunting, it can generate some stunning pictures of equilibrium uncertainty. Figure A.17 charts a selection.

In the first five of these cases, beliefs are usually between 10% to 90% certain. This guarantees significant learning-induced volatility provided S^2 is large relative to the switching propensities. However, $S^2 \gg \lambda_{12} + \lambda_{21}$ is precisely what generates the last case, where people are usually near-certain about the regime.

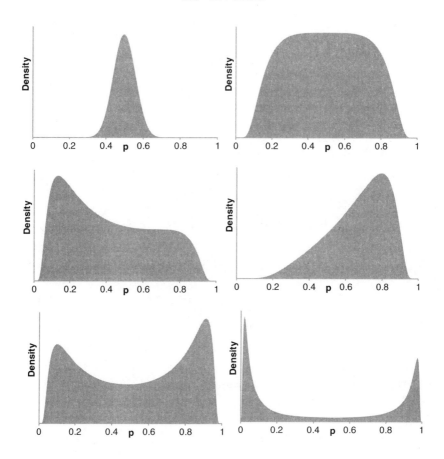

Figure A.17
Stationary Distributions of Beliefs

This deserves more investigation. For simplicity, I will focus on the special case of equal switching probabilities. I will denote the common value by λ and the ratio S^2/λ by Q. Note that Q indicates the expected profits if one recognizes a gamble of Sharpe S lasting for expected time $1/\lambda$ and applies a full Kelly criterion to bet S.

With symmetric switching, the log stationary distribution simplifies to a constant less twice $\log(p(1-p)) + \dfrac{1}{Qp(1-p)}$. This is maximized at $p(1-p) = \frac{1}{Q}$. At those points, (A11.19) simplifies to $\dfrac{\lambda}{2\lambda - \mu_1 - \mu_2 + E}$, which for typical parameter ranges is close to ½.

Hence, the learning-induced volatility is likely to be significant even in the chart that looks like it won't be. The only case where it isn't involves very tiny S. Then people stay very uncertain, as in the first chart, but the uncertainty makes little economic difference. If people have good economic cause to learn, learning will add significant volatility.

Simulations

Let me close with a picture of learning. Before presenting results, let me note that equation (A11.18) needs adjustment in discrete application to avoid generating negative probabilities. To keep simulations from causing extra volatility or other spurious patterns, I took two extra precautions. First, I updated hourly rather than daily. Second, I used the log-odds form of Bayes' rule before calculating the regime switches. If we define $\omega \equiv \ln\left(\dfrac{p}{1-p}\right)$, the analogue to (A7.10) is

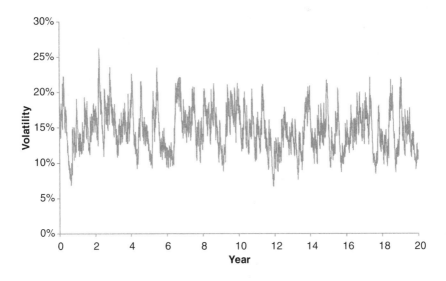

Figure A.18
Volatility for Simulated Prices

$$d\omega = -\lambda_{12}(1 + e^{\omega})dt + \lambda_{21}(1 + e^{-\omega})dt + S\frac{dx - \frac{1}{2}(\mu_1 + \mu_2)dt}{\sigma}. \qquad \text{(A11.21)}$$

At last we're ready for the application. Suppose regime 1 is very stable and reassuring. The expected life is 15 years ($\lambda_{12} = \frac{1}{15}$) while the dividend growth rate matches the discount rate ($\mu_1 = 0$). Regime 2, by contrast, is extremely unsettling but very short-lived. Dividends in regime 2 on average halve in a year ($\mu_2 = -0.7$), but the regime itself is expected to last only three months ($\lambda_{21} = 4$). In either regime, the volatility σ of dividends equals 3%.

The dividend ratio $\frac{y}{v}$ looks relatively stable for this model, ranging between 1.0% and 1.1%. Nevertheless the average price volatility at 15% is five times dividend volatility. Figure A.18 presents a 20-year simulation, with volatility charted as an EMA with a six-week average lag. Price volatility rarely falls below 8% and in 5% of cases exceeds 20%. Also note the pronounced GARCH-type behavior.

Different parameter combinations generate different patterns. For example, if dividend volatility triples to 9%, average market volatility increases only 100 bps, but the range of variation halves. The higher σ slashes the information content of any given observation and therefore makes the market more cautious in its beliefs.

Indeed, simulations suggest that volatility signatures are like fingerprints. No two are exactly alike. Here again uncertainty opens new vistas. Further exploration falls beyond the scope of this book.

REFERENCES

Abel, Andrew B. 1990. "Asset Prices Under Habit Formation and Catching up with the Joneses." *American Economic Review* 80(2): 38–42.

Aftalion, Albert. 1927. "The Theory of Economic Cycles Based on the Capitalistic Technique of Production." *Review of Economic Statistics* 9(4): 165–170.

Al-Jahri, Mabid A. 2004. "Remedy for Banking Crises: What Chicago and Islam Have in Common: A Comment." *Islamic Economic Studies* 11(2): 23–42.

Allais, Maurice. 1948. *Économie et Intérêt: Exposition Nouvelle des Problèmes Fondamentaux, Relatifs au Rôle Économique du Taux de l'Intérêt et de Leurs Solutions.* Paris: Librairie des Publications Officielles.

Altman, Edward I. 1968. "Financial Ratios, Discriminant Analysis and the Prediction of Corporate Bankruptcy." *Journal of Finance* 23(4): 589–609.

Atkinson, Thomas R. 1967. *Trends in Corporate Credit Quality.* National Bureau of Economic Research, Studies in Corporate Bond Financing. New York: Columbia University Press.

Bansal, Ravi and Wilbur J. Coleman II. 1996. "A Monetary Explanation of the Equity Premium, Term Premium, and Risk-Free Rate Puzzles." *Journal of Political Economy* 104(6): 1135–1171.

Barro, Robert J. 1979. "On the Determination of the Public Debt." *Journal of Political Economy* 87(5): 940–971.

Barro, Robert J. 2006. "Rare Disasters and Asset Markets in the Twentieth Century." *Quarterly Journal of Economics* 121(3): 823–866.

Barsky, Robert B., Miles S. Kimball, F. Thomas Juster, and Matthew D. Shapiro. 1997. "Preference Parameters and Behavior Heterogeneity: An Experimental Approach in the Health and Retirement Study." *Quarterly Journal of Economics* 112(2): 537–579.

Basel Committee on Banking Supervision. 2004. *International Convergence of Capital Measurement and Capital Standards. A Revised Framework.* Basel: Bank for International Settlements.

Basel Committee on Banking Supervision. 2005. *An Explanatory Note on the Basel II IRB Risk Weight Functions.* Basel: Bank for International Settlements.

Baxter, Rodney J. 2007. *Exactly Solved Models in Statistical Mechanics.* Mineola, NY: Dover.

Bayes, Thomas. 1764. "An Essay Towards Solving a Problem in the Doctrine of Chances." Published posthumously in *Philosophical Transactions of the Royal Society of London* 53: 370–418 and 54: 296–325.

Beck, Stacie and David R. Stockman. 2005. "Money as Real Options in a Cash-in-Advance Economy." *Economics Letters* 87(3): 337–345.

Bernardo, José M. and Adrian F. M. Smith. 2000. *Bayesian Theory.* Chichester, UK: John Wiley.

Bernoulli, Daniel. 1738. "Specimen theoriae novae de mensura sortis." *Commentarii Academiae Scientiarum Imperialis Petropolitanae* 5: 175–192. Translated by Louise Sommer as "Exposition of a New Theory on the Measurement of Risk." *Econometrica* 22(1): 22–36.

Bernstein, Sergei N. 1928. "Sur les fonctions absolument monotones." *Acta Mathematica* 52: 1–66.

Black, Fischer. 1985. "The Future of Financial Services." In R. P. Inman, ed., *Managing the Service Economy: Prospects and Problems.* Cambridge, UK: Cambridge University Press, 223–231.

Black, Fischer and Myron S. Scholes. 1973. "The Pricing of Options and Corporate Liabilities." *Journal of Political Economy* 81(3): 637–654.

Blanchard, Olivier, Giovanni Dell'Arricia, and Paulo Mauro. 2010. "Rethinking Macroeconomic Policy." IMF Staff Position Note 10/03, Washington, DC: International Monetary Fund.

Bogoliubov, Nikolai N. 1946. "Kinetic Equations." *Journal of Physics USSR* 10(3): 265–274.

Bollerslev, Tim. 1986. "Generalized Autoregressive Conditional Heteroskedasticity." *Journal of Econometrics* 31(3): 307–327.

Boltzmann, Ludwig. 1886. "Das Zweite Gesetz von Thermodynamik." Address to a formal meeting of the Imperial Academy of Science. Translated by S. G. Brush and reprinted in Ludwig Boltzmann, *Theoretical Physics and Philosophical Problems,* 1974. Boston: Reidel.

Borio, Claudio and Philip Lowe. 2002. "Asset Prices, Financial and Monetary Stability: Exploring the Nexus." BIS Working Papers No. 114, Bank for International Settlements, Monetary and Economic Department.

Born, Max. 2005. *The Born-Einstein Letters 1916–1955, Friendship, Politics and Physics in Uncertain Times.* New York: Macmillan.

Bossone, Biagio. 2002. "Should Banks Be 'Narrowed'?" Public Policy Brief No. 69. Levy Economics Institute, Annandale-on-Hudson, NY: Bard College.

Bragg, William L. and Evan J. Williams. 1934. "The Effect of Thermal Agitation on Atomic Arrangement in Alloys." *Proceedings of the Royal Society* A145: 699–730.

Brigo, Damiano, Andrea Pallavicini, and Robert Torresetti. 2010. *Credit Models and the Crisis: A Journey into CDOs, Copulas, Correlations and Dynamic Models.* Chichester, UK: John Wiley.

Briotti, M. Gabriella. 2005. "Economic Reactions to Public Finance Consolidation: A Survey of the Literature." Occasional Paper No. 38, Frankfurt: European Central Bank, October.

Broadbent, S. R. and David G. Kendall. 1953. "The Random Walk of *Trichostrongylus retortaeformis." Biometrics* 9: 460–465.

Brown, Morton B. and Robert A. Wolfe. 1983. "Estimation of the Variance of Percentile Estimates." *Computational Statistics and Data Analysis* 1:167–174.

Brzeźniak, Zdzislaw and Tomasz Zastawniak. 1999. *Basic Stochastic Processes.* London: Springer-Verlag.

Campbell, John Y. and John Cochrane. 1999. "By Force of Habit: A Consumption-Based Explanation of Aggregate Stock Market Behavior." *Journal of Political Economy* 107(2): 205–251.

Chantrill, Christopher. 2010. Available in www.usgovernmentspending.com/federal_debt_chart.html, using data from www.gpoaccess.gov/usbudget/fy11/hist.html and www.treasurydirect.gov/govt/reports/pd/histdebt/histdebt.htm.

Chin, William and Marc Ingenoso. 2007. "Risk Formulae for Proportional Betting." In Stewart. N. Ethier and William R. Eadington., eds., *Optimal Play: Mathematical Studies of Games and Gambling.* Reno, NV: Institute for the Study of Gambling and Commercial Gaming, University of Nevada, 541–550.

CIA. 2010. *The World Factbook.* Washington, DC: Central Intelligence Agency.

Cifuentes, Arturo and Gerard O'Connor. 1996. "The Binomial Expansion Method Application to CBO/CLO Analysis." *Structured Finance Special Report.* New York: Moody's Investors Service, December.

Cochrane, John H. 2004. *Asset Pricing,* rev. ed. Princeton, NJ: Princeton University Press.

Cochrane, John H. 2005. "Money as Stock." *Journal of Monetary Economics* 52(3): 501–528.

Cogley, Timothy and Thomas J. Sargent. 2008. "The Market Price of Risk and the Equity Premium: A Legacy of the Great Depression?" *Journal of Monetary Economics* 55(3): 454–478.

Constantinides, G. 1990. "Habit Formation: A Resolution of the Equity Premium Puzzle." *Journal of Political Economy* 98(3): 519–543.

Cover, Thomas M. and Joy A. Thomas. 1991. *Elements of Information Theory.* New York: John Wiley.

Cox, John C., Jonathan E. Ingersoll, and Stephen A. Ross. 1985. "A Theory of the Term Structure of Interest Rates." *Econometrica* 53(2): 385–407.

Dacorogna, Michel M., Ramazan Gençay, Ulrich A. Müller, Richard B. Olsen, and Olivier V. Pictet. 2001. *An Introduction to High-Frequency Finance.* San Diego, CA: Academic.

DasGupta, Anirban and Steven. P. Lalley. 2000. "The Riemann Zeta Function and the Range of Brownian Bridge." Technical Report No. 00-10. West Lafayette, IN: Purdue University, Department of Statistics, December.

David, Alexander. 1997. "Fluctuating Confidence in Stock Markets: Implications for Returns and Volatility." *Journal of Financial and Quantitative Analysis* 32(4): 427–462.

David, Paul A. 1991. "Computer and Dynamo: The Modern Productivity Paradox in a Not-too-Distant Mirror." In *Technology and Productivity*. Paris: OECD.

David, Paul A. and Wright, Gavin, 1999. "General Purpose Technologies and Surges in Productivity: Historical Reflections on the Future of the ICT Revolution." No. 31, Oxford University Economic and Social History Series, Economics Group. Oxford, UK: Nuffield College, University of Oxford.

de Finetti, Bruno. 1931a. "Funzione caratteristica di un fenomeno aleatorio." *Atti della R. Academia Nazionale dei Lincei*. Serie 6, Memorie, Classe di Scienze Fisiche, *Mathematice e Naturale* 4: 251–299.

de Finetti, Bruno. 1931b. "Probabilism: A Critical Essay on the Theory of Probability and on the Value of Science." Translated in *Erkenntnis* 31:239–261.

de Finetti, Bruno. 1937. "La prévision: Ses lois logiques, ses sources subjectives." *Annales Institute Henri Poincaré* 7: 1–68.

DeLong, Bradford. 2001. *Macroeconomics*. New York: McGraw-Hill.

Dennis, Brian and Ganapati P. Patil. 1984. "The Gamma Distribution and Weighted Multimodal Gamma Distributions as Models of Population Abundance." *Mathematical Biosciences* 68: 187–212.

Douady, Raphael and Nassim N. Taleb. 2010. "Statistical Undecidability." Working Paper Series, Social Sciences Research Network, October 12.

Dowd, Kevin. 2001. "Estimating VaR with Order Statistics." *Journal of Derivatives* 8(3): 23–30.

Dudley, Richard M. 2002. *Real Analysis and Probability,* 2nd ed. Cambridge, UK: Cambridge University Press.

Duffie, Darrell and Larry G. Epstein. 1992. "Stochastic Differential Utility." *Econometrica* 60(2): 353–394.

Eichengreen, Barry and Kris Mitchener. 2003. "The Great Depression as a Credit Boom Gone Wrong." BIS Working Paper No. 137, Basel: Bank for International Settlements, Monetary and Economic Department, September.

Ellis, Luci. 2008. "The Housing Meltdown: Why Did It Happen in the United States?" BIS Working Paper No. 259, Basel: Bank for International Settlements, Monetary and Economic Department, September.

Emery, Kenneth, Sharon Ou, Jennifer Tenant, Adriana Matos, and Richard Cantor. 2009. "Corporate Default and Recovery Rates, 1920–2008." Special Comment, *Global Credit Research*. New York: Moody's Investor Service, February.

Engelhardt, Gary V. and Anil Kumar. 2009. "The Elasticity of Intertemporal Substitution: New Evidence from 401(k) Participation." *Economic Letters* 103(10): 15–17.

Engle, Robert F. 1982. "Autoregressive Conditional Heteroskedasticity with Estimates of the Variance of UK Inflation." *Econometrica* 50(4): 987–1008.

Epstein, Larry G. and Stanley E. Zin. 1989. "Substitution, Risk Aversion, and the Temporal Behavior of Consumption and Asset Returns: A Theoretical Framework." *Econometrica* 57(4): 937–969.

Epstein, Larry G. and Stanley E. Zin. 1991. "Substitution, Risk Aversion, and the Temporal Behavior of Consumption and Asset Returns: An Empirical Analysis." *Journal of Political Economy* 99(2): 263–286.

Feller, William. 1951. "The Asymptotic Distribution of the Range of Sums of Independent Random Variables." *Annals of Mathematical Statistics.* 22: 427–432.

Feller, William. 1971. *An Introduction to Probability Theory and Its Applications*, vol. 2, 2nd ed. New York: John Wiley.

Fender, Ingo and John Kiff. 2004. "CDO Rating Methodology: Some Thoughts on Model Risk and Its Implications." BIS Working Paper No. 163, Basel: Bank for International Settlements, Monetary and Economic Department, November.

Financial Stability Forum. 2009. *Report of the Financial Stability Forum on Addressing Procyclicality in the Financial System*. Basel: Financial Stability Board.

Fisher, Irving. 1933. "The Debt-Deflation Theory of Great Depressions." *Econometrica* 1(4): 337–357.

Fisher, Irving. 1935. *100% Money*. New York: Adelphi.

Fisher, Ronald A. 1930. *The Genetical Theory of Natural Selection*. Oxford, UK: Clarendon.

Fisher, Ronald A. 1936. "The Use of Multiple Measurements in Taxonomic Problems." *Annals of Eugenics* 7: 179–188.

Friedman, Milton. 1959. *A Program for Monetary Stability: The Millar Lectures Number Three*. New York: Fordham University Press.

Friedman, Milton. 1992. *Monetary Mischief: Episodes in Monetary History*. New York: Harcourt Brace.

Friend, Irwin and Marshall E. Blume. 1975. "The Demand for Risky Assets." *American Economic Review* 65(5): 900–922.

Frisch, Ragnar. 1933. "Propagation Problems and Impulse Problems in Dynamic Economics." In *Economic Essays in Honor of Gustav Cassel*. London: George Allen & Unwin 171–205.

Frisch, Ragnar and Harald Holme. 1935. "The Characteristic Solutions of a Mixed Difference and Differential Equation Occurring in Economic Dynamics." *Econometrica* 3(2): 225–239.

Frisch, Uriel. 1996. *Turbulence: The Legacy of A. N. Kolmogorov*. Cambridge, UK: Cambridge University Press.

Fuhrer, Jeffrey C. 2000. "Habit Formation in Consumption and Its Implications for Monetary Policy Models." *American Economic Review* 90(3): 367–390.

Gabaix, Xavier. 2010. "Variable Rare Disasters: An Exactly Solved Framework for Ten Puzzles in Macro-Finance." Working Paper, New York University, Stern School of Business.

GAO. 2010a. "The Federal Government's Long-Term Fiscal Outlook: January 2010 Update." GAO-10-468SP. Washington, DC: U.S. Government Accountability Office.

GAO. 2010b. "State and Local Governments' Fiscal Outlook: March 2010 Update." GAO-10-358. Washington, DC: U.S. Government Accountability Office.

Garman, Mark B. and Michael J. Klass. 1980. "On the Estimation of Security Price Volatilities from Historical Data." *Journal of Business* 53(1): 67–78.

Giesecke, Kay, Francis A. Longstaff, Stephen Schaefer, and Ilya Strebulaev. 2010. "Corporate Bond Default Risk: A 150-Year Perspective." NBER Working Paper No. 15848. Cambridge, MA: National Bureau of Economic Research, March.

Gilbert, Daniel T. 2006. *Stumbling on Happiness*. New York: Random House.

Gleser, Leon J. 1989. "The Gamma Distribution as a Mixture of Exponential Distributions." *American Statistician* 43(2): 115–117.

Gneiting, Tilmann. 2010. "Making and Evaluating Point Forecasts." Preprint, arXiv: 0192–0902v2.

Gneiting, Tillman and Adrian E. Raftery. 2007. "Strictly Proper Scoring Rules, Prediction, and Estimation." *Journal of the American Statistical Association* 102(477): 359–378.

Goldberg, Dror. 2005, "Famous Myths of 'Fiat Money." *Journal of Money, Credit and Banking* 37(5): 957–967.

Good, Irving J. 1950. *Probability Theory and the Weighing of Evidence.* London: Charles Griffin.

Good, Irving J. 1979. "Turing's Statistical Work in World War II." *Biometrika* 66: 393–396.

Gordy, Michael B. 2000. "A Comparative Anatomy of Credit Risk Models." *Journal of Banking and Finance* 24(1/2): 119–149.

Gordy, Michael B. 2003. "A Risk-Factor Model Foundation for Ratings-Based Capital Rules." *Journal of Financial Intermediation* 12(3): 199–232.

Green, Jerry. 1987. "'Making Book Against Oneself,' The Independence Axiom, and Nonlinear Utility Theory." *Quarterly Journal of Economics* 102(4): 785–796.

Greenig, Douglas S. 1986. "Nonseparable Preferences, Stochastic Returns, and Intertemporal Substitution in Consumption." Princeton University Undergraduate Thesis.

Gruber, Jonathan. 2006. "A Tax-Based Estimate of the Elasticity of Intertemporal Substitution." NBER Working Paper 11945, Cambridge, MA: National Bureau of Economic Research, January.

Guo, Xin and Q. Zhang. 2004. "Closed-Form Solutions with Perpetual American Put Options with Regime Switching." *SIAM Journal of Applied Mathematics* 64(6): 2034–2049.

Hamilton, David T. and Richard Cantor. 2006. "Measuring Corporate Default Rates." Special Comment, *Global Credit Research.* Moody's Investor Service, November.

Hamilton, James D. 1989. "A New Approach to the Economic Analysis of Nonstationary Time Series and the Business Cycle." *Econometrica* 57(2): 357–384.

Hardy, Godfrey H. 1908. "Mendelian Proportions in a Mixed Population." *Science* 28: 49–50.

Hardy, Mary R. 1999. "A Regime-Switching Model of Long-Term Stock Returns." *North American Actuarial Journal* 5(2): 41–53.

Hausdorff, Felix. 1921. "Summationsmethoden und Momentfolgen." *Mathematische Zeitschrift* 1(9): 74–109 and 2(9): 280–299.

Heston, Steven L. 1993. "A Closed-Form Solution for Options with Stochastic Volatility with Applications to Bond and Currency Options." *Review of Financial Studies* 6(2): 327–343.

Hewitt, Edwin and Leonard J. Savage. 1955. "Symmetric Measures on Cartesian Products." *Transactions of the American Mathematical Society* 80: 470–501.

Hickman, W. Braddock. 1953. *The Volume of Corporate Bond Financing Since 1900.* National Bureau of Economic Research, Studies in Corporate Bond Financing. Princeton, NJ: Princeton University Press.

Hoffman, Philip T., Gilles Postel-Vinay, and Jean-Laurent Rosenthal. 2007. *Surviving Large Losses: Financial Crises, the Middle Class and the Development of Capital Markets.* Cambridge, MA: Harvard University Press.

IMF. 2008. *World Economic Outlook.* Washington, DC: International Monetary Fund, October.

IMF. 2010. Time Series Data on International Reserves and Foreign Currency Liquidity, available at www.imf.org/external/np/sta/ir/IRProcessWeb/topic.aspx. Washington, DC: International Monetary Fund.

Ising, Ernst. 1925. "Beitrag zur Theorie des Ferromagnetismus." *Zeitschrift für Physik* 31: 253–258.

Jorion, Philippe. 1997. *Value at Risk: The New Benchmark for Controlling Derivatives Risk.* New York: McGraw-Hill.

Kashyap, Anil K. and Jeremy C. Stein. 2004. "Cyclical Implications of the Basel II Capital Standards." *Economic Perspectives,* Federal Reserve Bank of Chicago, 1Q: 18–31.

Kelly, John L. 1956. "A New Interpretation of Information Rate." *Bell System Technical Journal* 35: 917–926.

Kendall, Maurice and Alan Stuart. 1972. *The Advanced Theory of Statistics,* vol. 1: *Distribution Theory,* 4th ed. London: Charles Griffin.

Keynes, John M. 1936. *The General Theory of Employment, Interest and Money.* London: MacMillan.

Keynes, John M. 1937. "The General Theory of Employment." *Quarterly Journal of Economics* 51(2): 209–223.

Kiff, John. 2005. "The Basic Math of Default-Mode Credit Loss Distributions." May 22 version, unpublished, Ottawa: Bank of Canada.

Knight, Frank H. 1921. *Risk, Uncertainty and Profit.* Boston, MA: Hart, Schaffner & Marx.

Kolmogorov, Andrei N. 1936. "Sulla Teoria di Volterra della Lotta per L'Esistenza." *Giornale dell' Instituto Italiano degli Attuari* 7: 74–80.

Kotz, Samuel, Tomasz J. Kozubowski, and Krzysztof Podgórski. 2001. *The Laplace Distribution and Generalizations: A Revisit with Applications to Communications, Economics, Engineering and Finance.* New York: Birkhäuser Boston.

Kreps, David M. and Evan L. Porteus. 1978. "Temporal Resolution of Uncertainty and Dynamic Choice Theory." *Econometrica* 46(1): 185–200.

Kurz, Mordecai. 1974. "The Kesten-Stigum Model and the Treatment of Uncertainty in Equilibrium Theory." In M. S. Balch, D. L. McFadden, and S. Y. Wu, eds., *Essays on Economic Behavior Under Uncertainty.* Amsterdam: North Holland, 389–399.

Kurz, Mordecai. 1994a. "On Rational Belief Equilibria." *Economic Theory* 4: 859–876.

Kurz, Mordecai. 1994b. "On the Structure and Diversity of Rational Beliefs." *Economic Theory* 4: 877–900.

Kurz, Mordecai. 1996. "Rational Beliefs and Endogenous Uncertainty." *Economic Theory* 8: 383–397.

Kurz, Mordecai. 1997. "Asset Prices with Rational Beliefs." In M. Kurz, ed., *Endogenous Economic Fluctuations: Studies in the Theory of Rational Belief,* Studies in Economic Theory No. 6. Berlin: Springer-Verlag, 211–250.

Kurz, Mordecai and Andrea Beltratti. 1996. "The Equity Premium Is No Puzzle." Working Paper No. 96-004, Stanford University Department of Economics, February.

Kurzweil, Ray. 1998. *The Age of Spiritual Machines: When Computers Exceed Human Intelligence.* New York: Viking.

Landes, David S. 1999. *The Wealth and Poverty of Nations: Why Some Are So Rich and Some So Poor.* New York: W. W. Norton.

Li, David X. 2000. "On Default Correlation: A Copula Function Approach." *Journal of Fixed Income* 9(4): 43–54.

Liptser, Robert S. and Albert N. Shirayev. 1977. *Statistics of Random Processes*, vols. 1 and 2. New York: Springer-Verlag. Translation of *Statistika Sluchainykh Protsessov*. 1974. Moscow: Nauka.

Lo, Andrew and Jasmina Hasanhodzic. 2009. *The Heretics of Finance: Conversations with Leading Practitioners of Technical Analysis*. New York: Bloomberg.

Lo, Andrew and Jasmina Hasanhodzic. 2010. *The Evolution of Technical Analysis: Financial Prediction from Babylonian Tablets to Bloomberg Terminals*. New York: Bloomberg.

Lorenz, Edward N. 1963. "Deterministic Non-Periodic Flow." *Journal of the Atmospheric Sciences* 20: 130–141.

Lotka, Alfred J. 1925. *Elements of Physical Biology*. Baltimore, MD: Williams and Wilkins.

Lucas, Robert E., Jr. 1972. "Expectations and the Neutrality of Money." *Journal of Economic Theory* 4(2): 103–124.

Lucas, Robert E., Jr. 1978. "Asset Prices in an Exchange Economy." *Econometrica* 46(6): 1429–1445.

Luenberger, David G. 1979. *Introduction to Dynamic Systems: Theory, Models and Applications*. New York: John Wiley.

Magdon-Ismail, Malik, Amir F. Atiya, Amrit Pratap, and Yaser S. Abu-Mostafa. 2002. "The Sharpe Ratio, Range and Maximal Drawdown of a Brownian Motion." Technical Reports 02-13. Troy, NY: Rensselaer Polytechnic Institute, September.

Marcinkiewicz, Józef. 1938. "Sur une propriété de la loi de Gauss." *Mathematische Zeitschrift* 44: 612–618.

Markopolos, Harry. 2010. *No One Would Listen: A True Financial Thriller*. New York: John Wiley.

Markowitz, Harry M. 1952. "Portfolio Selection." *Journal of Finance* 7(1): 77–91.

Maronna, Ricardo A., Douglas R. Martin, and Victor J. Yohai. 2006. *Robust Statistics: Theory and Methods*. Chichester, UK: John Wiley.

Martin, Ian W. R. 2010. "Consumption-Based Asset Pricing with Higher Cumulants." NBER Working Paper No. 16153. Cambridge, MA: National Bureau of Economic Research, July.

Marx, Karl. 1887. *Capital*. Revised English edition of *Das Kapital*, 1867. Reprinted in 1986. Moscow: Progress Publishers.

May, Robert M. 1973. *Stability and Complexity in Model Ecosystems*. Princeton, NJ: Princeton University Press.s

McComb, William D. 1990. *The Physics of Fluid Turbulence*. Oxford, UK: Clarendon.

McKean, Henry P. 1965. "A Free Boundary Problem for the Heat Equation Arising from a Problem in Mathematical Economics." *Industrial Management Review* 6: 32–39.

Mehra, Rahnish, ed. 2008. *Handbook of the Equity Risk Premium*. Amsterdam: Elsevier.

Mehra, Rahnish and Edward C. Prescott. 1985. "The Equity Premium: A Puzzle." *Journal of Monetary Economics* 15(2): 145–161.

Merton, Robert C. 1974. "On the Pricing of Corporate Debt: The Risk Structure of Interest Rates." *Journal of Finance* 29(2): 449–470.

Mishkin, Frederic S. and Tryggvi T. Herbertsson. 2006. *Financial Stability in Iceland*. Reykjavik: Iceland Chamber of Commerce.

Moody's Investor Service. 2009. *Moody's Ratings Symbols and Definitions.* June.

Müller, Ulrich A. 1993. "Statistics of Variables Observed over Overlapping Intervals." Zurich: O&A Research Group, UAM1993-06-18, November 30.

Muth, John F. 1961. "Rational Expectations and the Theory of Price Movements." *Econometrica* 29(3): 315–335.

Nelsen, Roger B. 2006. *An Introduction to Copulas,* 2nd ed. New York: Springer.

Nelson, Scott R. 2008. "The Real Great Depression." *Chronicle Review* 55(8): 898.

OECD. 2010. OECD.Stat (database), .doi: 10.1787/data-00285-en. www.oecd-ilibrary. org/economics/data/oecd-stat_data-00285-en. Paris: Organisation for Economic Co-operation and Development.

Orphanides, Athanios. 2004. "Monetary Policy in Deflation: The Liquidity Trap in History and Practice." *North American Journal of Economics and Finance* 15(1): 101–124.

Orszag, Steven A. 1970. "Analytical Theories of Turbulence." *Journal of Fluid Mechanics* 41(2): 363–386.

Osband, Kent H. 1985. "Providing Incentives for Better Cost Forecasting." PhD diss., University of California, Berkeley.

Osband, Kent. 1992. "Economic Crisis in a Shortage Economy." *Journal of Political Economy* 100(4): 673–690.

Osband, Kent. 2001. *Iceberg Risk: An Adventure in Portfolio Theory.* New York: Texere.

Osband, Kent. 2002–2005. Finformatics. *Wilmott,* various issues.

Osband, Kent. 2008. "Knowledge of Ignorance Is Bliss." Keynote speech at Citibank Global Quantitative Conference in Athens, Greece, June.

Osband, Kent. 2009. "Insecuritization: How Flawed Statistics Helped Catalyze Financial Mayhem." *Wilmott,* January/February: 66–78 and March/April: 54–60.

Osband, Kent and Stefan Reichelstein. 1985. "Information-Eliciting Compensation Schemes." *Journal of Public Economics* 27(1): 107–115.

Parkinson, Michael. 1980. "The Extreme Value Method for Estimating the Variance of the Rate of Return." *Journal of Business* 53(1): 61–65.

Pastor, Lubos and Pietro Veronesi. 2009. "Learning in Financial Markets." *Annual Review of Financial Economics* 1: 361–381.

Patterson, Scott. 2010. *The Quants: How a New Breed of Math Whizzes Conquered Wall Street and Nearly Destroyed It.* New York: Crown Business.

Persaud, Avinash D. 2000. "Sending the Herd off the Cliff Edge: The Disturbing Interaction of Herding Behavior and Market-Sensitive Risk-Management Practices." First Prize Essay on Global Finance. Washington, DC: International Institute of Finance.

Persaud, Avinash D. 2008. "Sending the Herd over the Cliff. Again." *Finance and Development* 45(2): 32–33.

Poundstone, William. 2005. *Fortune's Formula: The Untold Story of the Scientific Betting System That Beat the Casinos and Wall Street.* New York: Hill and Wang.

Reinhart, Carmen M. and Kenneth S. Rogoff. 2009. *This Time Is Different: Eight Centuries of Financial Folly.* Princeton, NJ: Princeton University Press.

Ricardo, David. 1820. "Essay on the Funding System." In John R. McCulloch, ed., *The Works of David Ricardo.* 1888. London: John Murray.

Rietz, Thomas A. 1988. "The Equity Risk Premium: A Solution." *Journal of Monetary Economics* 22(1): 117–131.

Risken, Hannes. 1996. *The Fokker-Planck Equation: Methods of Solution and Applications*, 2nd ed. Berlin: Springer-Verlag.

Salmon, Felix. 2009. "Recipe for Disaster: The Formula That Killed Wall Street." *Wired* 17(3): 74–79, 112.

Samuelson, Paul A. 1958. "An Exact Consumption-Loan Model of Interest with or without the Social Contrivance of Money." *Journal of Political Economy* 66(6): 467–482.

Samuelson, Paul A. 1965. "Proof that Properly Anticipated Prices Fluctuate Randomly." *Industrial Management Review* 6(2): 41–49.

Sargent, Thomas J. 1979. *Macroeconomic Theory*. New York: Academic.

Sargent, Thomas J. and Neil Wallace. 1973. "Rational Expectations and the Dynamics of Hyperinflation." *International Economic Review* 14(2): 328–350.

Savage, Leonard. J., 1971, "Elicitation of Personal Probabilities and Expectations." *Journal of the American Statistical Association*, 66(336): 783–810.

SEC. 2008. *Summary Report of Issues Identified in the Commission Staff's Examinations of Select Credit Rating Agencies*. Washington, DC: Securities and Exchange Commission.

Servigny, Arnaud de and Olivier Renault. 2004. *Measuring and Managing Credit Risk*. New York: McGraw-Hill.

Shannon, Claude E. 1948. "A Mathematical Theory of Communication." *Bell System Technical Journal* 27: 379–423 and 623–656.

Shiller, Robert J. 1981. "Do Stock Market Prices Move Too Much to Be Justified by Subsequent Changes in Dividends?" *American Economic Review* 71(3): 421–436.

Shiller, Robert J. 2006. *Irrational Exuberance*. New York: Doubleday.

Shubik, Martin. 1999. *Theory of Money and Financial Institutions*. Cambridge, MA: MIT Press.

Simons, Henry. 1934. *A Positive Program for Laissez Faire: Some Proposals for a Liberal Economic Policy*. Public Policy Pamphlet No. 15. Chicago: University of Chicago Press.

Sismondi, J-C-L Simonde de. 1819. *Nouveaux Principes d'Économie Politique*. Translated as *New Principles of Political Economy*. 1991. New Brunswick, NJ: Transaction.

Sklar, Abe. 1959. "Fonctions de répartition à n dimensions et leurs marges." *Publications de l'Institut de Statistique de l'Université de Paris* 8: 229–231.

Smith, Elliot B. 2008. "'Race to Bottom' at Moody's, S&P Secured Subprime's Boom, Bust." Bloomberg News Service, September 25.

Soros, George. 1988. *The Alchemy of Finance*. New York: Simon and Schuster.

Steutel, Frederick W. 1969. "Note on Completely Monotone Densities." *Annals of Mathematical Statistics* 40(3): 1130–1131.

Stokey, Nancy and Robert E. Lucas, Jr. (with Edward C. Prescott). 1989. *Recursive Methods in Economic Dynamics*. Cambridge, MA: Harvard University Press.

Student [Gosset, William S.]. 1908. "The Probable Error of a Mean." *Biometrika* 6(1): 1–25.

Taleb, Nassim N. 2004. *Fooled by Randomness: The Hidden Role of Chance in Life and in the Markets*. New York: Random House.

Taleb, Nassim N. 2010. *The Black Swan: The Impact of the Highly Improbable*, 2nd ed. With a new section: "On Robustness and Fragility." New York: Random House.

Tarashev, Nikola A. 2009. "Measuring Portfolio Credit Risk Correctly: Why Parameter Uncertainty Matters." BIS Working Paper No. 280, Basel: Bank for International Settlements, Monetary and Economic Department, April.

Thomson, William. 1979. "Eliciting Production Possibilities from a Well-Informed Manager." *Journal of Economic Theory* 20(3): 360–380.

Thorp, Edward O. 2000. "The Kelly Criterion in Blackjack, Sports Betting, and the Stock Market." In Olaf Vancura, Judy A. Cornelius, and William R. Eadington, eds., *Finding the Edge: Mathematical and Quantitative Analysis of Gambling.* Reno, NV: Institute for the Study of Gambling and Commercial Gaming, University of Nevada, 163–214.

Tirole, Jean. 1985. "Asset Bubbles and Overlapping Generations." *Econometrica* 52(6): 1499–1528.

Vasicek, Oldrich. 2002. "Loan Portfolio Value." *RISK*, December, 160–162.

Vazza, Diane, Devi Aurora, and Nicholas Kraemer. 2010. *Default, Transition, and Recovery: 2009 Annual Global Corporate Default Study and Rating Transitions.* New York: Standard & Poor's, Global Credit Portal, RatingsDirect, March.

Veronesi, Pietro. 1999. "Stock Market Overreaction to Bad News in Good Times: A Rational Expectations Model." *Review of Financial Studies* 12(5): 975–1007.

Veronesi, Pietro. 2000. "How Does Information Quality Affect Stock Returns?" *Journal of Finance* 55(2): 807–837.

Veronesi, Pietro. 2004a. "Belief-Independent Utilities, Aversion to State-Uncertainty and Asset Prices." Working Paper, Graduate School of Business, University of Chicago, January.

Veronesi, Pietro. 2004b. "The Peso Problem Hypothesis and Stock Market Returns." *Journal of Economic Dynamics and Control* 28(4): 707–725.

Volterra, Vito. 1926. "Variazioni e fluttuazioni del numero d'individui in specie animali conviventi." *Memorie della Reale Accademia Nazionale dei Lincei, Roma* ser. 6, 2: 31–113. Translated in an appendix to R. N. Chapman. 1931. *Animal Ecology.* New York: McGraw-Hill.

von Mises, Ludwig. 1940. *Interventionism: An Economic Analysis.* Translated from German and published in 1998 under the editorship of B. B. Greaves. Irvington-on-Hudson, New York: Foundation for Economic Education.

Wallace, Neil. 1980. "The Overlapping Generations Model of Fiat Money." In John Kareken and Neil Wallace, *Models of Monetary Economics.* Minneapolis, MN: Federal Reserve Bank of Minneapolis.

Weil, Philippe. 1989. "The Equity Premium Puzzle and the Riskfree Rate Puzzle." *Journal of Monetary Economics* 24(3): 401–422.

Weinberg, Wilhelm. 1908. "Über den Nachweis der Vererbung beim Menschen." *Jahreshefte des Vereins für vaterländische Naturkunde in Württemberg* 64: 368–382.

Weitzman, Martin. 2007. "Subjective Expectations and Asset-Return Puzzles."*American Economic Review* 97(4): 1102–1130.

Wilde, Tom. 1997. "*CreditRisk+: A Credit Risk Management Framework.*" Technical Document, London: Credit Suisse First Boston, October.

Wilmott Magazine. 2009. "The Riskperts." September–October.

Wilmott, Paul. 2006. *Paul Wilmott on Quantitative Finance,* vol. 1, 2nd ed, Chichester, UK: John Wiley.

Witt, Gary. 2004. "Moody's Correlated Binomial Default Distribution." *Structured Finance Rating Methodology*, Moody's Investors Service, August.

Witt, Gary. 2010a. "A Closed Form Distribution for the Sum of Correlated Bernoulli Trials." JSM Proceedings 2010: Paper Presented at the Joint Statistical Meetings Vancouver, Canada.

Witt, Gary. 2010b. "Statement Submitted by Request to the Financial Crisis Inquiry Commission." Washington, DC: U.S. Congress, June 2.

Wolpert, Robert L. 2009. "Extremes." www.isds.duke.edu/courses/Fall09/sta104.02/lec/104wk05.pdf. Department of Statistical Science, Duke University, Durham, NC.

Yoshizawa, Yuri. 2003. "Moody's Approach to Rating Synthetic CDOs." *Moody's Structured Finance Rating Methodology*, New York: Moody's Investors Service, July.

Zhou, Wei-Xing and Didier Sornette. 2006. "Is There a Real-Estate Bubble in the US?" *Physica A: Statistical Mechanics and Its Applications* 361(1): 297–308.

Zumbach, Gilles. 2007. "The RiskMetrics 2006 Methodology." New York: RiskMetrics Group, March.

INDEX